MEN OF THE WEST

MEN OF THE WEST

Life on the American Frontier

CATHY LUCHETTI

W. W. Norton & Company

New York • London

Title page photo: Jefferson Square Barbershop, San Francisco, California, 1906.

Copyright © 2004 by Cathy Luchetti

For information about permission to reproduce selections from this book, write to Permissions,
W. W. Norton & Company, Inc., 500 Fifth Avenue, New York, NY 10110

Manufacturing by South China Printing Co. Ltd.
Book design by Chris Welch
Production manager: Amanda Morrison

Library of Congress Cataloging-in-Publication Data

Luchetti, Cathy, 1945–
     Men of the West : life on the American frontier / Cathy Luchetti.
          p. cm.
Includes bibliographical references and index.
     ISBN 0-393-05905-7
     1. Frontier and pioneer life—West (U.S.)—Pictorial works. 2. Frontier and pioneer life—West (U.S.)
3. West (U.S.)—Social life and customs—19th century—Pictorial works. 4. West (U.S.)—Social life and customs—
19th century. 5. Men—West (U.S.)—Pictorial works. 6. Men —West (U.S.)—History. 7. Pioneers—West
(U.S.)—Pictorial works. 8. Pioneers—West (U.S.)—History. 9. Cowboys—West (U.S.)—Pictorial works.
10. Cowboys—West (U.S.)—History. I. Title.
     F596.L85 2004
     978'.02'081—dc22

                                                                                                                2003020698

W. W. Norton & Company, Inc., 500 Fifth Avenue, New York, N.Y. 10110
www.wwnorton.com

W. W. Norton & Company Ltd., Castle House, 75/76 Wells Street, London W1T 3QT

1 2 3 4 5 6 7 8 9 0

Failure never yet disheartened the American nature,

or squelched its individual members.

—J. ROSS BROWNE

To Peter,
with Love

CONTENTS

❖❖❖

Part 4   The Marryin' Kind

Part 5   Amazing Grace

Part 6   Men at Work

Part 7   Native Americans

ACKNOWLEDGMENTS

I N WEAVING TOGETHER a new look at the men who explored, settled, farmed, and otherwise made their livelihoods in the American West, I acknowledge the vast body of work that has gone before—so vast, indeed, that for the past twenty years many historians have shunned the subject of "men in the West" in favor of the less studied area of frontier women. But time again has turned the balance, and a new curiosity arises about frontier men. What did America mean to them? What were their lives like? For helping answer these questions and for his many contributions concerning western men and his suggestion that a woman's perception of the "men" subject would lend a fresh insight thanks go to Dr. Richard Dillon, historian and author. Thanks also to Robert Chandler of the Wells Fargo Historical Services for useful and humorous historical incidents, herein included.

Thanks to Barbara V. Quinn of Radcliff, Kentucky, for sending me the book *The Quiet Conquest*, written by her mother, Barbara Levorsen. Thanks to JoAnn Levy for several valuable journal and diary recommendations and to author and historian Harriet Rochlin for her advice. Author Necia Dixon Liles offered me many suggestions, as well as a copy of her work on Israel Shipman Pelton Lord, *A Doctor's Gold Rush Journey to California*. Bob Hawley's support and ideas have also been of great value.

Illustrative photographs, integral to this effort, have come from historical societies, museums, universities throughout the West, the Library of Congress, and the National Archives. Thanks in particular go to Ellen Harding of the California State Library for her assiduous help in locating specific photographs in the collection, her title and placement research, and her useful suggestions. Many thanks to Susan Snyder of the Bancroft Library for her suggestions and to Todd Arrington of the Homestead National Monument in Beatrice, Nebraska, for providing inspiring information about the monument and Nebraska. The photo selection in the book would be far less varied without the help of archivist Jim Bradshaw of the Nita Stewart Haley Memorial Library in Midland, Texas; Tom Shelton of the Institute of Texas Cultures; and author Jeff Kunkel of Oakland, curator of the McDaniel Collection.

Thanks to Frank Cutler for western inspiration, to Dennis Graves for his invaluable outlaw references, and to Tim Post of Ketchum, Idaho, distant relation to Jim Bridger, for his observation "In the old west, there weren't many people, but there were just as many fools." Thanks to Steve Thaw of Moraga, California, for supplying the unpublished Rinehart family record, from which quotes have been taken by permission. As always, I appreciate the support of Anne Edelstein, my agent; and thanks to Amy Cherry, my editor, for her vision in suggesting the book, and to the Book Club of California for a generous grant. Last, but first in memory, is Alice Hamburg, my friend and supporter throughout the making of this book, a stalwart pioneer who died at the age of ninety-six.

Introduction

DRIVEN BY DREAMS

MEN IN THE AMERICAN WEST

If never permitted by my destiny to accomplish great things, I could at least die attempting them.—Hubert Howe Bancroft

✦✦

Men in this part of the world [turn] up virgin soil and whistle cheerily at their work . . . they are hopeful and happy.—J. Ross Browne

✦✦

To experience the feeling of "something bigger," it helps to be by ourselves.—C. S. Price, Wyoming

✦✦

I always had a way of just going ahead, at whatever I had a mind to.
—Davy Crockett

FOR GENERATIONS, MEN had been driven to achieve an ideal, to follow vague yearnings, lunatic notions, and leftover dreams of a golden age, always searching for their concept of an earthly paradise. To some, the desire was anchored in wealth; for others, land; and for some, the prospect of freedom. Whether French, Spanish, or English, nearly every nationality yearned for such a paradise and sent emissaries—always men—in search of its existence to the Western Hemisphere. There the discontented proletariat of the Old World could become entrepreneurs and farm owners of the New. "The rich stay in Europe; it is only the middling poor that emigrate," noted J. Hector St. John Crevècoeur in 1759.

By the early 1800s the Western world had caught the excitement of the American frontier, a place so fantastical that "even the dogs are polite," or so believed the English novelist and naval commander Frederick Marryat, describing Monterey. "The horses, which are always grazing about, run up to you [in] welcome . . . [and], strange to say, the Americans are almost honest." General E. D. Townsend claimed to see woolly mammoths, Welsh-speaking Indians, and "strange sea monsters" galore.

The land too was fantastical. Mountain man John D. Young saw a Rocky Mountain peak "appear to raise out of the earth just as a ship raises out of the water at sea," "in a very strange freak of nature," while, freakishly, the "prairie dog, owl and rattlesnake" all "burrowed together" in the same hole. Even "fish crossed casually the high snowy peaks of the Continental Divide," he claimed, fascinated by the fact that a stream could be on one side, then suddenly on the other. "Truly grand sights" were in store for the men who flooded west in ever-increasing numbers.

"Strangers . . . swarm the land, spreading themselves over it in every direction," observed James Hall, drawn by adventure, hyperbole, and wild expectation. "Let freedom's holy banner be planted

upon the farthest ice-bound cliff!" rang out a typical slogan, making emigration synonymous with patriotism and whetting the nation's imagination as it quested for more land. Even "the risk of the undertaking," seemed, to western critic J. Ross Browne, "to give it a charm."

America was also a nation divided, not only by issues of slavery and reform but simply by its own great, unthinkable geographical excess. From New England to the sprawling Mississippi, towns, ports, farming centers, and cities sprang up, heeding the call of manifest destiny. Beyond lay the Great American Desert, a plain so maddeningly desolate that it stretched unbroken from Canada to New Mexico, a land where, said Francis Parkman in 1846, "No living thing was moving . . . except the lizards." Such vastness turned men into legends, as with Jim Bridger, Joe Meek, Jedediah Smith, and Jim Beckwourth. That same horizon was home to mythic men whose nations predated European and American exploration and invasion:

Crazy Horse, Dull Knife, Red Cloud, Chief Joseph, Geronimo, Cochise, and countless more.

Western men were generally young, highly energetic, heavily armed, and accountable to no one. As they forged their way across the country, the results of their heedlessness was seen in diminished herds of buffalo, trees felled, grass cropped rootless, and streams deeply muddied. Trees and rocks were marked in passing with epitaphs, mottoes, friendship verses, rhymes, and simply graffiti, in evidence since colonial times, including names, initials, faces, human figures, obscenities, initials, dates, and animal images. Some epithets, such as cattle brands, were brief, while other lovelorn missives were emblazoned on beech, alder, poplar, or aspen trees, young passion captured in block letters for generations to see. Shepherds or cowhands scrawled an aimless "hello," while other missives were frenziedly pornographic. One, inscribed into the trunk of an aspen in the Wasatch Mountains of Utah, said merely, *"Paso por aqui"* (I pass by here). Carvings could commemorate a kill, with one western birch bearing the legend "Z. Taylor 1835 Deer Hunt," while a Tennessee beech announced that "D. Boon Killed A. Bar in the year 1760." Thirteen years later "D. Boon" claimed another kill, dated 1773.

All history is selective, and to many, the West was a rowdy amalgam of raider and trader, lynch law and outlaw, a land governed by gunplay and gambling, ruled by prejudice, and captive to wild and colorful excess. There men could shape destiny to their own imaginings. The West was also a land of contradictions, where a buffalo slayer known as Buffalo Jones slowed in his killing task and grew pensive and after a while tried to save the species he had butchered. Indians seen as savage displayed skills of diplomacy and peacemaking more refined than those of the "civilized" whites. In the tough land, compassion and reason were also found, as ranchers, farmers, teachers, lawyers, inventors, healers, and scientists became husbands, fathers, and kin. Desperadoes aside, the greater body of western men held court behind cracker barrels, sang psalms, helped their neighbors, worked hard, and were disarmingly honest. Why else would "a gentleman . . . call on the county treasurer . . . and voluntarily pay over his poll tax? We do not state this to play upon public credulity," said a Sacramento newspaper on August 21, 1855. "It may be a fact, but it is very strange."

Who were the men of the West? To scholar Carl Becker, writing in the 1900s, they were "primarily men of faith . . . individualists . . . and idealists because they have faith in the universe, being confident that somehow everything is right at the center of things. [They] are ever inventing God anew, and must be always transforming the world into their ideal of it. . . . These qualities are not only Puritan, they are American." To historian Frederick Jackson Turner, the western man combined "coarseness and strength with acuteness and inquisitiveness," had a "practical, inventive turn of mind…a masterful grasp of material things . . . restless nervous energy . . . and the buoyancy and exuberance that come from freedom." Said British traveler James Hall: "The people . . . are high minded, spirited lovers of liberty, tenacious of their honour, and quick in their resentments; they equally loathe everything in the shape of oppression, encroachment, or dictation; they claim the same right of instructing their officers, and exercise the same power of dismissing them on the

slightest provocation. . . . They have generous feelings, which must always form a part of the character of a free, brave and enlightened people."

Frontier men, though shy of etiquette and belles lettres, could still expound in literary language, and many had a deep and unexpected appreciation of the West's natural beauty. "The mind falters," wrote a correspondent from the *Cincinnati Gazette,* "at the green oceans which roll across the Great Plains." Physician Israel Lord of California wrote: "No description, no paintings can give or convey an adequate idea of the beauties of the delightful valleys that branch off from the main one. . . . I have seen . . . a crimson poppy so very, so exquisitely beautiful, that I cannot remember ever to have seen its equal.

Men of all kinds were thrown together out West. Lacking community, history, place, or family, men might judge quickly, appraising one another by the most apparent virtues. "I liked him from the beginning" decided J. Ross Browne about an "overflowing, generous, genial" physician he encountered near Aurora, Nevada. "Whatever he did [was] with all his heart and soul . . . without regard to reason, expense, or the everlasting fitness of things." British traveler Robert Hall called his new acquaintance, General Presby Neville, "the kindest of human beings [with] a thousand tendrils about his heart, that continually entwined themselves in the little world around him. . . . No man was too great for his friendship, none too insignificant for his kindness."

The suspicious and distrustful also found much to support their view. James Wilkinson dined one day with Manual, a "Black Spaniard," and wrote to his friend Zebulon Pike at Cantonment Missouri, July 16, 1806: "I have seen too much of the World to fall in love with Strangers, particularly men of fine European & Asiatic languages, found in the wilds of the Missouri—the natural question is, how came so many accomplishments & useful qualities buried alive. . . . If I am Cynical I have cause for it." Henry Washington Carter worried as he eyed a fellow traveler: "I thought to myself, it may be possible that he has some sinister motive, he may be contemplating robbery and murder." To allay fears, men carried weapons and letters of introduction, which secured friendship and accommodation in a wild and strange terrain, validating their trustworthiness in a land where strangers bedded down together, never knowing what the night would bring.

When John Young Nelson told a friend of a proposed journey to Salt Lake City, the man's father-in-law was offered as a contact. "If I liked he would give me a letter of introduction to him, and I could stay there a week whilst I had a look around to find something to do." Wrote General E. D. Townsend, traveling down the coast of California by stage in 1855: "I had a letter of introduction to Mr. Banning. As soon as he knew who I was he was very polite." Even Constable Charles Stephens, chasing horse thieves, came to the small town of Moapa with credentials. "I went over to the storekeeper with my letter of introduction, credentials, etc. and made myself known to him." Indians were frequently identified as friendly by their "papers." An Osage chief, traveling in 1806 with several others, was identified by Zeb Pike as friendly and "from a nation . . . immediately under the protection of the United States: I do therefore, request all persons, to give them every proper assistance; and protection; & not to throw any let, or hindrance, in their way." Men might bring passports as they moved from state to territory but usually used written introductions instead.

Those without letters relied upon their own enterprise to make their ways. "All is work and excitement and proving ourselves men," wrote John Evans Brown, part of a male fraternity whose members were initiated through fighting, wrestling, warring, and bearing arms of all kinds. Such male bravado, according to historian Ruth Mather, quickly verged into the "nineteenth-century phenomenon of desperadoism," lived by "the morally bankrupt and the lawbreakers [who] left old vices for new, finding sanctuary beyond the call of civilization." To be "game" was to rise to any challenge, even as criminal behavior spread throughout the West. Often such rowdiness was hailed as manly and heroic; any male with a swagger and a gun could be the source of his own folklore. A fifteen-year-old boy in the mining town of South Park, Colorado, according to Mather, "believed that he could not be anything till he had shot somebody."

In this, he had the assistance of Samuel Colt, originator of the deadly, though cumbersome, Colt revolver, whose fame was established when fifteen Texas Rangers shot nearly forty Comanche Indians in a battle on the Pedernales River, thanks to the speedy new armaments. Captain Samuel H. Walker wrote to Colt in admiration, bragging of the "satisfactory skirmishes" and allowing Colt a "large share of the credit. Without your pistols we would not have had the confidence to have undertaken such daring adventures." Walker's only complaint: The gun was not heavy enough to use as a club after he exhausted his ammunition. Colt replied by seeking Walker's public endorsement, part of the newly minted world of advertising.

I have hard so much of . . . your exployets with the Arms of my invention that I have long desired to know you personally & get from you a true narrative of the vareous instances where my arms have proved of more the ordinary utility. . . . I hope yur will favour by with a minute detail of all occasions where you have used & seen my arms of ordinary construction. . . . I have no doubt that the hints which I may get from you & others . . . in the field that they can be made the most complete thing in the world.

Despite family and religious boundaries, the social life of many men fell into hard drinking, heavy smoking, and barroom bravado, particularly during a long winter. The more rural the setting, the more sordid the scene, with men huddling under ice-soaked canvas tents or, nearly snow-blind, bleary, and bleak, crouched in the questionable shelter of a crumbling frame shack.

One recourse was drink. "Liquor at that time was used as commonly as the food we ate," said carpenter Elbridge Boyden. "Every second house that you'd pass was a pub and its no harm to remark that they were the best built places in the city," noted sourdough miner Michael MacGowan, describing Alaska's tiny Klondike town of Dawson. "Some of them were open night and day and I'm telling you it was sweet whiskey they sold—it cost a[n English] pound a glass." At every dance, liquor "set the meaner elements of the heterogeneous mass well in motion," chided the *Winfield* (Kansas) *Courier* on February 1, 1873. Once drinking commenced, "halters to teams were cut, whips stolen, the road strewn with fence posts, three or four fights ensued, pistols [were] drawn and [all was] bedlam." The article concluded: "We have told enough; numerous other things happened that won't do to tell."

Typically, men fought. "A couple of men in a train just over the stream had a quarrel last night. One struck at the other with a large knife, and then both took their rifles and went out to shoot each other. But it all ended as it began, in nothing," observed Dr. Israel Lord of a wagon train party in 1849. Fights arose over women, money, pride, and property, in no particular order. Like the flat prairie vistas, living without boundaries was the basis of frontier life, making every event, from a scant debt to kinship revenge, a cause for combat. "He owed me nine dollars," complained cowhand Oliver Nelson about a companion. "When he came, we had it around and around all over the cabin: he reached for his gun, but didn't quite get it, and heaved an ax, which buried itself in the floor; I

grabbed a [Dutch] oven in each hand from where I'd hung them on the door in September, and chased him around the roof in the south room. Finally he wrote me out an order on a merchant in Supply." Unfortunately, when Nelson presented the order to the merchant, he was turned down. Meanwhile his opponent had slipped away, leaving Nelson without money or satisfaction.

❖　❖　❖　❖

WHY SUCH VIOLENCE? General rootlessness and a surfeit of six-shooters, Sharps and Henry rifles, Spencer carbines, Winchesters and Remingtons contributed to the disorder. Moreover, although many men came west to settle, many hoped to make fortunes and

Texas rodeo cowboy, 1880s.

then leave. This lack of allegiance to state, territory, or town allowed men to indulge in Sabbath breaking, profanity, low morals, drunkenness, and general instability.

While actual laws were routinely broken, unwritten "codes" remained inviolate. Women should not be hurt or killed, killings should be justified, hospitality in the wilderness was demanded, men could kill in defense of life and property, and a man's opponent deserved a fair chance. To kill an unarmed man, to shoot him in the back, and to stage an ambush were cowardly acts. But high standards were no guarantee of longevity, as Langford Peel discovered in Helena, Montana, in 1867. He quarreled with an enemy, Bull, and

drew his gun. Seeing that Bull was unarmed, Peel gallantly told him to "go arm yourself. Come back fighting." Bull followed his advice, crept back to the saloon, and ambushed Peel, killing him in a craven act that drew general disdain but no jail sentence.

A strange formality, an old-fashioned, even awkward etiquette, governed the shoot-out. Wyatt Earp was known never to draw until after his enemy. Sheriff Billy Breckenridge never shot at a man unless he had already been shot at. If one man ran out of shells, his opponent should hum, tap his boots, or spit if necessary, waiting for him to reload to commence firing. When Eldorado Johnny went gunning for the ubiquitous Langford Peel, he went to a barbershop, shaved, had his hair coiffed and his boots buffed; donned his Sunday clothes; and then challenged Peel. Good grooming aside, Peel shot out the door, guns blazing, and quickly killed Johnny.

One reason fighting was so common was there were so many divisions among western men. Cowmen hated sheepmen because range cattle couldn't feed on the sheep's nubbed-down grazing spots. Farmers hated cattle drives, during which sod was pounded, crops were crushed, and the thunder of hooves was so loud the crockery cracked and crocheted tidies fell off the sideboards. Blood kin often hated one another, could cite every grudge down through time, and rallied with weapons at the least reminder. The usual causes of male feuds were often simple and trifling, and flamed into violence at the least provocation. The Civil War, when families separated over the slavery issue, also furnished both cause and condition for feuds. Men raised during times of war were long accustomed to bloodshed and bushwhacking. Backwoods America was chiefly settled by ex-army men sporting testy, violent natures, whose frontier lives had few of the usual restraints of civilization.

Nor were men restrained from bigotry, which sprang up in times of tension, when races mingled, or when competition surged. "The d-d Yankee, the chivalric Southerner, the long bearded miner, Jew and Gentile are mixed in the throng, giving a peculiar life and style to . . . San Francisco," reported the *American Israelite*. "The antipathy manifested toward the Jew was perpetual." Suspicion and hostility turned to anti-Semitism, and in 1854 a firing squad in Los Angeles executed a mock Judas in a plaza, reported the *Hebrew*. In a farcical moment a Jewish man and his Catholic wife wanted their son circumcised. "All [her] relatives rushed into the room to prevent by force the act, yet were prevented by the wife, who publicly stated that she consented to the circumcision." Tension between Anglo Americans and Spanish Americans was ongoing, and violence against the Chinese common. As for black Americans, they were accepted as long as they conformed to expectations. "We had a very nice dinner," wrote Rosa Newmark, "and had a colored man to cook the poultry."

✢   ✢   ✦   ✦

PHILOSOPHER CARL BECKER believed that "the American cares for material things because they represent the substance of things hoped for. He cares less for money than for making money; a fortune is valued not because it represents ease, but because it represents struggle, achievement, progress." Would frontier men have agreed? When a boom mentality prevailed, men imagined their own success and then wrote home about it. While some actually earned fabulous amounts—"When I think of how much money I am making it seems like a dream," wrote gold miner Carlisle Abbot—others simply lied or admitted their losses. Henry Washington Carter on his yearlong journey to California in 1857 "had been unemployed for some time, dollars were getting scarce, there was something wrong in the exchequer, there was a tightness in the chest. I began to understand what people mean when they talk about 'coming out at the little end of the horn.' "

Westerners were frequently in debt as they sought to build farms or establish small enterprises. Miners were particularly impoverished, with typical wages of about eight dollars a day. Many, such as farmer John Grannis, lived out the American dream in a fretful state of poverty. He wrote on September 14, 1865: "To Day is my 36th Birth Day. Age is advancing with rapid strides. The Meridian of life is passed and my fortune is not made yet." In 1828, American colonist to Mexico Stephen F. Austin noted that the majority of the immigrants to Texas owed debts to their mother country, having left with the hope of paying for their failures.

To compensate, many insolvent men fabricated success in their letters home, writing spellbinding accounts of their earnings—or at least their potential—until finally, they had no recourse but shamefaced admission of financial defeat. Typical was Andrew Phelps, writing from Pleasant Valley Ranch, California, in 1854:

> I would write to Mr. Arnold and see if he would not loan me a thousand dollars, but then I had a delicacy about doing so knowing that I have always wrote home how well I was off and also making money. . . . I have always told the truth and have made money our property that is the ranch and what belongs to it is worth ten thousand dollars, but ever since the mill started we have had one thousand dollars of borrowed money which we have had to pay five per cent per month interest on (and sometimes more) which you see has more than doubled the interest we have

paid every month. But the principal is still the same this would have been all paid off long ago if the mill had run this winter for we have loggs enough, besides those in the woods all ready for hauling. . . . [Thus] I had never sent any [money] home to you.

All that has been wanting to have made me a rich man by this time has been ready money and that I have never had in sufficient quantity since I have been here. . . . I will tell you that story when I come home this summer.

Samuel Emlen wrote to his father in August 1877 from Pagosa Spring, Colorado, with a similar request. "I dislike very much to breach this subject of money to you, especially as I know in what position you are financially at this time. Yet I don't see what else I can do. I don't see the least chance in the world for making a raise here. Nor of getting anything to do that would keep me here. In case you see a way out of the difficulty. I suppose a draft on Denver would be the best way to send the money. I could negotiate that."

For some men, the way to success was through teamwork. When the seemingly impossible happened—trails carved across Appalachia, the Missouri navigated, the Rockies conquered, the transcontinental railroad built—such efforts were evident. "It was a busy and lively sight," wrote Ferguson, a young surveyor, helping lay the Union Pacific line in1865. Bright campfires, busy troopers, the men sweating with picks, shovels, wheelbarrows, teams and scrapers, plowing and filling and laying out the grade for the track, caught his fancy. He was a part of history, part of an effort that brought together hundreds of young Irish from New York and other eastern cities and young Civil War veterans. The gold boom enticed men to work together. Colorado's California Gulch was bone dry, the nearest stream was five miles distant, and in order to sluice gold, each miner had to cooperate, working on the ditch one day per week, thus putting a thousand men to work each day—a tremendous undertaking. Throughout, they made joking fun of one another, anything to keep spirits up. "The miners are like little boys, who can hardly wait to share their secrets with others. . . . They all had a good time making fun of me and slanging all I said for two or three weeks, then it began to die out and we were all soon passably good friends," wrote H. C. Bailey in 1853.

Danger drew together the disparate, the rowdy, the crazed, and the sound, as well as men of sundry energies and talents. Assembled might be a fast runner, a good shot, a navigator, one fearless in rough water, another intrepid when it came to heights; skills were endless and wide-ranging. Men at risk respected the partners who saw them through. To hoist a drowning man from a roiling cataract created instant kinship, apparent in the Lewis and Clark party, whose members meshed like smooth running gears as the disciplined unit crossed the continent with rifles and a vision, managing, cooperatively, to survive each grueling day with "a great deal of Satisfaction," as noted by Joseph Whitehouse in 1804. With every day that they remained alive, the members were "all chearful and in good spirits."

Although early frontiersmen were illiterate, some overland travelers, homesteaders, and miners were literate enough to know they were a part of history and recorded their impressions for future generations. They rarely wrote of their feelings. More often it was a constant tracking of route and weather, faithfully entered in diaries and daybooks. "To-day I bought this book, in which I intend to note down, from time to time, such happenings as may seem to have some meaning for the future," wrote Henry Brokmeyer in 1856. "I thought I would put down the thoughts and happenings as they occur, for I have not time to sort them, and yet I want to preserve them for my own use." Men were shy of their companions, determined to be seen as strong and successful, and would never show their journals to anyone unless they were filled strictly with travel details, the categorization of flora, supply lists, directions, map coordinates, and descriptions of terrain. "At 3 p.m. the therm was at 55 degrees, and at 8 pm In the Evening 28-degrees. The day has been very fine mild and of an agreeable temperature," William Dunbar noted. At night the journal keeper hunkered quietly over his task, the pages lit by flickering firelight, every nuance of a limited education strained to write about his role in history. Pens flew as men turned pensive or romantic, combing their impressions for suitable sentiments or often spicing up their musings with lyrical verse "borrowed" from popular poets of the day. In polite society, men were judged on clever, graceful words, and every heartfelt lyric was seen as marvelous, particularly if self-composed. The desire to communicate touched everyone,

and even the barely literate kept faithful, if slightly misspelled, accounts. "I am writing a lot more in this diary than when I started it," California gold prospector Carlisle Abbot shyly admitted. "And saying things I would not care to have anybody read. I think I will burn it up soon. . . ." Abbot's need to record far outweighed any embarrassment at his grammatical shortcomings or even a loathing to make known his apparent sentimentality. Like others, he understood that he was a part of history, and he wanted to commemorate the event.

Men often kept small diaries, one for each year, adding daily descriptions. Enciphered diaries were secret chronicles, kept private by their authors through the use of codes. Often the most encoded

Introduction

21

diaries held nothing more secret than details of an errant sex life, as did those of William Thomas Prestwood, a southern gentleman of the planter class who settled on the Pee Dee River in upper South Carolina and kept thirty-three diaries over his lifetime. From 1783 to 1859 he recorded his activities: He taught school; surveyed land; wrote deeds, wills, letters, and sermons; mapped the area of Macon County, North Carolina; fiddled at dances; pulled flax; kept daily meteorological records; dug graves; studied nature; studied Greek, astronomy, navigation, and the use of logarithms; shucked corn; made tool handles; taught singing; served on juries; tanned leather; rolled logs; picked cotton; mined gold; split rails for "worm" fences; carved gravestones; and was elected as a county surveyor. He was also a compulsive and insatiable lover who finally married and raised a family of six boys and one girl but still continued extramarital escapades.

"Work was the order of the day," wrote Hubert Howe Bancroft. "Work, by which means alone men can be men . . . by which alone there can be culture, development, or a human species fit to live on this earth." In fact, a man's work granted recognition. He was known by his labor, his dependability, his ability to get things done.

↛ ↛ ↚ ↚

THERE ARE TWO kinds of people: those who like the sheltered life and those who cannot endure it; those who think the world as they know it is well enough and those who dream of something better or, at any rate, something different. The men of the West were the latter restless ones. Drawn by land, by the possibility of making it rich, or just by temperament, they all had their singular reasons to leave home, but they jointly left their mark on their creation of a place that is both physically real and the product of legend.

Part 1

ON THE MOVE

Photo on previous page: Hunter, Colorado, ca. 1900s. Photo by Collier.

1

THE BUCKSKIN BRIGADE

❖❖

I worked with my hands till the bears got fat, and then I turned out to hunting, to lay in a supply of meat.—*Davy Crockett*

✦

The solitary Trapper . . . sits under the shade of a spreading pine whistling blank verse and beating time to the tune with a whip . . . while musing. . . .—*Osborne Russell*

✦

If we lived through a few more days in this awe-inspiring country, it was going to make a mountain man of me yet.—*Andrew Garcia*

✦

The ordinary food of a trapper is corn and buffaloe-tallow . . . [but often] he is forced to devour his peltry and gnaw his moccasins.—*James Hall*

T HE EARLY FUR traders, mountain men, and trappers were the first Americans to make their homes in the West. They were a rowdy and fearless bunch, alcohol-soaked, pleasure-loving coureurs de bois, or free traders, who plied the Indians with firewater and delighted in firing their muskets aimlessly into the air while ridiculing all easterners, the "dressy polite people" at the heart of civilized America, said Philip St. George Cooke.

A motley and bedraggled crew, many had honed their skills in the deep gloom of the Alleghenies in the 1830s, long before civilization's push farther west. The winding paths and deep ravines of these mysterious mountains proved irresistible to them. Like Daniel Boone, they craved nature's solitude and fled at the first curl of chimney smoke, the telltale sign of an encroaching neighbor. Not just skittish about civilization, they were also enterprising businessmen, often fur company employees, and, like Daniel Boone, employees of land-speculating companies, sent to move the frontier back through the Ohio Valley to the Old Northwest and beyond.

In pre–Civil War years only canoes and flatboats had navigated as far north as Lake Erie; the entire western half of the continent was virtually unknown. Eager to trap, explore, and risk danger, the mountain men bushwhacked their way across recondite terrain, blazing trails into the upper Missouri and, farther, into Oregon and California. The distances covered in a three-month spring or fall hunt in the 1830s might be thousands of miles.

Many were ex-army scouts and spies, who had learned to shoot, wrestle, duck, dodge, paddle, swim, and zing tomahawks through the air with split-second speed and accuracy. During the Indian wars of 1798 to 1865, the forests north of the Ohio teemed with Shawnees, Delawares, Wyandots, and Miamis, or Maumees, and a

drinking grog, re-creating the wild abandon of their boyhoods in the backwoods. Wiry as brambles, they could march for days through unbroken wilderness with scarce water and a handful of parched corn for food, existing without game, since a rifle crack in the silent forest could alert Indians.

They were gaudily attired, encased in well-greased deerskin shirts and sporting bright handkerchiefs, and their usual armament was a Kentucky rifle, the first small-caliber American firearm, so long its barrel swung crazily from side to side when aimed at game 150 yards distant. Laden with bullet molds, powder horns, tinderboxes, razor-like axes, and gleaming knives, good trappers, like a traveling tinker, were always prepared. Trapper Osborne Russell, writing in 1853, described the trappers' needs:

> Six Beaver traps a blanket with an extra pair of Mocasins his powder horn and bullet pouch with a belt to which is attached a butcher Knif a small wooden box containing bait for Beaver a Tobacco sack with a pipe and implements for making fire with sometimes a hatchet fastened to the Pommel of his saddle his personal dress is a flannel or cotton shirt (if he is fortunate enough to obtain one, if not Antelope skin answers the purpose of over or under shirt) a pair of leather breeches with Blanket or Buffaloe skins with his long hair falling loosely over his shoulders completes his uniform.

So provisioned, they bartered and bestowed trinkets, keeping up a steady flow of hardtack, powder, lead, and liquor to smooth commerce with the local tribes. Saving enough alcohol for barter after their own personal consumption posed a problem. At the annual trappers' rendezvous at Henry's Fork on the Green River, it was a "riotous debauch," "one continued scene of drunkenness, gambling, and brawling and fighting, as long as the money and the credit of the trappers last," wrote the frontier traveler George Frederick Ruxton. The maxim if "one Small drink would Stimulate the whole Sistom, imagine the joys of a full cask" was often heard. At Fort Simpson, part of the Hudson's Bay Company, alcoholic revelry broke out in occasional "small wars," according to the company's daybooks. "Outside the locked gates there were milling Indians and muskets, knives

Father Shepherd, the hermit; an old resident of Colorado, near Telluride.

good scout had to be more stealthy than his enemy, keeping keen track of fresh footprints, alert to the click of a cocked gun, the fear of ambush always in mind. Bravery was key; the mountain man had to nerve himself to wheel suddenly when pursued by Indians and take direct aim, hoping the Indians would scatter even though his gun might lack ammunition. Mountain men also were competitive, fueled by regional jealousies. Men from Pennsylvania or Kentucky vied wildly with one another, shooting, tossing, running, lifting, and

and pike poles. There were whoops and yells and attempts to batter down the fence. Then the fort was demolished by means of that twenty-five gallon barrel of rum." Huge tankards of potent backwoods concoctions, tangleleg and tarantula juice, flowed freely, the latter favored by everyone—trappers and Indians—and highly intoxicating. The "juice" was two quarts of alcohol, a few burned peaches, and a plug of black tobacco, fermented and fortified with red pepper and served up with another frontier favorite, boudins, briefly roasted buffalo intestines, still warm from the kill, the odiferous contents slightly fermenting. Revelries broke forth wherever the mountain men gathered, but no stopover had the same cachet as Brown's Hole, a bar built in 1822 at the confluence of Wyoming, Colorado, and Utah, where a yearly "Great Rendezvous" drew men from all over the West who spent their profits of $130 a year to drink, gamble, regale one another with stories, fight, and shed drunken tears over such deep concepts as loss, beauty, and life itself.

Best known of the early explorers were William Clark and Meriwether Lewis, America's greatest pathfinders, who left St. Louis in May 1804 and traveled by keel boat and pirogue up the Missouri River, determined to find a northwest passage, a series of rivers that would traverse the mountains to the Pacific Ocean. As the first white men to travel the western half of North America, they floated, portaged, and bushwhacked eight thousand miles in twenty-eight months, losing only one of their thirty-three-man party, the Corps of Discovery. The exploit carried out the mandate of President Jefferson: to extend the boundaries of the American fur trade, to discover and catalog the geography of yet unclaimed reaches of the continent before the Spanish or the French.

Lewis and Clark were educated men, who had honed their backwoods skills traipsing through the scrub wilderness surrounding their family plantations in Virginia. Although more tame than the bear-infested Northwest, the dense thickets and uncharted terrain gave both men backwoods savvy. As military men, backwoodsmen, and gentlemen they were a rare combination for the times.

The success of the expedition threw open the West for exploration by wild and free backwoodsmen such as Jim Beckwourth, Jedediah Smith, Bill Sublette, and Kit Carson, who bushwhacked, portaged, floated, and rode into the wilderness, from Canada to Montana and beyond. Prim admonitions against crossing the Rockies only fueled their urge to roam, and hunters, adventurers, wanderers, and trappers straggled toward the flanks of the Wind River range and beyond, to the dark, towering lofts of the Rocky Mountains, a hulk of granite guarding the nation's four great rivers—the Missouri, the Platte, the Columbia, and the Colorado.

The wilderness invited a steady stream of misogynists, misfits, and flint-eyed loners, mainly Scotch-Irish backwoodsmen bent on seizing an empire from the Indians and avoiding the snares of settled society. The exploits of these unruly hordes shocked and titillated the populations of Europe and the East Coast. So recondite were these scraggly men, so far from the pale of refined interaction, that their bearded, shaggy images and rowdy reputations earned them the term "savages" in the popular press. They were, wrote British traveler James Hall, "rude, fierce and repulsive" and stirred up endless antagonism by their apparent cruelty. They seemed, in fact, like backwoods monstrosities, their vices grossly exaggerated in novels, travel books, and folktales. They were "children of Nature," as well as "good hunters . . . capable of bearing bodily fatigue in pretty considerable degree," although "very similar in habits and manners to the aborigines. . . . They fight for the most trifling provocations, or even sometimes without any. . . . Their hands, teeth, knees, head and feet are their weapons, not only in boxing with their fists . . . but also tearing, kicking, scratching, biting, gouging each others eyes out by a dexterous use of a thumb or finger, and doing their utmost to kill each other, even when rolling over one another on the ground."

Their scrawled accounts tell stories of great cruelty and prejudice—so much so that many of them died violently and early, their passing marked by only the wry eulogy "Gone under, maybe."

꙳　꙳　꙳

LIKE NATTY BUMPPO, the Daniel Boone–like character in the *Leatherstocking Tales,* the mountain men passed back and forth between civilization and the wilderness, marking both environs by rude comments, hawked tobacco, and endless rounds of alcohol. With packs stuffed with pelts and trinkets for trade, they sold the valuable skins to agents who shipped them east via the interior river routes or through the port of New Orleans. "We were in a sort of panic," recalled roving trapper John Young Nelson, "yet went in for enjoying ourselves thoroughly." Often the panic was a series of grueling days. For example, one morning in 1824, on a typical beaver-trapping expedition, James O. Pattie's group "scrambled along under the cliffs, sometimes upon our hands and knees, through a thick tangle of grapevines and underbrush," crisscrossing one river thirty-six times. Often hungry, Pattie and his fellow trappers melted away into mere skeletons, moving "slowly and painfully." Starving, they devoured the last beaver, killed a buzzard, and enjoyed a lone sea otter for both breakfast and supper. "One morning we killed a raven, which we cooked for seven men. It was unsavory flesh in itself, and would hardly have afforded a meal for one hungry man. The miserable conditions of our company may be imagined, when seven hungry men, who had not eaten a full meal for ten days, were all obliged to breakfast on this nauseous bird."

Wiry and hardened, like Osborne Russell, they claimed to go "for 65 days without eating." They strode over passes and peaks, melting snow in their hats for water and huddling at night in the still-steaming carcass of a slain elk or buffalo to keep warm, calling it "tolerably comfortable." Keen-eyed and wary, with skins as cracked and furrowed as buffalo hides, trappers were physically rock hard, despite a penchant for fever, colds, intestinal disease, and the incessant racking up of knife wounds and bullet holes. Trapper John Young Nelson was typically sanguine at a self-inflicted wound. He had fumbled his own revolver and shot himself through the left wrist. The bullet traveled up through his mouth and lodged in the frontal bone that shaped the forehead. Alarmed but still in control, he took a deep breath, sneezed, and caught the bullet as it fell out.

Grizzlies roused from the berry bushes raged as they treed the terrified men, seemingly impervious to the hail of frantic musket shot. Yet the survivors were matter-of-fact. Philip St. George Cooke laconically noted in his journal, "I find the curiosity of our men with respect to this animal pretty much satisfied." To John Young Nelson, "the flesh of the animal was highly relished," and he and his party "feasted on it until nothing but the bones was left." Bears, as well as Indians, were the stuff of the fur-trading frontier, and any man who ventured west must be prepared. "That I had 'bear fright' goes without saying," wrote hunter John R. Cook. Mountain man Pattie, exploring the upper Mis-

souri (western Kansas) in the 1820s, "counted, in the course of the day, two hundred and twenty white bears (grizzlies)." On one expedition, trapper Peter Lebeck, slightly inebriated and accompanied by Delaware Indians, crossed paths with a huge grizzly wolfing down a pile of acorns. Startled, Lebeck hesitated too long and was grabbed in a death grip. The tree beneath which he was buried is inscribed, "Peter Lebeck killed by a bear Oct. 17, 1837."

For the earliest trappers, bears were terrifyingly common. The single shot made before reloading had to be deadly accurate, striking directly through the brain, or else mayhem ensued. A good day was a day without a grizzly confrontation, but most days in the early West proved bad indeed. To Pattie, "the next moment would bring us face to face with a bear, which might accost us suddenly." Once he saw a "bear devouring a horse, still alive," and shot the bear, wounding him. He also witnessed a bear attacking a man. The other men with him tried to free the man from this terrifying attack:

The enraged bear . . . tore up the ground around him with his claws. Some of the men came so near, that the animal saw them, and made toward them. They all fired at him but did not touch him. All now fled from the furious animal, as he seemed intent on destroying them. In this general flight one of the men was caught. As he screamed out in his agony, I, happening to have reloaded my gun, ran up to relieve him. I placed the muzzle of my gun against the bear, and discharging it, killed him. Our companion was literally torn to pieces. The flesh on his hip was torn off, leaving the sinews bare, by the teeth of the bear. His side was so wounded in three places that his breath came through the openings; his head was dreadfully bruised, and his jaw broken. His breath came out from both sides of his windpipe. . . .

Besides bears, the mountain men shared the wilderness with the Indians. Trappers might barter with them, in one case, noted by John Young Nelson, using a "tin pannikin holding about two-thirds of a pint" of whiskey as the standard measure. Everything was calculated by the pannikin—so many cups of coffee or alcohol for so many buffalo robes.

A natural sympathy sprang up between the coureurs de bois and

the Indians. "From the moment they came into camp they exercised a charm over me . . . and I determined at all risks to [live] among them," said John Young Nelson. So taken was he that he strolled into an encampment of four hundred Sioux, picked a tepee and walked in to seat himself in front of Spotted Tail, the chief of the tribe. Unaware of his gaffe, Nelson simply sat. He refused to leave until finally giving up, the Sioux offered him a blanket. Charmed, he followed the Indians on their wanderings and was formally adopted as Sioux.

Mountain man Jim Beckwourth and his companion, Harris, were starving to death in the Platte River wilderness in Arkansas in 1823 until rescued by Crow Indians. "I had not proceeded half a mile ere I . . . saw two Indians approaching with demonstrations of friendship. I explained to them that [we] were nearly starved to death. One started off like a race horse along the trail . . . after about three hours the rattling of hoofs was heard, and we discovered a troop of Indians approaching at full speed. They brought with them a portion

The Buckskin

Brigade

29

Unidentified cowboy, ca. 1900s.

of light food of corn meal made into a kind of gruel, of which they would give us but a small spoonful at short intervals."

Beckwourth later became an adopted Crow Indian. He wintered with them in the Wind River Mountains and persuaded them not to attack Americans. "I saved more life and property for the white man than a whole regiment of United States Regulars could have done in the same time."

Part of life's lesson in the wilderness was tolerance, particularly when it came to coexistence with the Native American. In the mountain "schoolroom," men who were generally ignorant, steeped with prejudice, and spoiling for trouble learned, over time, that existence often meant dependence, most particularly upon Indian women, who comforted and cooked for them, bore their children, and served as a connection to family members who knew the prime trapping areas, were skilled hunters, and often would do the white man's trapping for him in the winter.

William Clark had anticipated meeting "warlike nations of savages, of gigantic stature, fierce, treacherous and cruel; and particularly hostile to white men." But the drowsy Mandan settlement of the Dakotas proved less than formidable. Pity sprang up as he saw the children's ailments; he treated one boy's abscess, another, whose "feet [were] frosed." He gave one Indian, feverish with smallpox, tiny bites of stewed fruit and tea, and one with pleurisy, he sweated and bled. In 1806, Clark treated the small son of their Indian guide and companion Sacagawea: "[He] is dangerously ill. His jaw and throat is much swelled. We apply a poltice of onions, after giving him some creem of tartar &c. This day proved to be fine and fair which afforded us an opportunity of drying of baggage which had gotten a little wet." After a few weeks Clark could feel relieved that the various treatments were working. "The Child is recovering fast. I applied a plaster of sarve [salve] made of the rozen of the long leafed pine, Beaswax and Bears oil mixed which has subsided the inflammation entirely, the part is considerably swelled and hard."

Mountaineer James O. Pattie, was "afflicted with pity and horror" when a marauding tribe of Pawnees started to burn a young Indian captive. The child was too small to be dangerous and too trivial as a means of revenge; why not sell the boy to him? Pattie "showed . . . a roll of bright red cloth" and offered the Indians ten yards. Grudgingly the child was released. Puzzled, the Pawnees wondered at Pattie's odd behavior. Why bother to save a child? What was his motivation?

→ → ← ←

THE WRITINGS OF the frontiersmen often reveal shy and sentimental leanings, fierce loyalty to fellow trappers, courage, thriftiness, and a surprising lyricism when it came to nature's bounty. "I was upwards of 6,000 ft. above the level of the lake," wrote trapper Osborne Russell, and "below me was a dark abyss silent as the night of Death. I set and smoked my pipe for about an hour and then laid down and slept until near daylight—My Chief object in Sleeping at this place was to take a view of the lake when the Sun arose in the Morning." Russell would detour miles out of his way to admire a sunset or view a natural wonder. Philip St. George Cooke, part of a military group sent to protect the trappers' trade routes in the early 1800s, saw a landscape "where grandeur is softened by beauty." Jedediah Smith, religious and brooding, found biblical inspiration in wild and tangled nature and quieted himself by psalms while his rowdy companions caroused and fell unconscious from bouts of tangleleg, the potent drink with pepper and rum. "I saw a number of Goslings to day on the Shore," mused William Clark, struck when he "walked to the hill, from the top of which I had a butifull prospect of Serounding country." John R. Cook "saw four beavers" while lost in the outback of New Mexico. "They were disporting in the stream, and seemed as delighted as little children could be when the first snowflakes of the season came." Andrew Garcia "kept getting all the more joyful" as he traveled. "I began to think I was a combined lark and nightengale. I started to liven up the surrounding country [the Musselshell River] with my melody." Mountain men were simply entranced by the beauty of the unfettered wilderness.

Yet in this wilderness, hostile Indians lay in wait, determined to keep their hold on their land and push back the intruding white armies. Osborne Russell, surrounded by eighty armed and furiously firing Blackfeet Indians, lived to describe his ordeal:

We were completely surrounded we cock[ed] our rifles and started thro their ranks into the woods which seemed to be com-

Hunters with mountain lion, ca. 1915.

pletely filled with Blackfeet who rent the air with their horrid yells, on presenting our rifles they opened a space about 20 ft. wide thro which we plunged about the fourth jump an arrow struck White on the right hip joint I hastily told him to pull it out and as I spoke another arrow struck me in the same place but they did not retard our progress. At length another arrow striking thro My right leg above the knee benumbed the flesh so that I fell with my breast across a log. The Indian who shot me was within 8 ft. and made a Spring towards me with his uplifted battle axe. I made a leap and avoided the blow and kept hopping from log to log through. A shower of arrows flew around us like hail, lodging in the pines and logs. After we had passed them about 10 paces we wheeled about and took [aim] at them. . . . I was very faint from the loss of blood and we set down among the logs determined to kill the two foremost when they came.

Mountain men, no matter how rough, were deeply loyal, going to any means to protect a friend as well as to offer kindness to strangers. Although a mountain man might plunge directly into debauchery, he was loath to lie or show meanness of spirit, both unthinkable offenses in the West's "unwritten code." Nor would a mountaineer invade private property, even a humble campfire, without asking. In the mountains, a man's cookpot defined his temporary property, and visitors had to pull up fifty feet short and shout out loud before advancing.

Abandoned sites, however, were approached by a different etiquette. "We were soaking wet and half-frozen and it was almost dark when we reached the mouth of Slate Creek," recalled Osborne Russell. "By good fortune we found a big log cabin on the flat, locked up and nobody at home. It was no time to stand on ceremony, so we broke open the dooor and took possession." With "plenty to eat, a good fire, a tight shanty, and room for all" they were safe from driving sleet, shrieking wind, and crashing, falling trees. The next day they composed a written apology to the cabin's owner; the code must be followed. "[We] gave out names, address and why we burst [the cabin] open."

An occupied cabin, on the other hand, assured hospitality. A log house, usually cramped and small as a shed, "would always admit one more to share in all the comforts," recalled James Haines of Illinois. "I guess we stopped at forty cabins [and] never failed to get an invitation to grub, never were allowed to pay a cent, and I want too put it down right here that bigger hearted, more generous or more hospitable men than there are in the mountains never lived on earth."

A British traveler to early Ohio was offered hospitality by a "half-naked, ill-looking fellow" who took James Hall to a cabin "of the earnest kind, consisting of a single apartment constructed of logs, which contained a family of seven or eight souls. After drinking a bowl of milk . . . I asked to know his charge for ferrying Me over the water, to which he good humouredly replied, that he 'never took money for helping a traveler on his way.' 'Then let me pay you for your milk.' 'I never sell milk.' 'But,' said I, urging him, 'I would rather pay you, I have money enough.' 'Well,' said he, 'I have milk enough, so we're even; I have as good a right to give you milk as you have to give me money.' "

Hospitality, bravery, compassion: sometimes they all ran together and seemed the same or separated out, like flat cream, leaving men conflicted and edgy about the true nature of their obligations. One truth, however, prevailed: To give was to get, and the life saved today might be a man's own tomorrow. Ideally, the strong helped out others, as when a backwoods Samaritan, welcome as an angel, appeared to William Timmons, who lay half frozen, dying of exposure, and hopelessly lost. Somehow his horse had made it to a remote mountain cabin, stopped, and allowed Timmons to slide out of the saddle.

An old trapper with long white whiskers came out and looked at me. Without asking a question he took me into a spare room where there were a few sacks of feed and, on them, some empty feed sacks and horse blankets. He made a bed and took off my calfskin coat, overshoes and boots. Next he massaged my face, nose, ears and feet. He handed me a little coffee [before] he went out and took care of Buck. Then, after assuring me that my horse was all right he said, "I can't take you to the fire—heat drives frost in. I don't know where you are frozen. But I've got some beaver oil—it draws out the frost. I'll rub you with it."

He did—first face and ears, then hands and feet, till my body had been oiled from head to foot and I went to sleep. In a few hours he woke me. He had killed snowbirds and made a little broth. That and coffee were all he gave me until the next afternoon, when I had a coffee-soaked sour-dough biscuit and sugar. Later he gave me some root tea; he said he always had some to keep his own system in shape.

After I'd been oiled for forty-eight hours he put me in his room and bed and let me eat solid food. For two weeks I stayed with the trapper—doing as he said. He was an old frontiersman, that doctor, and he knew just what to do. I came out of it without any ill effects, and I was a more steadfast believer in prayer [after].

Mountain men who admired the Indians were saddened by their constant ill-treatment. "When I first joined this band [of Paiutes]," wrote John Young Nelson, "I found them a set of innocent, harmless children. When I left them they were, as I have said, completely demoralized, and the result was brought about by that arch-fiend, drink. For this they have to thank the white traders, who cheated them out of all their hard-earned savings in the way of skins and other products for this vile compound, the ruin of their homes, the cause of much heartache, illness, trouble and death."

"Innocent" and "harmless" they might be, but Young had no trouble scalping a Ute Indian he had killed when challenged to do so by two Canadian trappers. "I am not particularly squeamish, but I must confess it was with no feelings of pleasure that I set about the task. . . . I made a fearful mess of my initial subject. The great knack is to get the scalp-lock away from the skull, and this is only to be done . . . by making a deep incision with a sharp knife round the base of the lock, twisting [it] round the wrist, then giving it a strong jerk, when it comes away readily enough. . . . I had seen the Sioux lift scalps over and over again; but I had never had the curiosity to watch them sufficiently close to acquire the artistic touch necessary."

⤞ ⤞ ⤝ ⤝

THE MOUNTAIN MEN were the earliest white men to go west in numbers. But their time had to pass. Ever changeable, the wilderness shrank, and the demand for furs diminished, forcing the trappers

from the beaver trade into riding for the pony express, hunting buffalo, trading with Indians, stealing horses, and occasionally becoming lawmen. Some married, some moved, and many worked as guides or bullwhackers, but most, like John Young Nelson, found that working in town, "tied up like a hobbled horse," was a threat to their restless spirits. Even though time passed pleasantly, he could take no more. "I used to look out over the prairie and wish myself upon it," Nelson said. "At length I could stand it no longer, and I told Ackley I must leave him, as indoor life did not agree with me. . . . I told him I was sorry to go, but I should go mad if I stayed." Jim Beckwourth returned—briefly—to his family in St. Louis: "All my clothing consisted of dressed antelope deer, and the skins of mountain sheep, highly ornamented by my Indian wives. My long [black] hair descended to my hips, and I presented more the appearance of a Crow than that of a civilized being. My sister gazed at me for a moment with a searching look, and then exclaimed, my God, it is my brother!"

To some, the wilderness was impenetrable and bewildering, without familiar signs or markings. But as the frontier progressed, a maze of trails and tracks, some indistinguishable from animal tracks, crisscrossed the West. Outfits of trappers, soldiers, hunters, and adventurers crossed up the Panhandle into central-west Texas to the Clear Fork of the Brazos; from the Staked Plains down to the Rio Grande in New Mexico or north to the Arkansas River.

Settlements spread through the thick, majestic woodlands of the Alleghenies as eighteenth-century settlers pushed west. The forest was one to be destroyed since its foliage hid lurking dangers, was home to wild animals, and was a barrier to cultivating the land. The mountain men shunned this vision; it physically sickened them to see the bare clearings and ramshackle log cabins.

The trappers were part of a far-reaching economic enterprise: fur trade and land speculation. But as explorers they opened the entire region beyond the Mississippi, thus allowing the wealth of the continent to be tapped. They became a colorful part of American folklore and helped guide the government in its westward explorations. In essence, they opened the West to the domesticity they wanted to leave behind.

2

WAGONS WEST!

MEN ON THE OVERLAND CROSSING

Traveling with a family across this American desert is the very hardest business I have ever followed.—*Richard Martin May*

✦

My genius certainly does not lie in driving oxen nor have I as yet been able to find in what it does lie.—*Hugh Brown Helskell*

✦

We were bewildered for a long time. . . . Finally we concluded that we should . . . pursue a straight course west by the compass.
—*John D. Young*

✦

Very often we could not tell whether [the trails] were made by deer or Christians."—*John D. Young*

A S WHITE-TOPPED wagons crossed the bleak and solitary plains, it seemed as if the entire East Coast were changing locale, first heading across the Alleghenies, then veering off toward the Great Plains, pausing briefly at the Rocky Mountains before striking out for the Pacific coast. "Roads were crowded with emigrants of every description," noted British traveler James Hall, amazed at the steady stream of travelers jostling down trails and byways of the Allegheny Mountains in the 1820s. "Now a gang of forty or fifty souls, men, women and children; and now a solitary pedestrian, with his oaken staff, his bottle, and his napsack; and once a day, a stage-load of tired travelers, dragged heavily towards the west . . . half-clad beings, of every age and sex, slowly winding up the mountain path . . . [like] gipsy bands."

Overland parties of the 1840s, bound for California and Oregon, were far more organized. Guidebooks proliferated, listing routes, time schedules, needed supplies, maps, and the dangers of a journey once known only to fur traders and scouts. Wagon-bound emigrants would forge twenty miles a day for three months, at best. "A Company is now being formed at Fayetteville, Arkansas, consisting of Vigorous, Enterprising and Substantial citizens of Washington and adjoining counties with the intention of paying a visit to the gold mines of California and securing a portion of the rich deposits of that region," announced the *Arkansas State Democrat* on February 9, 1849.

"We are now eight teams in company," wrote traveler Edmund Booth at the beginning of his passage in 1849. "All from Dubuque, and Jackson & Jones counties. Eighteen men, four women, two small children, and over eighty head of cattle . . . yesterday we had a bad hill to climb up. We put on five to eight yoke to each wagon and it reminded me of cattle climbing a tree. . . ."

The trains traveled various routes. The mountains of southern

"Westward Ho." Photo by Snelson.

Arizona, seldom blocked by snow, were more navigable than the high passes of the Rocky Mountains, and many followed this, the Gila Trail, from New Mexico to the banks of the Colorado River. The Cherokee Trail, approximately thirteen hundred miles long, threaded its way through Arkansas, Missouri, and Oklahoma to converge at the Neosho River and, after crossing two-thirds of Kansas and Wyoming, tied the historic Santa Fe Trail to the Oregon-California Trail, the gold seeker's highway from 1849 through 1862. Other wanderers, California bound, sailed around Cape Horn, disembarked, and jogged by muleback over slippery, tropical mountain passes to Panama, where they sailed on to California. The tropics proved menacing: ovenlike heat, malaria-carrying mosquitoes, intestinal maladies, and attacks by outlaws. Going to California was no easy task, no matter how it was done.

Emigrants generally followed a guide, someone who had made the trip before and was judged honorable and dependable and able to anticipate danger. "One slight error of judgment has resulted in the massacre of several hundred people," wrote Oliver Nelson. "A guide must be always on the alert, and . . . know by intuition the state of the surrounding country, the proximity of an enemy."

Horses, mules, or oxen pulled wagons that weighed over a thousand pounds, each laden with clothes, furniture, quilts, pillows, tools, and food—a hundred or more pounds of flour and bacon, ten pounds of coffee, and hefty supplies of sugar, salt, crackers, beans, candles, jerked meat, and grains. The traveler needed a "good medium two-horse wagon, with wooden or wrought iron axles—no cast iron or pot-metal spindles—falling tongue, and two lock chains," for reasons cited by Colorado-bound John D. Young: "Oh the hardships of going up and down those bluffs I shall never forget. We had to use double teams going up hill and then take hold of the wagons and help. Every ten yards we would block the wheels and take a breathing spell and so on resting at intervals till at last we gained the top feeling very thankful indeed." "A day's travel," wrote William Byers and John H. Kellom in their *Hand Book to the Gold Fields of Nebraska and Kansas,* "should commence from six to seven o'clock a.m., continue five hours, rest two, again travel five hours, and camp for the night. Of course this rule cannot always be adhered to, but it should be so far as practicable. Don't travel Sundays. Your cattle need rest, and so do you."

A community of twenty-five Trappist monks and eleven students, fleeing French oppression, migrated to Cahokia, Illinois, to settle on four hundred acres of land, donated by a wealthy citizen. Dom Urban Guillet, like others, found the trail daunting:

We left Kentucky by land, to the number of three religious, eight children and their teacher, and forty animals—horses, oxen, and

cows. . . . The weather was very fine for three weeks, but so hot that the dust and the scarcity of water made us suffer very much. Our best horses became ill upon leaving and remained two days lying down without eating or drinking. Towards the middle of our trip several of our mounts tired out, developed saddle sores and refused to give further service, thus forcing us, one after another, to walk. A wheel broke into twelve pieces. Twice the wagon was upset by the terrible roads and once it broke down. A large number of rascals going to Louisiana often accompanied us. They stole from us when they could and they dried up the springs. Their animals, to which they could give no grain, fell on ours during the night. The peasants along the road here and there seemed to have

given one another the word to sell their supplies at three times the value. These delays . . . so exhausted our purse that at the end of the trip we were reduced to dividing one small biscuit among four and I lacked nine sous to pay for crossing the river. . . . Finally without bread or money, we arrived at Cahokia.

Wear and tear were anticipated, but ingenuity was needed to keep clothes from falling into rags and tatters. "I have worn one hole in my Pants; and I must git Some Buck Skin and Patch them," wrote a worried James Sawyer Crawford in 1849. The aforementioned *Hand Book to the Gold Fields of Nebraska and Kansas,* 1859, noted: "Your ruffled shirts, standing collars and all kinds of fine clothing had better be left in your trunk, or wardrobe at home . . . adapt yourself at once to woolen and leather; provide yourself with woolen under-clothes, woolen overshirts . . . woolen shirts. . . . You are going to a region of the country where the rise and fall of temperature in the twenty-four hours is great."

By day the emigrants sweltered; by night they tossed with fears and longings. "I have thought more about home since last night than I have during the same period of time since I left. I dreamed of home last night. Saw friends—but this morning sorrow returned and the voice in my dreaming ear melted away," wrote William H. Quesen-bury. What they faced was a world so unfamiliar that comprehension faltered. Gone were the well-watered slopes of the East, replaced by bleached plains and deserts so vast that no figure could be seen, and nothing heard but awesome silence. Breathtaking and lonely, it was a new kind of vista, in which pure joy came from traveling in the shadow of towering peaks, beneath scattered clouds. "Oh, what a solitude," cried Israel Lord. "Not a bird or beast or sign of one. Not even a cricket or a worm." John R. Cook, bound from Santa Fe to Bean Creek, a tributary of the Rio Grande, in 1874, exclaimed: "The mountains were grand! The scenery sublime and awe-inspiring! Near . . . camp was a place where we could gather mountain dewberries and huckleberries at the same time. Not more than fifty feet away we could make snowballs and [throw them] at the saucy magpies. We had grass in abundance for our saddle-horses and pack burros," while delighting in the "beautiful rivulet bordered with watercress and fringed with quaking-asp." James Sawyer Crawford, in Red-bud Creek, Oklahoma, loved the "world of Prairie; you may See here as far as your eyes will let you look. [It is] butiful."

Everything struck the emigrants as wonderfully foreign, from cougars to stampeding herds of buffalo. Plant life too seemed aston-ishing, from lush wild plums, cherries, and summer grapes to arbors of sheltering willow. Cattail, scouring rush, Mexican poppy, shaggy portulaca, Indian grass, and wild blue rye waved in the wind, fluid as an ocean wave. John Pyeatt, at Echo Summit, Utah, thought it "appierd strange" to be "so near the snow and have grass but this is the case in the valies and on these snow mountains whear the snow is off thear is grass and one of our company says he was whear he could getheer snow with one hand and pluck flowers with the other

the same time." Even starting a fire proved distinctive to overland travelers Overton Johnson and his friend William Winter. They tried the traditional way, with rock and flint, and finally, "after many attempts . . . at length sprinkled powder into the crown of a hat, together with whatever dry combustibles we could find, and dis-charg[ed] a pistol into it. To this we added the dry Willows which we had collected, and soon had a comfortable fire."

Friendships grew in this wild place. The rigors of the trail bred camaraderie. "My room is filled with jolly fellows, laughing, talking, singing & reading poetry aloud," wrote General E. D. Townsend. "Wagons were drawn up by the river-banks in pleasant groves of willow," wrote J. Ross Browne of his emigrant train, camped in Nevada's Ruby Valley. "The camp fires sending up cheerful clouds of smoke, and the merry voices of children making a sweet accord with the lively strains of flute and violin." After supper, William G. John-ston and his party would "while away the tedium of the darkened hours by singing songs."

John D. Young, who thrilled to the outdoors, also enjoyed the warmth of companionship: "We were comparably comfortable. We cooked some fresh venison that we got that day, made some warm biscuit and a good cup of tea and had a most comfortable supper with the storm howling madly around us on the highest range of the Rocky Mountains. After supper we built a huge fire, sat closely around it and enjoyed ourselves by talking and singing for a couple of hours. The time passed as joyous and lighthearted as if we were at a splendid hall in the city."

Camp fare, though simple, seemed delicious. One night Young's party roasted trout, ducks, venison, and buffalo in leftover bacon grease, breathing in the homey scent of the bacon fat. "For dessert [we] made warm biscuits and tea . . . a most comfortable meal."

Israel Lord, traveling with a wagon train and out scouting one night to find water, came across a "grand encampment" in a deep val-ley and gazed down, bewitched by a scene in which "lamps, candles and huge bonfires burned night to day [as] a group was laughing and swearing and gambling, [a]nother trying a criminal for a murder recently committed [and] a hundred males and a half a dozen females [were] dancing cotillion on the base rock to the music of flute and hautboy and clarinet and violin and horn."

Gold fever: prospectors going to a new goldfield, 1889. Photo by J. C. H. Grabill.

At first dawn the camp stirred, men groaned, and figures pulled themselves out of wagons and from sleeping bags. Breakfast now done, the men faced a hard reality. Most of them were amateurs in the saddle, unsure of firearms, insecure about their roles, the route, even their ability to face danger with dignity. Shopkeepers, teachers, and tradesmen had little experience with guns, and few were skilled enough to provide needed game for survival. The myth of the heroic frontiersman was vastly overblown, and many first-time travelers were inept bumblers. "The emigrant will not be counseled by experienced persons," wrote the *Cherokee Advocate,* on October 22, 1849.

"Gun accident—again!" wrote W. G. Johnston in 1849. "John Fuller accidentally shot and killed himself wilst removing a gun from a wagon. The mode was the usual one—the muzzle was towards him, and went off of itself." Later that day he saw a Mr. Harper "putting his pistols into their holsters and discharg[ing] its contents through the palm of his left hand. We dressed the wound as best we could until more skillful surgical attention can be secured." When such legends as General Custer, supposedly a skilled marksman, shot his own horse in a moment of confusion, what was the amateur capable of? Anything, according to emigrant David Demarest. "This morn-

Homesteaders in the Loup Valley, 1886. Photo by Solomon Butcher.

ing I was shot in my right hand by mistake. The ball passed in at the knuckle joint of the first finger and came out below the little finger within an inch of the wrist. We had two Doctors in our party, so I had the best of care."

Guns aside, other dangers lurked for the unlucky or the unwary. "Joe and myself were standing on the feed box, getting down to help the horses. Joe caught his foot in a rope and dove head first into the stream," recounted John D. Young. "The water was as cold as ice and the morning frosty but there was no pity for him, [we] all had a hearty laugh at his expense."

Accidents and poor health were routine, as Oliver Mack Lipe reported in the *Cherokee Advocate* on July 30, 1849. "I have been extremely lucky I have had no accidents. . . . I could have been purfectly happy could my dear family be with me, I am now in perfect health, perfectly well of the fall off my horse and a sore mouth with which I was afflicted for a few days. . . ."

Casualties were multiplied when Indians attacked, a threat that kept every man on edge, particularly those unfamiliar with the terrain, the times, and the temperament of Indians. Emigrant Lorenzo Dow Stephens was nearly paralyzed with terror when a warning sounded and suddenly "Indians began to pour in from different quarters . . . the[y] flocked in, the doors were barred, rifles were ready for the scrap, when a pack train hove in sight." Rather than a dreaded attack, "It was an emigrant train from Arkansaw, and being the first one from that direction, from a distance, it was natural to infer they were Indians."

Along with Indians, oxen and mules were maligned and hated. Diaries were filled with accounts of man versus mule encounters. "The custom of swearing at the mule is often inherited and has become . . . habitual," complained William Haney. "To-day while one of our party was trying to manage a wild mule, the rope slipped out of his hands and caught his feet," wrote David Demarest. "After much exertion on the part of the company, the mule was caught and the poor fellow released." John D. Young "was just dozing off" when he felt a warm breath on his face one night. "I started, opened my eyes instantly and saw a sight that startled me so much that I yelled out. It was the mule looking into my face with his nose just touching mine. The poor fellow wanted companionship but you can-

not imagine how horrible looking it was just as I opened my eyes to see by the bright moonlight his great goggle eyes looking into mine. I gave him a box in the head and sent him off."

Fear, surprise, and misreckoning ruled, causing a passing sentry to be seen as an Indian, or a cow mistaken for a bear. When General E. D. Townsend journeyed through California in 1855, his party was startled awake by the cry "[H]ere's a coyote—he is trying to get in the wagon!" The alarmist, Willie, insisted that a coyote lurked behind the wagon wheel. When Townsend stoked up the fire, light flickered over the scene. "I asked him if he saw the coyote still & he said 'yes, right by the wheel!' I then discovered that he wanted me to shoot one of our best mules, which was lying very quietly to rest himself with his head near the ground. Being of a grey color, his head did look, with its long ears, something like a coyote." But the scare unsettled Willie, who asked for a revolver "to protect himself from all ravenous beasts." He was soundly refused.

＋　＋　＋

LIKE TRAVELING VILLAGES, each train instituted its own rules and command. Leaders sprang up, and men were judged as just or just not worth it, depending upon their actions under stress and their general behavior. Because of proximity and interdependence, crimes were addressed quickly; it was unhealthy to let disputes fester. "Thefts are of very rare occurrence," confided John D. Young. "The infliction of immediate punishment . . . is the invariable rule of our society on the plains, the offender being caught is instantly tried by a jury picked upon the road. The witnesses both for and against are heard and if not proved he is discharged . . . if guilty he will be punished according to the enormity of the offense. For horse or mule stealing or murder he is hung to the nearest tree. If a less grievous crime he is tied to a tree or wagon wheel and receives from ten to one hundred lashes on the bare back." In one wagon train dispute, a "Dr. White shot Dr. Tompsons horse. He was a vicious horse . . . and White had told Tompson twice that he was biting & scaring his horse up & that he would not suffer it. . . . [White] shot him just behind the shoulder, and he soon died. Tompson said he would retaliate. White told him, " 'if my horse is a vicious horse doing you any mischief kill him if otherwise & you shoot him you will have to bear the consequences.' "

Group justice, even vigilantism, prevailed, as witnessed on a wagon train passing through Laramie, bearing an orphaned pair of teenagers, left in the care of their westward-bound uncle. The girl was nearly seventeen, the boy a year younger. According to guide John Young Nelson:

One morning the news went round the camp that this girl was very ill, followed shortly by the statement that another stranger, this time a diminutive one, had joined the outfit. At length the news leaked out that the guardian uncle was the cause of the commotion . . . and a . . . scandal sprung up. . . .

At noon we camped for dinner, and in the stillness of the prairie a rifle shot denoted that something was going on . . . the brother of the girl had taken his gun, walked up to his uncle, and shot him through the heart. That afternoon we dug a grave . . . and laid the body in it. We had no wood to make a coffin, but we stuck a cross over the head of the grave.

The boy gave himself up with the words, "hang me if you think you should," but he was soundly acquitted. . . . All he said was that he had to do it.

In fact, having to do it validated much lawless action and was often condoned on principles of manhood, justice, and plain good sense. Included were sexual peccadilloes, which were rampant. On the Cherokee Trail, an emigrant, Davis, recorded the actions of a fellow traveler, Hoge, who was "true to nothing but his old and vicious instincts. He is forever wheedling around the English woman . . . Mrs. Caroline Hail, and there are many gross and scandalous reports in Camps about them, which I forbear to put on paper." Drinking, though not condoned, was also common. "The Devil seems to take

full possession of three-fourths of all that come on to the route," wrote Israel Lord. "Within one hundred miles after leaving the Missouri River and when they reached the South Pass all restraint seems to be at an end. They are by turns, all together, cross peevish, sullen boisterous, giddy, profane, dirty, vulgar, ragged, mustachioed, bewhiskered, idle, petulant, quarrelsome, unfaithful, disobedient, refractory, careless, contrary, stubborn, hungry and without the fear of God and hardly of man before their eyes." They were, Lord concluded, "half-animalized." Another account appears in the *Cherokee Trail Diaries.*

Sunday April 1 Yesterday Mr. G. Backus had the business tact to get drunk at the Fremont and make himself the laughing stock of all. While in that state, three of our men tried to get him to his room when he drew a knife and stabbed Mr. Pillet in his right thigh. The wound was not dangerous.

26th. . . . several of our men and teamsters [have taken] advantage . . . to get gloriously how-come-you-so, with the prospect of two or three knocked downs before morning.

27th. One of the teamsters returned drunk and wanted to fight one of our men who showed two revolvers, at which he backed out and went home.

Overland travel, grueling at best, was the training ground for an even more hardscrabble life to come, noted Israel Lord in 1849. "Men frequently lie down by the road side, with black parched lips and dry swollen tongue and wait till some passing team can spare a cup of water, or until the sun goes down," perhaps having ignored the sound advice never to leave the vicinity of a spring without storing a twenty-four-hour supply of drinking water.

Inevitably, when supplies dwindled, men and beasts both suffered. "One lean ox" wrote Lord, "was trying to swallow an iron cask hoop, rolling his tongue over and over it and then around his head." Mules pulled apart bags, leather thongs, and picket ropes, "anything they could get their teeth upon," while starving men behaved in kind. "Every few miles we see a creature with some portion cut out of its carcass. They generally cut from each side of the backbone. It is a great saving to eat cattle that die of themselves. It saves the time of killing and dressing; besides, they are good for nothing but to eat." A story was told of a Methodist preacher, trying to cross the Great Desert without water, who lost his way and saved his life by drinking the blood of his horse.

Hunger drove men to ingest familiar-looking plants. Wild plants, particularly anything resembling parsley, seemed alluring. Those who sampled the root of the wild parsnip, which grew abundantly in the plains, "vomited freely . . . and the effects vanished." In 1849, John A. Dawson of St. Louis, Missouri, fell dead by the side of the road, driven by hunger to eat the parsnip's poisonous root.

Ultimately, to eat was to hunt, and men learned to aim and fire with gusto and occasional skill. "It will bee two weeks Tuesday since we left home & we have not eatin but one ham and two thirds of one midling of our Bacon," wrote James Sawyer Crawford from Red-bud Creek, Oklahoma. "Their has not been any game killed on our rout yet Except Some Turkeys." In California, "the birds are very numerous," noted Israel Lord. "Desirous of examining one, I brought my revolver (a five inch barrel) to bear upon him and winged him at seventeen paces. I believe it was a very good shot." Oliver Nelson "got to killing deer" one November, outwitting his game with devious baiting maneuvers. "I would knock off china berries at a certain place so they would learn where to find them. About sundown I would take up a position three hundred yards from the trees, and when they came to pick up the berries I would shoot one. . . . Later I would get another shot at the same bunch. I had no place to sell them, so killed only to keep a supply of meat."

At some places game abounded. Fish flipped and collided in the shallows, easily lured by lantern light to the stream's edge where they could then be speared. Grouse, swans, geese, ducks, and smaller fowl flapped, floated, and spiraled over swamps and meadows. "It's incredible the number of these birds that appear after the first rains," marveled J. Ross Browne in the California foothills. "Twenty or thirty teal duck at a single shot is nothing unusual." Game was for slaughter, and regrets were few, although some men did pause to consider the effects of their hunting. Browne noted the continuous erosion of Native American food supplies and wondered how they would live. On the islands in Mono Lake, California, thousands of screaming gulls laid eggs, thick as a white carpet. The Indians once feasted upon the eggs, "but the white man," he wrote, "having a better right, of which gunpowder is the proof, has ordered the aboriginal egg-hunters to keep away." The only food left to the Mono Indians was "a curious and rather disgusting deposit of worms" that rimmed the lake, lying in a "solid oily mass . . . about two feet high by three or four in thickness." When sun-dried, mixed with acorns, berries, and grass seed, and patted into a breadlike mass, it was tasty and nutritious, although scorned by settlers.

Buffalo were plentiful when the first wagons crossed the plains. The mighty beasts, raw power thundering across the plains, were an awesome sight. "Between Pawnee Fork and Cow Creek (Kansas) . . . they literally formed the whole scenery, and nothing but dense masses . . . was to be seen in every direction, covering valley and bluff, and . . . blocking up the trail," recalled George Frederick Ruxton. Huge and lumbering, they fell defenseless from rifle fire and were judged so stupid that according to Oliver Nelson, "in central Texas in the early '70's the buffalo bulls would sometimes follow the milk cows right up to the settlers' corrals, and they'd have to drive them away." Often, after a few shots had been fired, "the poor things would all lay down," wrote hunter John Cook, in a mass behavior called a killing bed. Cook observed his friend Lew's hunting:

> He would shoot all he could take care of, then slip away. The live ones would leave, and the next day he would get another kill at them. The hunters used a Sharps .50, called a Long Tom. They kept bar lead and black powder; molded their bullets, put the powder in the shell and rammed it tight with a wood stick and a small mallet, wrapped the bullet with heavy paper and pressed it in. One man in the outfit did the shooting; several others would do the skinning and cure the meat. Dried meat brought three cents a pound, hides fifty to seventy-five cents each. Good shots got five to ten dollars a day, or they were paid by the hide ten to twenty cents a head.

So excessive was the carnage, so blatant the greed, that the settlers became conscious of the loss. Travelers began to note the diminished herds—a single hunting trip might net many thousands of hides—and sympathies for the animal gradually gained, so much so that in 1870 the Texas legislature proposed a stringent law curtailing the killing of buffalo. This was followed by laws put into effect in Colorado, Kansas, and even the Indian Territory, where patrols of U.S. marshals drove professional hunters elsewhere to kill. Sympathies reversed, however, when General Phil Sheridan of Texas, head of the Southwest's military department, heard of the proposed Texas bill for buffalo protection. Weren't buffalo hunters "settling" the Indian question by eliminating their food source? "For the sake of lasting peace, let them kill, skin, and sell until the buffaloes are exterminated," Sheridan exhorted. From then on, a "hail of lead" greeted the shaggy beasts, said Sheridan, and the condoned killing continued.

"That vast sea of animals . . . caused us gladness and sorrow, joy

and trouble and anxiety," mused John Cook, as well as "independence for the next three years." He knew they were "ruthlessly slaughtering" the livelihood of the Indians, but it was "too late to stop and moralize. . . . We must have these 3361 hides . . . within three months [to pay expenses]." His companion, Hart, shaking off his glum look, went out and in two hours had killed sixty-three bison. "Many times we had in one killing more hides than the two ponies could pull to camp." Prime killing time was 8:00 A.M. until noon, but some good killings were made in the evening. If the carcass stayed unskinned overnight, it would bloat up so tightly that the skinner might fumble, slashing and ruining the hide. Cook estimated that "in 1876 155,000 hides went down the Missouri River on steamboats from Montana, that 170,000 went east over the Santa Fe Trail, and 200,000 were shipped to Ft. Worth, Texas." In addition, he claimed, for every hide that went to market, "one and a half more were destroyed on the range from various causes."

Cook fretted about the "ruthless slaughter of the thousands of tons of meat" and felt "blue" at the sight of wounded animals dying a lingering death. He hated that the beasts "went insane from intolerable, unbearable thirst" because their watering holes were crowded with hunters, while hundreds of kids and yearlings stood lost and bawling for their slaughtered mothers. Yet to comfort himself, he would call up Sheridan's plea for white hegemony and "picture . . . a white school-house on the knoll yonder where a mild maid was teaching future generals and statesmen the three R's." Killing buffalo was seen as loyalty. How could settlement occur amid the war whoops of the Kiowas or the Comanches?

Others also worried. Mountain man John Young Nelson "saw no fun in killing animals simply for the wolves and vultures to feed upon." If white men would only adopt the Indian principle of economy, "there would be thousands of buffalo and other animals on the western plains, where not one now is left."

Arguments mounted along with heaps of buffalo bones, thrust up like haystacks across the prairies. "We passed a pile . . . eight feet deep that would cover a fourth of a city block," wrote Oliver Nelson, in Oklahoma. "Later I learned they belonged to the freighter, George Laflin. He had nine piles near trails, waiting for the railroads to come through." Added Nelson: "Once a buyer offered me fifty cents a pair for all the buffalo horns I would bring in. I drove a day and picked up three hundred pair of good ones. The man just lost heart. I sold a few pair—one for $2.50, some for $1.00—later took the rest to my folks in Sumner County, and they gave them away."

All game, including the shaggy, recondite grizzly, was fair game to men with guns and a sporting instinct. Hunting the greatly feared grizzly measured a man's courage, speed, and ability to stand his ground—or to climb a tree, as did Henry Washington Carter:

We were just loading our pipes for a smoke when we saw a huge Grizzly walk out of the thicket into the clearance about 30 yards ahead. . . . Before I had time to take a proper survey of the situation, bang went the rifle and at the same instant the bear gave a bound and a groan. But he was only slightly wounded in the hind leg as his rapid strides to where I was standing plainly showed. I had crept along the edge of the woods so as to bring my revolver to bear . . . and now I thought it time to fire my shot. Singularly enough it hit him about two inches below the other in the same leg, but still he came on growling and foaming at the mouth. My situation was now getting desperate; I fired again and made towards a large pine tree distant about a hundred yards, and so I kept up a running fire, that is to say I fired and ran. Although three of my shots had taken effect he still came on, and as my shots became less frequent, I ran the faster, perceiving that my safety depended entirely upon getting to the tree, for we had already got into the wood and Dickens had been trying in vain to get into such a position as to shoot at the bear without hitting me. . . . I had now reached the foot of the tree. . . . I thought if I had to die I would die fighting, or in other words, "Never say die with a shot in the locker." . . . The animal was close upon my heels and you may depend I fired a desperate shot, when on turning round to take aim I found only a few yards between me and my Bearish friend, who would soon have me in his affectionate embrace unless I proved myself pretty good at climbing. . . .

I did some good climbing that time, at least I thought so when I looked around and found perhaps six inches between us. He certainly treed me and perhaps was just thinking that he had fought a good fight when Dickens fired . . . and the bear lay dead.

Colorado men in wagon, ca. early 1900s.

Then I came down from the tree. He measured from the tip of his nose to the end of his tail just 5 ft. 8 inches, and weighed as near as we could guess about 500 pounds.

Grizzlies were feared by all, and men were unsure how they would react in the face of danger. Overton Johnson and William H. Winter, part of a small hunting party accompanying an overland party, were startled to see three grizzly bears.

We approached near to them, and . . . fired at the largest one. It fell, and . . . we borrowed our companion's gun [to finish it]. Finding the first one still alive, we gave him the contents of the second gun. . . . We returned and were hastily reloading our firearms . . . when all three came rushing to the top of the hill, roaring furiously, and so loud that the answering hills and hollow caves were filled with the beastly thunder. They stopped within forty yards of

Fishing in Glacier Valley,
Unalaska Island, Alaska, 1900.
Photo by Wilfred McDaniel.

us, and in open view, rearing up on their hinder feet, the wounded one in the middle—which, as he stood, was about eight feet high—with the blood streaming from his mouth and down his side, snuffing the air on every side, to catch some tainted breath of us; but the wind was ours, and being blind with rage and pain, he did not discover us. Our companion became dreadfully frightened, so that he lost all reason, and commenced running around his horse, and exclaiming loudly, "Oh Lord! What shall we do?" We told him to mount; but he still continued running around his horse, bawling at the top of his voice: "Good God Almighty! What shall we do?" "Mount! mount!" said we again; but he paid no attention, and was making about the twentieth trip around his horse, crying aloud; when we gave a loud whoop, and the two

Bears that were not wounded wheeled and ran off, and the wounded one tumbled back down the hill. This set our partner a little to rights, and turning to us, with a look of most perfect simplicity, he exclaimed, in a half weeping tone, "Good God! We can't fight them three Bears." "You were frightened, were you not?" said we. "O, no, no, not bad scared," said he; "but stop—look here," he continued, "[you'll never] catch me in a bear fight again."

Exploits abounded, challenges arose, and men turned always to something even more daunting than before—namely, the trek. Whether from Gypsy desire, giddiness, or lack of money, numbers of men walked across the country rather than ride, striding routeless and rootless through desert, prairie, and gulch, strangers on foot in a forbidding terrain. One of those following his wanderlust was Charles Lummis, son of a Massachusetts minister and a photographer of the Southwest. Small, wiry, and ever alert—he hardly ever dozed—Lummis set out from Cincinnati, determined to stride across the continent. The near-impossible task took him 143 days to cover nearly thirty-six hundred miles, during which time he plunged through thin ice into a frozen lake, nearly died in a New Mexico snowstorm, and fell off a cliff in Arizona, resulting in a bent and broken arm. Lummis recounted this accident:

Here was a bad job—an ugly fracture. . . . I placed the discolored hand between my feet and tried . . . to tug the bone back in place but flesh and blood could not stand it. Ah! The strap of my discarded canteen! It was very long and broad and strong leather. . . . I gave it two flat turns about the wrist, and buckled it around a cedar tree. Beside the tree was a big squarish rock. Upon this I mounted, facing the tree; set my heels upon the very edge, clenched my teeth and eyes and fist, and threw myself backward very hard. The agony, incomparably worse than the first, made me faint; but when I recovered consciousness the arm was straight and the fracture apparently set. . . ."

He walked the remaining seven hundred miles to Los Angeles, his arm still in a splint.

The route from Illinois to California beckoned the trail-happy Stephen Mann, who "paid $100" for the feat. The *Evening Mail*, of Stockton, California, published his story in 1909.

Stephen H. Mann . . . walked all the way to California from Pike County, Illinois and paid $100 for the privilege. . . . He came with a train of ox teams and his contract for the privilege of walking to this state included a provision that he must take his turn at driving the teams of the man to whom he paid the $100. To be sure, the man provided the food for the trip, and as they were six months on the way, the man was not unreasonable, although the grub consisted mainly of bacon and hardtack, with buffalo steak now and then and such other fresh meat as the men of the company managed to kill.

They started from Illinois in the spring of 1852 with quite a large caravan. . . . Once [across] the Great Plains, there was no sign of civilization. Indians were seen early every day, and the travelers often came upon evidence of battles.

On Wednesday, May 16, 1849, two men, footsore and haggard, approached W. G. Johnston. They had traveled from Ohio to California without a horse, sleeping beneath an umbrella at night and with only enough food for thirty days, expecting to get fresh supplies at forts along the way. Another cross-country pedestrian, Henry Washington Carter, had a sense of the danger he faced:

I was now again undertaking a dangerous journey. Such a thing was never thought of as for a man to go through this country alone on foot. Everyone I spoke to about it seemed to wonder that I should think of doing it. . . . Only the day before the mail had been stopped on this very route by Indians and the driver killed but fortunately the two passengers . . . had escaped.

I left Las Cruces about 7:00 in the morning intending to walk on til I got to Franklin, a distance of about 50 miles. When I got to Ft. Filmore I went to the Suttlers store theater and laid in a supply of crackers and cheese . . . . I started off on the road to Franklin. It was then about 10 in the morning. The country through which I was now passing was wood and prairie alternately. I had been walking for about two hours when on making a curve in the road I came suddenly upon a Mexican man and woman. Now then thought I, here's danger perhaps. As soon as they saw me they held their shawls up so that I should not see their faces. . . . "Bona Dios," good day, said I. But they made no answer. That made the matter still more mysterious. . . . I didn't like their appearance at all, they were an ill looking couple. I thought would just step into the bushes and wait until they came by and watch their movements a little. I had not been in ambush thus long before they came along. They were in earnest conversation about something and stopped not very far from the place where I was. After a good deal of talk they again went on for some distance and then they stopped again and had another consultation, and finally turned round and retraced their steps and I so lost sight of them.

All America seemed to be on the move. Not only did men strike out on foot, but whole villages, with general stores, hostelries, and homes, might move "yonder" if the mood struck. "Today we passed two large rafts lashed together," wrote James Hall, traveling down the Ohio River. "Each raft was eighty or ninety feet long, with a small house erected on it; and on each was a stack of hay, round which several horses and cows were feeding, while the paraphernalia of a farm-yard, the ploughs, waggons, pigs, children, and poultry, carelessly distributed. . . . A respectable looking old lady . . . was seated on a chair; the men were chewing their tobacco. . . . In this manner these people travel at a slight expense. They bring their own provisions; their raft floats with the current. . . ." When the railroad bypassed LaFoon, South Dakota, the city fathers decided to put their town on wheels, migrating six-miles away to Faulkton, which adjoined the train tracks and was destined for commerce. The Reverend Bert Foster, an Episcopalian priest ministering in the inter-mountain region of Idaho, Utah, and Wyoming, noticed its departure when summoned to conduct a funeral for a miner. He "found that the town was gone . . . people had lifted the buildings bodily onto flat cars, and the railroad company had carried the whole business—houses, stores, and people—twelve miles farther north." The most lavish gift ever was from storekeeper Rufus Klimpton to his wife,

Celina: Her hometown Anglican church was "stolen" upriver, disassembled, and transported by barge to "give her a treat." Why not? he reasoned. Didn't he love her? And hadn't she longed for the church services of her childhood?

⇥ ⇥ ⇤ ⇤

HARDSHIPS WERE MANY, and nearly every diary confessed to the extremes of weather, sickness, want; at times it seemed too much for a man to bear. John Rankin Pyeatt, writing from the Indian Territory on April 28, 1849, noted: "James Carnahan has had the dieree [diarrhea] and was very sick a day or two but has got well and A B Crawford had the bowel complaint and has got well. . . . some others of the company have had it . . . but all have got well . . . the boys ar all in fine sperits." Furthermore, wrote Pyeatt, "we have lost A. B. Crawford's mair. We lost him the second night after we laf the rendiveus she is stolen no dout by the cherikees." Nevertheless, the overland route prepared men for what lay ahead, a life of hardship, often failure, and certain disappointment. Still, their time along the trail was filled with a sense of their own manifest destiny. "We in some respects resemble the Israelites in their march across the wilderness," noted Alonzo Delano. They understood their part in history and embraced the chance to be a part of it.

3

"Gold the Size of Beans" and the Mining Frontier

About every tent is a gambling house . . . it made my head swim to see the money flying around.—*Carlisle Abbot*

✣

You ought to see me now. I'm a beauty, my beard is long and flowing and I haven't had a bath in two weeks . . . I have fattened 6 lbs. and feel splendid.—*Robert Hunter Fitzhugh*

✣

Workingmen—the true heroes of the pick and shovel.
—*J. Ross Browne*

✣

I feel a need of Rest. A years hard work in the mine has made me feel ten years older.—*John Grannis*

GOLD FEVER DROVE men west. Their restless quest for the precious metal and the attraction of easy-to-outfit placer mining created an elemental force that swept tens of thousands into remote deserts and ranges, once known only to Indians and a few pioneers. The Americans, Europeans, Latin Americans, and Chinese who flooded the West as placer miners—men

equipped with nothing but high hopes, pick, shovels, and pans— sped up exploration and settlement beyond the Rockies from 1849 until several decades later. "It is astonishing how many people are coming to California. The hills are crowded with miners and prospectors," wrote miner Carlisle Abbot in 1851. "Sacramento is the liveliest place I ever saw. There are over five thousand people living there, mostly in tents, and not more than a dozen wooden houses in the place. Hundreds of people from San Francisco are coming up the river every day, and the bank is piled up with all sorts of goods and provisions for the mines. About every tent is a gambling house and it made my head swim to see the money flying around." In other territories as well, the gold rush created towns where there were none. In Nevada City, Israel Lord marveled at "diggings . . . on a magnificent scale . . . and 500 or 600 houses have sprung up like mushrooms. . . . [Here] all the ravines are dug up, and hundreds of shafts sunk and being sunk." Where nothing but "ditch and pump and bail and drain" once operated, streams were turned "from their beds and [conveyed the miners] to the diggings along the mountain sides, across broad valleys and deep ravines, over precipices and rivers."

As gold was depleted in one area, traces and veins sprang up in another, drawing hordes of argonauts from California to Canada's Fraser River, then to Nevada's rich silver deposits in the Comstock Lode. Crowds surged into Colorado for the Pikes Peak boom in

Spriggs, Lamb, and Dillon washing and panning for gold, Rockerville, Dakota, 1889. Photo by J. C. H. Grabill.

1859. Then, in 1883, almost simultaneously, rich veins were unearthed in Montana, the Black Hills of South Dakota, Leadville in Colorado, and Idaho Springs. Thousands of claims were registered, worked, then dropped. Gaudily named towns such as Boozeville, Drunkenman, Delirium Tremens, Poker Flat, Red Eye, Red Nose, Winesville, and Damn sprang up like mushrooms, then shrank away as the gold veins ran out.

Excited crowds filled the streets of Council Bluffs, Atchison, and Kansas City, trying to arrange passage west. Wagons of every description bumped through the noisy streets, "boom or bust" signs flopping, as they rushed to be first in the goldfields. A man unable to pay for his own rig might drive or escort a freight wagon. Thousands rode horseback or walked, bringing their belongings by handcarts or wheelbarrows or slung on their backs. "California or bust!" sounded out. In response, wagons hopelessly bogged down in mud or with broken spokes bore the grim message "Busted, by Thunder!"

Overblown accounts of vast riches flowed back to the settled East. Who could resist the lure? Wrote Edmund Booth from Chili Bar, California in 1850: "A few days since, another lump of 15 pounds was found . . . it is about half gold. These two lumps and the one of 22 lb. over a year ago were all at the foot of the same mountain. This mountain is known to obtain veins of gold in the quartz rock . . . all winter, after a rain I have seen Mexicans, and often Americans, walking along the street slowly & stooping over, looking for lumps which the rain uncovers. Sometimes they would scrape up the dirt in the road and wash it out for the stuff."

Stories of great strikes teased the men. "Your real gold hunter is the most careless fellow in existence," noted frontiersman John D. Young. "New reported discoveries will excite his imagination and carry him off even at midnight to secure a claim without making any provision for the difficulties and dangers of the way." Mark Twain wrote: "I expected to see masses of silver lying all about on the ground. I expected to see it glittering in the sun." But most men did not find the earth's elusive wealth or enough of it to become rich. "I went with my butcher knife," wrote Ephriam Green, prospecting outside Sutter's Fort, "and collected nine dollars worth." Those questing after gold had left home with such optimism they were shamed by their defeat, and their letters home maintained stunning denials of their own fiscal woes. "Times were so hard that many men lived on the pickings from the swill barrels of the hotels," recalled Isaac Mossman. "It was a beggar's revel," wrote Twain about the Comstock Lode. "There was no mining, no milling, no productive effort, no income . . . yet a stranger would have supposed he was walking among bloating millionaires." Recalled Alonzo Delano:

Daily men passed my camp on Mud Hill, who, fearing starvation in the mountains, were trying to gain the towns. . . . Some were sick, and scarcely able to drag themselves along. . . . Along the road there were no tents for public accommodation. When night came, the sick, the weary and hungered were obliged to lay on the wet ground, in the chilling rain; and when morning appeared, they still had fifteen or twenty miles to go, wading through the mire, or swimming deep sloughs, with an exertion for life which was enough to discourage a strong man. . . . Wherever we turned, we met with disappointed and disheartened men, and the trails and mountains were live with those whose hopes had been blasted, whose fortunes had been wrecked, and who now, with empty pockets and weary limbs, were searching for new diggings.

Despite failure, fantasies of wealth, glamour, and derring-do were rampant, and no man wanted his family to know how poorly he was really doing. Men spun out their own self-delusions in dress and rowdy western style, hopelessly romanticizing themselves. "Californians were anxious that their friends in civilized countries should

see just how they looked in their mining dress," wrote early San Francisco authors T. A. Barry and B. A. Patten. "[They posed] with their terrible revolvers, the handle protruding menacingly from the holster . . . when sitting for a daguerreotype to send 'to the States.' They were proud of their curling moustaches and flowing beards; their bandit-looking *sombreros*." To be rich, successful, daringly dressed, and well mounted, to dash along with flowing hair and glittering trappings: This was the measure of a man.

As for mining itself, any man with a pick or a shovel could dig a hollow in the ground, give it a grand name, and then, as the expression went, "take it to speculation," selling the rights to his claim with no proof of gold at all. A pure iron outcropping, less valuable than

Gold prospectors aboard the USS Senator, *heading to Nome, Alaska, 1900. Photo by Wilfred McDaniel.*

Unidentified Colorado prospector, ca. 1890.

gold, could still fetch a good profit, and in every argonaut's mind was the hope that a hammer would rise from a pile of smashed rock, iron ore clinging to it like metallic feathers. So insistent was the dream that men fell easily for treachery and deceit, often buying up bogus mining claims or mines salted with gold.

Most miners worked by contract, earning, in the heyday, between sixteen and twenty dollars a day and, in more paltry times, as little as a dollar.

✦ ✦ ✦ ✦

MORE LASTING RICHES might be found in friendship and loyalty, as men became partners, trusted and relied upon one another, and learned how slight were their ethnic differences. Men of all cultures and geographies met and mingled, from Sandwich Islanders to Chi-

nese. Italians, Chileans, French, and Irish passionately wielded pick and shovel at their claims or worked as machinists, surveyors, draftsmen, or as part of the population engaged in everything *but* mining, which included pimping, fleecing, and speculating. "At one time I had two partners, a Chilean and a Norwegian," wrote Edmund Booth, a deaf-mute who might very well have encountered prejudice of his own. "In all my California life I found the men good-natured, civil and kindly. We were all much alike. All away from home and all knew it." He continued:

On one occasion I met a Mexican. Kept an open eye on him as he was about to pass. He stopped suddenly and spoke. I made the sign of not being able to hear. He understood and pointed to his open mouth, meaning he wanted food. I swung around my pack, took out three or four big square crackers and gave him [them]. . . . As he took the crackers he made the sign of the cross . . . it was rather a pleasant adventure and I sat down to see what he would do on meeting my Chinese friends. He passed them with no sign. When they came up they scolded me in their way for going so fast. It was evident they regarded me as a protection to them.

Brotherhood did not always survive among the mining fraternity population. As the boom progressed—it was considered officially over by 1850, although subsequent, smaller discoveries energized men for several decades to come—competition bred anger and deep competition. Ranks of northern European immigrants jostled edgily with blacks, Hispanics, and, particularly, the Chinese, who flowed steadily into the country; customhouse figures assert that twenty-five thousand Chinese passed through the port of San Francisco in 1852 alone. Tensions grew from situations such as the mining failure of Alonzo Delano and party, who had been working the Ottawa bar but had to abandon it during a flood. According to Delano, "When the water was very low a company of Chinese took possession of it, and took out from fifty to a hundred dollars a day for many days. So that the harvest, which was almost within our reach, was reaped by others, and they foreigners and aliens." A new popular saying—"He treated me white"—linked honesty and ethical behavior with skin color.

In Sacramento a "tangled mass of men and rogues and Mexicans and Chinese and Chileans and Kanakas and horses and mules and asses and oxen and drays and lumber and flour and potatoes and molasses and brandy and pickles and oysters and yams and cabbages and books and furniture and almost everything that one could think of—except honesty and religion" impressed Israel Lord. Worse, some might "sing in French, and make noise enough for a nail factory." Like many, Lord believed "most foreigners . . . may be found swinging in a hammock at all times—the lazy vermin."

Not all settlers were xenophobes. So outraged was author Bret Harte at the attacks "upon the inoffensive celestials" that he expounded in the *Springfield Republican* in 1867:

The attack on these defenseless Chinamen was only the natural climax of a system of tyranny and oppression to which they had been subjected at the hands of the ignorant since their first immigration. . . . Regularly every year they were driven out of the mining camps, except when the enlightened Caucasian found it more convenient to rob them. . . . They furnished innocent amusement to the honest miner . . . and their Chinese tails, particularly when tied together, cut off or pulled out, were more enjoyable than the Arabian nights' entertainment. . . . To throw stones at a Chinaman was a youthful pastime of great popularity, and was to a certain extent recognized and encouraged by parents and guardians, as long as the stones went to their mark with accuracy, and did not come in contact with a superior civilization.

"The Chinese are the greatest curiosities," reflected General E. D. Townsend, fascinated by these foreigners who poured into the country and first thing rushed out to "provide themselves with one or more pairs of stout American boots." They were "frugal, amiable and harmless people [who] never give trouble." They paid high taxes on their gold and were content to work abandoned diggings, sifting through the tailings for stray traces of gold. Scorned by the Anglos, they clustered in crowded boardinghouses or cheap hotels and slept wall to wall with piles of other single males when staying in rural camps or village ghettos. There they scratched out abandoned claims, drank gallons of green tea, and cooked aromatic soups in "curious little black pots and dishes, from which they helped themselves with their chopsticks," observed John David Borthwick, a traveler in the goldfields.

Indians, on the other hand, became the flotsam of the gold camps, peaceable but "degraded," remnants of the early California tribes, dubbed by the whites with fantastical names, such as Crying Mother and Tar Face. They slouched about the mines, begging for bread,

Ed McDaniel holding gold amalgam (gold plus mercury) at Nome, Alaska, cabin, 1901. Photo by Wilfred McDaniel.

Unidentified men in front of a general store, Florence, Colorado, ca. 1890s.

dressed in castoff trousers, battered hats, and a ragtag assortment of multicolored scarves and shirts, and depended upon odd jobs or handouts to live. They were often kidnapped from their tribes by whites and used as slaves. The so-called Digger Indians of the coast offered little resistance when attacked, and the treatment they suffered was so reprehensible that even the gold rush population was appalled.

Black miners were also in evidence. Typical was a family of "free coloreds" who lived in Jackson, California, the father working as a bootblack and two of his eight children as servants, noted by present-day historian Ruth Mather. Most were recently emancipated from the South, while others were free agents from the North who had never been enslaved. No matter their technically free status, black miners on the gold rush frontier still encountered a strong plantation mentality—usually held by whites from the South. In Marysville, California, a white physician, Dr. Wells, was handed a glass of liquor at a bar at the same time a black man next to him was served. Testily the doctor announced, "I am not accustomed to drink with Negroes." The man replied, "Nor do I, often drink with mean rascally whites." A fight erupted; the black man was shot and "not expected to recover." Indeed, said observer Israel Lord, there were "all kinds of wickedness in these diggings—drinking, swearing, swindling, litigation, quarrelling and fighting," as well as bigotry and racial unease.

❧   ❧   ❧   ❧

LIFE ON THE mining frontier was thrown together however possible. The roof of a miner's hut, according to J. Ross Browne, could be "clapboard, or rough shingles, brushwood covered with sod, canvas . . . flour sacks, cast off shirts, coats and pantaloons, all sewed together like a home-made quilt." Some shacks even sported rawhide ceilings, which became "flabby and odorous" in dampness, then stretched tight in the sun. "Think of a canvas chimney!" Browne exclaimed, "sporting out over a hut made of stone, wood, scraps of sheet iron, adobe bricks, mud, whisky barrels, nail kegs, and even canvas."

Israel Lord was struck by the "want of order" in most camps. Ungraded streets, crooked footpaths, and wagon routes wound about, while the ground was littered with tents, bedrolls, and various, untidy paraphernalia. Worse was the waste: "Boxes and barrels, empty, or filled with all kinds of goods, in passable, indifferent, or bad order, or totally ruined, and wagons, lumber, glass bottles, machinery and plunder of all sorts, heaped and scattered about. . . . At one establishment alone, over 200 boxes of herrings [were] rotting in one pile, any amount of spoiled pork, bacon, cheese, moldy and rotten, pilot bread, and almost everything else. The destruction and waste of property here is almost, or quite equal to that of the plains, with not half the necessity, and a thousand times the recklessness."

Miners fretted and tossed from bedbugs, fleas, thick air, bronchial coughing as they crammed two to a bunk in overcrowded hotels, boardinghouses, or dorms, wrote Dr. Israel Lord.

The American House on K street. . . . There were two rooms. . . . Against each end wall was a double tier of berths, and on either side was [a] triple tier, and there were two berths to each tier. Thus within the narrow compass named, there were *accommodations* for forty men in rough, wooden bunks, arranged as the berths of a canal boat or sleeping car. . . .

The small stove served as a central point of attraction; and about it, pre-empting the chairs, were gathered some lodgers as though intent on keeping it warm; one or more of whom, with a view of drying their water soaked boots, held the soles of them against it, thus emitting the delightful odor of burnt leather. Others contributed by spitting tobacco juice upon the innocent stove, in spite of a regulation which possibly on account of some previous grievance had been painted on the pipe, "No spitting on the stove."

The clerk stood beside a pile of coarse blankets, one of which he delivered to each applicant for a berth upon payment of one dollar. The possession of a blanket, therefore, was equivalent to a ticket or certificate for the night's lodging. By ten o'clock, every bunk was taken, and most of them occupied. . . .

Privacy was at a premium. When homesteader and miner Ole Dovre of North Dakota set up his claim shack, the uninvited began to buzz around, hoping to share. "Two brothers with whom he had become friendly began hinting. . . . Finally they 'struck a bargain' and the men moved in. The first thing they did was to make [his] bed wide enough for two and for the third man they made a 'flat bed' . . . that could be set aside during the day. The brothers took turns sleeping on this [and] they also took turns cooking."

George Locke wrote home to his mother in February 1853 from

Unidentified Chinese men, ca. 1880s.

Chinese tea carrier at east portal of the Central Pacific Railway's tunnel 8, Sierra Nevadas.

washing; mended their own clothes, made their own beds and on Sundays cut their own hair, greased their own boots, and brushed their own coats; thus proving by the most direct positive evidence that woman is an unnecessary and expensive institution which ought to be abolished by law."

Yet no matter how successful the miners were in forgetting women, they still spent an inordinate amount of leisure time "reading yellow-covered novels and writing love-letters." Perhaps, Browne reckoned, it was to "fortify themselves against the insidious approaches of the enemy." Many men were married and tried to keep their wives and families close to mind.

Wrote miner and inventor J. J. Craven to his wife in May 1850 from Colma, California:

I have endured many hardships, suffering many times from cold and hunger, there being so much snow still on the mountains that we were not able to prospect and our animals giving out for this want of forage we were forced to retrace our steps toward the valey of Sacramento where I arrived wore out by the fatigue of my journey and suffering with the worst of all California disease. . . . I was not able to perform any laborious work and being nearly out of funds I was forced to look up some situation where I could earn my board accordingly I accepted an offer of $200 a month for my services in a laundry house in the place as clerk and bar tender where I shall remain a few weeks until I regain my strength and then for the mines[.] The dysentery has left me and I am in hopes soon to be myself again. . . . I have now $300 in lumps of gold weighing from 1 penny to 3 ounces. When I can smelt this to $1500 I shall be looking out for home[.] If I stay until fall I am in hopes to have more but I shall be governed by my health I should like to send you money but I dare not trust it with Strameyer. It is now late and I must close for the night[.] So good night My Kitty.

Craven turned his earnings to his advantage. He was an inventor who discovered that gutta-percha could coat telephone cables for underwater transmissions as well as be used for rain boots. Later in life he served in the U.S. House of Representatives.

Jackson Creek, California, describing his accommodations: "Now in the mines here there are thousands a running a bout each broke without a place to lay there head thank god I have a good house to retreat to when out of a claim I will point out the place where I reside at present . . . now just imagin a log cabin with a cloth roof on it and a fire place in it four feet long and you will imagin mine. . . . How would you like to be out here in such a place?"

The bachelor status of the miner was often idealized, as in the observations of critic and traveler J. Ross Browne: "These jolly miners were the happiest set of bachelors imaginable; had neither chick nor child . . . to trouble them; cooked their own food; did their own

Argonauts were their own best friends, their own employers, and usually their own cooks. Israel Lord wrote:

One strikes a fire, another prepares the wood, a third wets up the bread, or mixes the batter for pancakes . . . while a fourth assists the last in grinding coffee, washing dishes, etc. Only a small portion of the numerous messes which traversed the plain aspired to the luxury of a table; and as for civilized knives and forks, so genuine a sign of effeminacy was considered rather to compromise a man's character among the aristocracy of the plains; which spoons were put to unheard of uses if used at all, and tea spoons were returned [unused.] . . . Such cooking as I have seen would surprise any one who had not previously made a dirt pie, and accidentally got a little flour and stewed apple into it.

George Sharpe got up a very good supper. The Raisin cake was baked to a turn and frosted like the Shasta peak. Peas and potatoes would have made us glorious. [Usually ravenous after a hard day in the mines] they gorge themselves on beef and bread and stale butter and peppered pickles and stimulating sauces, like wolves or anacondas, and the last thing before going to bed, must have sardines at three to five dollars a box, or a pie at one dollar as its equivalent, and then they lie down like swine and groan and blaspheme in this slumber of victim of gluttony and drunkenness now of disease tomorrow and the doctor the day after.

No wonder the miner turned to drink. The daily danger of being "dropped down two hundred feet into the bowels of the earth in wooden buckets, then hoisted out by blind horses," wrote Browne, consigned their lives to fickle fate. Would the rope hold? What if the bucket gave way? The mouth of a mine shaft was the size of a washtub, "black and dismal," lit only by a flickering glow from a thousand feet below. The shaft was almost straight down, with ragged ropes and splintery, often rungless ladders, tied together down the side. A miner could be reeled down in a bucket and trust to fate or inch and slide his way down the skein of ladders, exposed every moment to a free fall.

Mining regions were home to the burrowing miner, the silver-tongued speculator, and another breed of man, the prospector, a grizzled, independent type who considered himself an adventurer in a fortuitous world, plying his skill in the discovery of silver ore or veins of gold. Pockets jingling with the last of his change, daunted by nothing, he traipsed and traversed the declivities and rugged pockets of the mountains, always seeking a new claim as well as the solo jaunt that took him there. Every new lead shimmered with allure—far more than the actual drudgery of working a mine. Every prospector hoped to realize a fortune, and such hope fueled the swindles and dishonesty of the ever-present mining speculators.

Rough, scraggly miners spent the day washing gold, sometimes running water from a river into a new channel. Flumes huddled close to the nearest stream, ideally three hundred feet from the head of the claim, five hundred feet long, eight feet wide, and sides three and one-half feet high. Robert Hunter Fitzhugh, an Alaskan miner, was one of a group of miners who "set up a dam diagonally from the head of the claim near the head of the flume, turning all of the water in the river through the flume. Then we built another dam at the foot of the flume to keep the back water out, and that gives us a stretch of five hundred feet of the river bed fairly dry." Miners rolled huge boulders clear of the stream, stripped the earth down to bedrock, smashed the rock with a huge hammer to find pay dirt, which they shoveled into a long sluice box, combed through the water to flush lighter particles to the top and heavier gold to the bottom, onto a smear of absorbent quicksilver. Incredibly, a single gold flake was so heavy it would settle in the streambed and not float downstream. At day's end the miner would squeeze out the quicksilver in a rag and scrape off random gold flakes. "A veteran gold washer," pointed out the miner John D. Young, "could put a grain of dust weighing only one cent into a bushel of earth, mix it up thoroughly and still find that small piece of gold." However, claimed Israel Lord, "[e]very time gold is weighed, something is lost, and the business streets of Sacramento will, in a few years, be worth digging up and washing for the gold. . . . In the large establishments, the dust is dipped about in tin pint cups. In a word, it is an article of produce, as easily got as wheat or corn in the States, and handled with much the same feeling, and comparatively with the same waste."

To obtain the precious glittering flakes, ore was stacked in a brick furnace, heated by intense fire. The molten ore shimmered with white heat, and the quicksilver evaporated away in a breath of mercurial vapor. Larger, more volatile particles of escaping mercury often poisoned the water. Worse, the workers in the reduction works, according to J. Ross Browne, who breathed in the noxious fumes of the plant, damaged the nervous system. The workers were "frequently salivated, and are liable to palsy, vertigo and other disorders of the brain." Mercury's effects were little known, but the tainted wells, streams, and rivers, as well as the addled behavior of anyone long exposed to the fumes, made it clear that men had been poisoned.

Paradoxically, such toxicity existed in terrain so beautiful—at least in California—as almost to defy description. Men faltered in their praise, unsure how to describe the sweeping fields of golden poppies, evening primroses, yellow heartseases, and wild roses. Every hillside resembled a bouquet, laced with delicate ferns and brooding pines. Creeks twisted and splashed though green vales, bouncing along though dark green tule lands or sliding over greenish serpentine cliffs. Just as the land presented a wealth of beauty, it also offered the prospect of gold. Wrote Browne:

Gold bearing earth lay to the depth of from four to six feet upon the top of rocks. Usually we cast aside as worthless a layer of sand, or sometimes sand mixed with earth; all below this was carried to be washed, and the nearer we approached the rock, the greater were the returns. When the surface was reached, it was scraped and swept with great care, for here the gold could be seen, lying in shining particles. . . . At the outset I tried rocking a cradle, thinking knowledge of that kind might some day become useful. It seemed at first sight quite simple, but on trial, I found it rather difficult to acquire the peculiar art of moving one arm forward and backward to do the rocking, and with the other to dip up water with which to drench the dirt in the hopper. Skill too was required to know the exact motion that would produce the best results. If shaken too violently, the fine gold would pass out over the cleats in the bottom of the cradle and be lost; and if not swayed rapidly enough, the dirt would become packed behind the cleats. The miner, too, required to learn his machine, as the height and curve of the rockers, the size of the cleats, and the slant of the cradle towards the stream had much to do with proper working. I was so much exposed to water, my feet constantly in puddles, and my clothes dripping with sweat, that I was glad to exchange cradle work for what was usually accounted severer labor—digging with a pick.

The drudgery and isolation of mining fell away when miners went to town, where a carnival-like atmosphere prevailed. "Such hooting, yelling and screaming I have not heard in a long time," exclaimed Young, when mining in Colorado. "All seemed to be enjoying themselves. . . . They were singing songs cracking jokes and passing round the whisky pretty freely. They appeared to be very friendly and always said, 'Stranger take a drink.' "

The miner's favorite was the circus, so popular an event that "circus day," which began in the settled Northeast, became an annual feature in most western towns. An article reported on Joseph Rowe and his fantastic pioneer hippodrome: "By far the most extensive and elegant organized equestrienne establishment that ever appeared in California . . . traveling through the State at an expense of fifteen thousand dollars a month." As an added incentive, "the seats are carpeted, and attentive and gentlemanly. Ushers to wait on Ladies and family." George Bartholomey and his Pacific Circus, another big top pioneer, played in San Francisco in 1856, having amazed crowds in tiny frontier hamlets throughout Oregon. By the end of the century circus troupes, including Ringling Brothers, were crisscrossing the country, some traveling to California through New Mexico and Arizona, others heading southwest with a retinue of trapeze artists, acrobat riders, a herd of elephants, a giraffe, elks driven to harness, camels, polar bears, ostriches, ponies, and, of course, some kind of monster. Men were delighted as children by the circus advertisements of "rare and curious wild beasts," such as Adam Forpaugh's hippopotamus, Samson, the giant elephant, and a snow-white buffalo. Moreover, a circus allowed even the most godfearing man to feast his eyes on a comely woman, scantily attired, such as the blindfolded M'lle Zola with the Forepaugh Circus, whose bright red bicycle balanced on a wire fifty feet in the air.

Payday brought crowds of unshaved, ragged miners onto the busy streets, drinking, shoving, fighting, and flirting with the stageloads of women who careered into town to earn their livings as dancers, hurdy-gurdy girls, crib girls, dance hall girls, and parlor house madams from the red-light districts, where bordellos bustled with women and their clients. One line of cribs, on Dupont Street in San Francisco, was "a narrow alley [that] ran like a slit through a wall. . . . In [each] shallow bay window . . . a woman sat, her glossy dark hair piled high. Her cheeks were painted; her eyes glazed; she wore a bright-colored Mother Hubbard gown. One sat at every window as far as the eye could see down the alley toward Kearny Street. They sat motionless, looking straight ahead," recalled young Harriet Levy, who often "rushed through the alley" with her father, bound for Mar-

ket Street. The women charged fifty cents to a dollar. So degraded was their trade that a foul oilcloth, draped across the end of the bed, was for men so hasty they never even shed their boots.

Prostitution existed as an art, a social service, and a thriving industry in nearly every major city of the West. It contributed substantially to local revenues and began in earnest during the gold rush, when "fancy ladies" came by wagon and muleback, by overland coach, and by ship from the States, Europe, and South America. The women set up shop in canvas tents or bar back rooms, pursuing the single largest occupation for women in the Comstock Lode.

More than a thousand girls worked the Barbary Coast in San Fran-

cisco between 1904 and 1917. A few of the madams and more successful prostitutes found money and a bit of fame. Virginia City's Julia Bulette rode daily in a lacquered brougham, its doors sporting a crest of four aces, her gentle smile both invitation and comfort to her many friends.

✧ ✧ ✧

BARS WERE A central gathering place for the miners. Saloons sprang up in hastily constructed tents, shacks, or crude Indian wickiups, vented on all four sides. For the rough miners, a saloon was refuge, eatery, hotel, bath and comfort station, gambling den, dance hall, bordello, barbershop, courtroom, social club, political center, post office, library, opera, city hall, trading post, and ice-cream parlor. Most important, it was a place to dispel loneliness as well as to frolic, fight, and dicker. Here a man could congregate with friends, read the paper, sit by a warm stove, and pass away the night in his own private club.

Men streamed into the Bucket of Blood saloon—a name so popular it appeared all over the West—as well as individual barrooms bearing such lively names as the Crystal Bar, the Smokery-Delta Saloon, and the Come In and Die, where men downed tangleleg, forty rod, tarantula juice, rookus juice, and Taos lightning. An addition of burned sugar with an occasional wad of tobacco thrown in turned barrels of alcohol into the brew of choice. Forty rod was named for the distance a man could travel away from the bottle before collapsing, a useful side benefit, since it knocked the drinker out before he resorted to gunplay. Whiskey, the staple of the day, was sold to miners in flask bottles.

As mining camps flourished, the saloons grew more elegant, sporting long, polished wooden bars, often more than fifty feet long. Some served fine foods; a few even boasted French chefs. A showy saloon might further emulate French style with large, dangling chandeliers and walls hung with paintings.

Drama prevailed. Even dismounting from a horse could be "trying to the newcomer's nerves," wrote Browne, "to sit quietly and see horse and rider dashing at full speed directly for you, as if both were bent upon dashing though the wall of the house, not [slowing] until within five feet of you, then stopped with a shock, as sudden as if struck by lightning."

Gawking passed time during the day. Empty boardwalks would suddenly fill with men, and shuttered windows popped open at any hint of an *event*. Nothing was too mundane to stir up interest; even a Sunday outing piqued curiosity. "I was not surprised that the entire population, without distinction of age or sex, crowded out from every door to enjoy the spectacle," wrote J. Ross Browne, who was simply starting off in a wagon and horse for a picnic by the Walker River. But curiosity and hospitality were closely linked, and, wrote Browne, "Not only do [the worthy citizens of Austin] feast every new-comer, but [they invite] him to explore their ledges [claims] and fill his pockets with specimens of chlorides, bromides and sulphuets." Such outreach was less forthcoming when it came to full-time residents.

    ✦ ✦ ✦ ✦

WITH THE COMPLEXITIES of frontier existence worked out, all that remained was a man's success or failure. For prospector John D. Young, "it took three days to make a tailing ditch and to divert the stream bed and three more days to reach pay dirt eleven feet below." The first day's work of washing pay dirt netted prospectors the magnificent sum of three dollars, about forty-three cents apiece. Over two weeks the amount might go as high as seventy cents a day per man. With their expenses of about a dollar a day, they at last concluded to call it quits. Young considered himself fortunate to find a buyer to pay five dollars for his claim.

David Demarest wrote of his financial straits:

Board is 21 dollars per week and lodgings 7 (per week) are like hog pens. So to live cheaper we put up a tent and sleep in a carpenter shop. I could get no work, but Beaching paid me 35 dollars Chateueuf went too selling coffee and cake—altogether we managed to make a living while here and have a little left to start to the mines with in the Spring. Mining in the aggregate is a losing business and must eventually . . . leave the operatives in debt. . . . The truth is, the whole operation is deeply, irretrievably in debt, hopelessly in debt now, and so profoundly sensible are people here of it that they are loath to give notes for this indebtedness, anticipating that the courts at home will never give judgment on obligations which accrued here.

It was no different in Alaska. "I don't know what has gotten into the people in the states," wrote Robert Hunter Fitzhugh. "They are all going crazy out Alaska and it is going to result in more misery and tragedy than gold. There is gold up there . . . no doubt, but 9 out of 10 of the people who go in will spend about $1000 in getting a few hundred in gold and the vast majority will get nothing. Yet hundreds of thousands go in without knowing the first thing about roughing it and will fall by the wayside. I am glad that I will be ahead of the great rush. *I am afraid of it.*"

Yet some did find success. On a good day a miner such as John Grannis might gross as much as two hundred dollars. Being particularly thrifty, Grannis reinvested his profits in additional claims and lent his idle funds out on interest, continuing to work hard at mining all the while.

Successful or not, many men stayed on, leading to the settling of such cities as Virginia City, Nevada City, and Sacramento, among many others.

Part 2

ROUGHING IT

❖

Photo on previous page: Soldiers fighting over horsemeat, ca. 1885.

4

GAMBLERS, LAWMEN, AND OUTLAWS

It seemed like all Billy's chums were either hung, shot or had run away.
Ben said, "Bill, you been keepin' bad company."
—*Oliver Nelson*

Bob and I still clung to the old Texas style which is, never kill one of
your own beéves when you can get somebody else's.
—*Charles A. Siringo*

He did not need to tell anyone he was a bad one, for hell was
written all over his face.—*Andrew Garcia*

In the afternoon I visited the state house—a large stone building to be
3 stories high & also the penitentiary, quite massive. Both will be a credit
to the country—there is something American about them.
—*James Ross Larkin*

WESTERN MEN, SUFFERING from one manner of turpitude or another, sought excitement in the gambling dens and saloons of small settlements or rallied for a round of dogfights, gambling, bloodletting, or general carousing in larger, urban settings. Geared up for wickedness as well as for gold, villains and outlaws kept pace with "every variety of crime, folly and meanness," said physician Israel Lord. Frontier men were "beer drinkers, shiftless, and habitual lynchers," and women of refinement were warned away recalled John D. Young, in Denver. "One thing was very odd looking to me," he added. "Although the street was crowded . . . there was not a lady to be seen. I suppose there was not a dozen of them in the city. I never saw one on the street during four days that I stopped there."

Maverick outlaws, such as Wyatt Earp, Clay Allison, Tom Horn, Boon Helm, Billy the Kid, and Henry Plummer, rampaged, while others, perhaps less driven, turned to idle or petty crimes, pure vandalism. "A house was burned on J St. last night," noted Israel Lord, "the work of an incendiary." The flames drew a crowd of twenty-five hundred onlookers, according to historian Necia Dixon Liles.

In Illinois "the laws of the land were not much in evidence," noted traveler James Haines. "Differences of opinion were discussed at house raisings and like gatherings. Serious quarrels were settled at elections by personal combat. Social intercourse was frank to a degree [to seem] rude and vulgar."

Towns sprouted up like windblown seeds, and saloons were quick to follow. Tucson, described by soldier John Spring, was typically filled with "cursing tramsters, rollicking soldiers, and rustling gamblers." In local taverns tables groaned under piles of silver and gold, while fast-fingered monte dealers presided, day and night. "Brag and poker were also played," noted Israel Lord. "It seems to be a perfect mania . . . [in which] common laborers, mechanics, etc. will risk a whole day's earnings on the turn of a card, as if it was a pleasure to get rid of the stuff; and if they do curse, it is because they are chagrined at guessing wrong, rather than at losing their money. . . . [By]

morning, the floor around and under the [monte] table is covered with cards, two or three deep, at least half a bushel of them. Sometimes they played only one hand, and threw the pack away; then they would play several and again one of them would, in a fit of irritation, hurl two or three unsoiled packs on the floor at once."

Frontier taverns were well-stocked male sanctuaries, luring men to drink and cavort amid lavish displays of glasses, bottles, cigars, and liquor as fine as in the largest liquor taverns in Chicago. Tables invited the unwary, and the unlucky, to games of crap, roulette, blackjack, poker, and monte, as well as faro, which, if fairly dealt, gave the customer an almost even break. "I saw the probate judge of the county lose thirty Denver lots in less than ten minutes, at cards, in the Denver House on Sunday morning, and afterward observed the county sheriff pawning his revolver for twenty dollars to spend in betting at faro," wrote a visitor to Denver in 1859. Saloon success was traced by John Young Nelson in the genesis of Dog Town (Kansas):

It consisted of two stores, a few bawdy-houses, and four whiskey saloons. Hal Gay and I went down there, and putting our capital together, started a whiskey bar. This brought the number up to five.

All the soldiers from the fort used to patronise us. . . . Every one, far and near, came to our place, which we called the Robber's Roost. . . . I had never had so much cash in my life—it just came pouring in. As business increased we provided for the demand by establishing monte, poker, faro, dice, roulette, and every game calculated to take the fancy. In fact so popular did our place become that we built quite a big gambling saloon, in which many a poor fellow lost not only his money but his life.

The shootings became so frequent that we had to establish a grave-yard at the back of our place a hundred yards or so out on the prairie. . . .

Our game was to get the emigrants in to drink and gamble. Once they were there we could look after them, but they were a bit shy, and wanted coaxing in. . . .

Hal would disguise himself, rubbing a lot of dirt in his hair, over his face and hands, and putting on some dirty ragged clothes . . . he went down to talk to some of the men, and brought them up to the town. He then strolled along to the Robber's Roost, and invited them in to have a drink. Once in, it was not long before he got them into the gambling saloon, where he began to play, and invariably won by an arrangement he had with the banker, who was in our employment.

Having won a pile he stood more drinks, and . . . soon strangers started in. . . . The more they gambled the more drinks I sold. Finally things became so warm and the shootings so frequent, I suggested we clear out before we got into trouble.

Ironically, the men returned to gamble under the new owners, lost their money, got "skinned out" in a common gambling stratagem used in Denver, according to Nelson, to "decoy the unwary." One man, the decoy, would dress in rough miner's clothes and straggle up to the table, looking confused and amateurish, wager five dollars on a card, and win. And "then the fun began": "He doubles it. It wins again. He increases his bets always winning and at last says he will not risk any more and agrees to give his place to anybody else. Some greenhorn lays down a twenty on the winning card and in a moment the cards are turned up again and he has lost."

The confidence games resulted in a complete *loss* of confidence, at least for the losers. As "thousands of dollars were changing hands at every turn of the cards," battered spirits were assuaged by the bar girls, "women . . . gaudily dressed trying to decoy the poor greenhorn into their toils," said John Young Nelson. Like many, he soon "grew weary of the . . . wretched sight of that abode of crime." He was disturbed to see men so careless of their money. "They got it so easy. It seemed to burn in their pockets till it was all gone."

"Public opinion [in Denver] was very strongly opposed to gamblers," wrote John D. Young. "They were sure to be punished if caught in the least unlawful act." Often lynch law replaced the sanction of legitimate government, and officers of the court, sworn to do justice to all men, could respond to the will of the people when lynch law was in effect. One trial in Denver, described by John D. Young, "was to take place at seven in the evening at Denver Hall and the citizens were invited to be present by large posters stuck on the streets." About a thousand people were present at the trial, that of a young gambler who had defended himself in a gunfight, had killed his attacker, and been angrily "arrested" by Denverites. The judge ordered the prisoner to step forth. "He was a young well dressed man tall and good looking. His face was pale as death and his eyes were fixed and staring wildly over that vast throng to find some gleam of compassion . . . but there was no such signs among the crowd. A low savage murmur spread across the hall and as he heard it he knew it was his death warrant and he fell fainting into a seat." Unhappily, the shooting had been a fair match: Both men had faced each other, and drawn for their guns, one had died, and one had been arrested. Probably the trial would not have occurred except that the defendant was a gambler. When the case came back from the jury, said Young, "the single word written on it [was] 'guilty.'" When the judge asked what punishment he should give, "there arose one loud fierce yell, 'hang him, hang him.' The judge did not pass the sentence—and thus could never be accused of murder. Instead the will of the people was done."

✦ ✦ ✦ ✦

MEN IN MINING camps fashioned their own judicial organizations. In Colorado the gold miners had special law and order problems. Camps lacked any law enforcement, and to fill the need, miners handled claim disputes at miners' meeting. The sheriff would post the necessary notices, a meeting would assemble, a president would call it to order, and a trial would ensue. After the testimony, a vote would be taken by voice, and the decision would be final. If a claim was jumped, then a man was justified in shooting the claim jumper dead. Miners adopted codes of law for each camp or district, to limit claim size and appoint claim recorders. So effective were these informal codes they were later embodied in the federal Mining Law of 1866.

But there were few to back up the codes or the law in much of the territory. Violent men and outlaws could terrorize and commit crimes a long time before anyone tried to hold them accountable. Perhaps one of the most awful stories of vengeance and retaliation was that of Overton, a half-breed who had killed his father, stolen his horse and sundries, and set up for himself. He drifted from tribe to tribe as an interpreter in the 1830s, sometimes working with the Americans, then committing some outrage and being driven out of society. Wearing boots and spurs, a laced coat, and a long sword, he rode the hills, calling himself Colonel Overton, making enemies everywhere. Numerous robberies made him the terror of the mountains around Santa Fe. Everyone—Canadians, British, Americans, and Comanches—were after him. One day a Comanche hunting party spied him riding a spirited stallion. Observer Matley Watson wrote:

The chase was a long one. Overton . . . reached a platform covered with fine pine trees, and thought himself safe . . . he spurred his horse, already covered with foam . . . and to his horror and amazement, found that between him and the valley was a horrible chasm, twenty-five feet in breadth and two hundred feet in depth. . . . What could he do? His tired horse refused to take the leap, and he could plainly hear the voices of the Indians encouraging each other in the pursuit.

Along the edge of the precipice there lay a long hollow log, which had been probably dragged there with the intention of making a bridge across the chasm. Overton dismounted, led his horse to the brink, and pricked him with his knife . . . he fell from crag to crag into the abyss. The fugitive crawled to the log and concealed himself under it, hoping that he would escape. He was mistaken, for he had been seen; at that moment, the savages emerged from the wood and a few minutes more brought them around the log. Now certain of their prey, they wished to make him suffer a long mortal agony, and they feigned not to know where he was.

"He has leaped over," said one; "it was the full jump of a panther. Shall we return or encamp here?"

The Indians then began a conversation. One protested, if he could ever get Overton, he would make him eat his own bowels. Another spoke of red-hot irons and of creeping flesh. No torture was left unsaid, and horrible must have been the position of the wretched Overton.

"Since we are here, we had better camp and make a fire; there is a log."

Overton now perceived that he was lost. From under the log he cast a glance around him. . . . He understood that the savages had been cruelly playing with him and enjoying his state of horrible suspense. Though a scoundrel, Overton was brave. . . . He resolved to allow himself to be burnt, and thus frustrated his cruel persecutors. . . .

Leaves and dried sticks soon surrounded and covered the log . . . the Indians watched in silence. Overton burst out from under the fire, and ran twice round within the circle of his tormentors. They were still as the grave, and not a weapon was aimed at him, when, of a sudden, with all the energy of despair, Overton sprang through the circle and took the fearful leap across the chasm.

Incredible as it may appear, he cleared it by more than two feet; a cry of admiration burst from the Indians; but Overton was exhausted, and he fell slowly backwards. They crouched upon their breasts to look down—for the depth was so awful as to dizzy the brain—and saw the victim, his clothes still in flames, rolling down from rock to rock till all was darkness.

Had he kept his footing on the other side, he would have been safe, for a bold deed always commanded admiration from the Indians, and they would have scorned to use their arrows.

❧ ❧ ❧

THE WEST TEEMED with desperadoes, drifters, and cowboys, their guns and their kerchiefs low-slung, ready to fight at the hint of an insult. John D. Young described his first glimpse of a wild western town when he arrived in Denver:

I heard an altercation in a saloon across the street. There was only a few words when I heard the simultaneous report of two pistols. I got very much excited and was rushing to see what was

Gamblers,

Lawmen, and

Outlaws

Unidentified California men "after the picnic."

murder being committed. I asked him if there was no punishment for crimes there. He said yes and that they would probably hang that fellow that killed the other just now.

Samuel Clemens, coming to Nevada to work as a newspaperman, "was introduced to several citizens" in Carson City, including a man named Harris:

"Excuse me a minute [said Harris], yonder is the witness that swore I helped to rob the California coach—a bit of impertinent meddling."

Then he rode over and began to rebuke the stranger with a six-shooter, and the stranger began to explain with another. When the pistols were emptied, the stranger resumed his work (mending a whiplash) and Mr. Harris rode on by with a polite nod, homeward bound, with a bullet through one of his lungs, and several through his hips. And from them ran little rivulets of blood that coursed down the horse's sides and made the animal look quite picturesque. I never saw Harris shoot a man after that but it recalled to mind my first day in Carson.

With violence rampant and men all dressed similarly, it was difficult to tell true outlaws from armed pranksters bent on having amusement, and some offenses seemed downright silly. In the state of Washington territory, a small gang raided hen roosts, stole corn, and finally, according to Smith Tryo, an early settler in the Dungeness Valley, "drove a band of sheep right past the door in the broad daylight. . . . Jack Tucker was caught red-handed. . . . He was arrested and tried. In court his defense was that the sheep were trying to bite him. He was found guilty and sentenced to 30 days in the county jail. But since there was no jail . . . he simply lived with the sheriff at the expense of the county for a month."

⤞ ⤞ ⤝ ⤝

THE WEST IN fact was defined by violence, often springing from social inadequacy, human error, or simple shortfall of character. Its prevalence in American society, mostly male, had been intensely analyzed by nineteenth-century Europeans trying to understand the

the difficulty when my friend Collier caught me by the shoulder and very coolly told me I must not go near them. . . . He said it was only a man shot and that we had better get out of the way as very probably there would be more shooting. I asked him with astonishment if that was the way they done things here. He said that was nothing unusual that scarcely a day passed without a

workings of the American mind. The presence of "true evil" was suspected by British traveler James Hall. He commented on the Harpers, a family famed for the incredible atrocity of their adventures on the Kentucky frontier in the 1790s, as they spread death and terror in their wake. "Their first recorded victim was a young gentleman, Langford, who stopped to breakfast at a public house in the Kentucky wilderness and noticed that the Harpers looked hungry, and were unable to pay. Langford generously invited them to eat and, and upon paying, carelessly showed a quick glint of silver from his wallet. Days later, his body lay near Big Rock-Castle River, the silver stolen."

Yet "plunder was not their object," recalled Hall. A "deep-rooted malignancy against human nature" had led to the invidious murders. The Harpers destroyed without the prospect of gain. "Females, children and servants no longer dared to stir; unarmed men feared to encounter a Harper, and even hunters flinched at the sound of a breaking twig, imagining one of the Kentucky barbarians nearby."

Each stealthy attack was always slightly different. A black child, riding to the mill with a bag of corn, was seized; his brains were dashed out against a tree, while his grain was left untouched. In another incident, two travelers approached a house and asked for shelter. Shortly after the Harpers drifted in, signaling the terrified woman to be silent. For amusement, they decided to impersonate

Unidentified men in front of a Colorado cabin.

"Good times" near Siskiyou County, California, ca. 1880s.

Methodist preachers, and each would sleep with one of the strangers, as was the custom in overcrowded way stations. "One crept into a bed on the lower floor . . . while the other retired to the loft with another. Both the strangers became their victims." The Harpers then "consummated the foul tragedy by murdering their hostess and setting fire to the dwelling."

They were pursued, and one of them was wounded by a man named Leiper. While waiting for the arrival of Stegal, the husband of the murdered woman, the wounded Harper brother was queried by Leiper, a slow-spoken and easygoing man who was genuinely curious about Harper's motivation. "You must die at any rate," said Leiper calmly. "Tell me why you have killed so many?" Harper replied that he "hated his species" and had sworn to destroy them without regret. The only death he lamented was the murder of his own child. "It cried," he complained, "and I killed it: I had always told the woman, I would have no crying." As his gruesome tale ended, Stegal rushed up and decapitated Harper; the head was "placed in the fork of a tree, where it long remained a revolting object of horror."

Unhappily similar were the Benders, a family that wreaked murder and mayhem in Osage Township, Kansas, in the 1870s. William Bender, his wife, son, and daughter erected a crude house on the highway running from Independence, Missouri, to the Osage Mission in Kansas. Inviting travelers in, they would entertain them, lead them to a private room separated by a wagon sheet from the main family, and, in several cases, murder them. When discovered, the family fled Kansas and were never caught.

Cruelty was indiscriminate, and Indians were usually considered fair game for poor treatment, even if it led to death. The observations of Thomas Knight of California confirmed history's record of the treatment of the California Indians by the Kelsey family:

The Kelseys built a sawmill at Sonoma, run by water. There were a great many Indians in the Clear Lake region, a very good spot, and when I lived in Napa Valley I used to employ them to work for me. I treated them well, and never had any trouble with them. Other white men employed them also. The Kelseys would sometimes go out and get 50, 60 or a hundred of these Indians, and bring them to their place, and make them work for them. They treated them badly, and did not feed them well. They should have given them a bullock once a week or so to eat, but failed to do so. The Indians were kept so short of food that they occasionally took a bullock and killed it themselves. On such occasions, if the Kelseys failed to find the special offenders they would take any Indian they might find at random and hang him by his thumbs, so that his toes just touched the floor, in an adobe house they had on the premises, and keep him there two or three days sometimes with nothing to eat, and some of the other Indians would go and slyly feed them. Sometimes they would kill an Indian outright on the spot for some small offense. In driving them in to their place, they would shoot any of the old, or infirm ones by the wayside. At the time of the Red Bluff excitement, the Kelseys went up into the Clear Lake region, and got some 80 Indians, and drove them to Red Bluff to make the valuable mines. . . . On getting them there, a long distance from their homes, it was ascertained that that . . . there was no gold there. The Kelseys then and there abandoned these Indians, who were in a hostile country, with nothing to eat, and then were killed or starved, and finally only some eighteen of them ever got back to their homes. In revenge they murdered Andy Kelsey, who was in the Clear Lake country, tending a large herd of cattle. The government troops then went up and killed a large number of these Indians. Then they arrested the Kelseys for their inhuman treatment of the Indians . . . but they escaped punishment.

Even youngsters learned early the price of toughness, seeing every day the value in it. One boy believed "he could not be anything till he had shot somebody," wrote Mark Twain, stunned by a youth who could grab a revolver, shrug himself into a long-tailed coat and slouch hat, and stalk the streets, trying to provoke a shoot-out. At each encounter the boy's nerve failed; face-to-face combat was for more seasoned men. Finally he hid in a stable and "shot the first Chinaman who entered," thus murdering his way into his idea of frontier manhood.

For those less inclined to kill, there was always the ongoing pastime of banditry, which was a way of life in most small towns. Almost anyone, particularly the tough characters who plied the rustling trade for a living, could fall outside the law at one time or another. Bandits and "bad" elements ranged freely about, so much so that in Gaines County, New Mexico, no one blinked when a man galloped by and tossed his revolver into the wet adobe wall of a house under construction. As the builders continued to slap up the adobe, he was confident that the evidence against him would remain walled up in the baked mud structure, never to be used against him in court.

In Grant County, South Dakota, everyone knew the James brothers, marauders who lived in a two-mile stretch of woods between Northfield and Waterford. A few days before their historic robbery of the Northfield bank, young Julia Amsden opened the door to a young man, well dressed in a serge suit, who had run up to her house, she said, "seemed very excited," and begged threads and a needle to mend a tear in his trousers. Alone but fearless, she handed him the sewing supplies. She discovered later that he was a notorious outlaw as well as a man in charge of his own couture.

The road to rowdiness differed from one man to another, provoking the timeless question of what prompted evil: nature or nurture? Texas outlaw John Wesley Hardin emerged from his childhood experiences—frequent public hangings, neighborhood gunplay, and daily knifings—with an outlook that led to his lawless path. Son of a religious and conservative family, he grew up hunting for sport, a common pastime. But unlike other boys, he committed his first violent crime at the age of fourteen, stabbing a classmate over a verse of poetry inscribed on the schoolhouse wall, referring to what, no one knows: " I love Sal, and Sal loves mutton . . ." The classmate drew a knife first, but Hardin stabbed back, "almost fatally in the breast and back." The next year he committed his first murder, shooting a black man, then running. The farther he ran, the more he killed, shooting oxen, whiskey bottles, Mexicans, ex-slaves, Indians, whites—nearly anyone or anything that he encountered. Finally captured in 1878, he spent years in prison studying law and the Bible and, after his release, passed the bar examination in Texas. Although he was now launched on a lawful course, his past finally caught up with him. In 1895, while prosecuting a case in El Paso, Texas, he was assassinated by an old enemy, who approached from behind and shot him, execution-style. Why such mayhem? Historians speculate that in spite of its law-abiding aspect, the Hardin family preached a strong

Unidentified man, ca. 1880.

regional hatred of the North, causing the boys to grow up as relentless rebels on the Texas frontier of their youth. Another Hardin son was hanged by vigilantes.

To stay alive on the frontier took luck and vigilance. Eyes must rove and the mind stay pleasantly alert yet uninvolved. Being circumspect was everything. Cowboy Jim Oberly, inured to danger, was riding home from a line camp one cold February day in 1883 when a bullet suddenly whizzed through his hair, leaving a hole in the crown of his Stetson. There was no report, no smoke, and no damage, so he simply shrugged, sped up a little, and rode on. In fact, rid-

ing on was judged the safest approach to any incipient danger, as experienced by retired army guide, ex-trapper, and mountain man John Young Nelson, who was stepping along one night, minding his own affairs, when he glanced casually in the window of a gambling house to see how it was "getting on." Horrified, he glimpsed "two men with their bowie knives drawn, standing over a man who was stretched out on the floor." Nelson quickly skirted away but was pursued by one of the murderers, who was swinging a bowie knife. Nelson tried to warn him off but failed. To save himself, he stabbed the man "in the bread basket." A second murder had occurred.

"In those days the settlement of these matters was usually decided by a majority. I did not know what friends he had," wrote Nelson, "but a glance told me that . . . discretion was the better part of valor, [so] I tramped off and made tracks for Provo City, a Mormon town up the Jordan River." Although he believed he should have been "thoroughly exonerated" by the law, Nelson feared that "the law of six-shooters ruled," and if he returned, the murdered man's friends would try to avenge his death. "Revolvers were called into requisition to settle all matters in dispute."

The six-shooter ruled—for a while. Six-shooter law gave rise to vigilantism, an equivalent brand of violence that proved a strong force in America's legal history. James Hall, commenting on the district of Kentucky after the Indian wars, wrote:

Among the early settlers . . . Lynch's Law . . . was a way of trying causes. . . . Its operation was as follows: when a horse thief, a counterfeiter, or any other desperate vagabond infested a neighborhood, evading justice by cunning or by a strong arm . . . the citizens formed themselves into a "regulating company," a kind of holy brotherhood, whose duty was to purge the community of its unruly members. . . . Squire Birch . . . established his tribunal under a tree in the woods, and the culprit was brought before him, tried, and generally convicted; he was then tied to a tree, lashed without mercy, and ordered to leave the country.

Schemers, quacks, outlaws, card sharks, and the most shiftless of the population had had their way. Far from civilization, they had felt free to scheme, take unfair advantage, press grudges, and be lawless at will; legal institutions were weak, officers of the law scarce, and punishment was spotty. Many homicides had simply never come to trial. Vigilantism was society's effort to gain control of haywire criminality. Faced with incessant crime, citizens had little choice but either to ignore the ongoing mayhem or else to act on their own. When cowboy Oliver Nelson rode into Denver in the 1860s, "it was a common thing to find four or five fellows swinging of a morning. . . . They were made to mount the hand rail [of the bridge over the creek] and the noose being slipped over their necks they jumped or were pushed into eternity."

The vigilance committee was to blame. The miners, storekeepers, and merchants of the frontier West considered themselves peaceful, yet in the Denver area alone, they hanged more than 150 men in one year. No matter how many swung, more were waiting in their stead. "I was always prepared to meet [Indians]," wrote Nelson, "but these murdering cut throats . . . would pot at me for the mere devilment of the thing, and would have killed me if they could, just for the sake of killing."

Vigilantes often performed their acts secretly. Some who took part in multiple hangings felt remorse. When Captain James Williams of Montana committed suicide, many believed he was prompted by his conscience. Vigilante officer Nathaniel Langford confessed that he and others "knew full well that when the Federal courts should be organized, they themselves would be . . . held accountable before the law for any unwarrantable exercise of power." Most were solid citizens. They loved their wives and families, paid for schooling, read Scripture, respected civic authority, yet believed that they could enforce these values with their own system of justice.

✧ ✧ ✧ ✧

NOT ALL JUSTICE was handled vigilante fashion. A typical justice court was headed by a justice of the peace and a sheriff, with powers to collect taxes, deputize citizens, and form a posse. The average justice of the peace had little education, knew less law, and often worked without any written material, including a copy of the statutes. Justices excelled in assigning fines; how else would they get paid? William Balfour of Tascosa, Texas, recalled a justice of the peace named Scotty.

> There was no appeal in his court. A man came once and got drunk, then became boisterous, and was put in jail over night. The next morning Scotty held court, coming in with his law book. He asked the man his name and the fellow told him and he entered the case. Then the court's deliberation was very short. Scotty asked him:
>
> "Do you have any money?"
>
> The man said "no." Then Scotty said:
>
> "Get the hell out of here and across the river, and don't come back until you have some. . . . " As Justice of the Peace, he was death on six shooters. When a man was arrested he found out whether he had any money or not.

As the frontier matured, county, district, and federal courts were established, men of education and forbearance were involved, civility and good sense ruled, and criminals were brought to lawful justice.

"Persons meet in saloons, bagnios, and gambling places with deadly weapons upon their persons; they drink, gamble, dispute when half intoxicated, banter each other, and at last draw out their weapons for fancied causes and slay each other," said William Timmons. "I remembered [some advice]. 'These fellows all carry guns. Dress like they do. Get a gun. A gun carries respect anyway.' "

An innocent gesture was often misread by men already jumpy and suspicious. Dr. Henry Hoyt recalled strolling one moonlight night with his friend Billy the Kid. There was a baile across the street, and Hoyt challenged Billy to a footrace to the dance hall. "As we neared the door I slacked up, while Billy kept on at full speed through the door. Mexican adobe houses, for some reason, have a threshold about a foot high, and as the Kid flew through, the heel of one of his boots caught on it, landing him full length in the middle of the ballroom. Quicker than a flash his prostrate body was surrounded by his four pals, back to back, with a Colt forty-five in each hand, cocked and ready for business [at] the Kid's unconventional entrance."

Deputy Marshal William Foley and Frank Smith, a blacksmith and a former deputy, had been drinking together in the Palace Saloon. Smith departed around three in the morning, followed a few minutes later by Foley. When Foley reached down to adjust his

Two men being hanged, California, ca. 1870.

trousers, Smith, who was lingering outside, was alarmed by the gesture and drew his gun. Foley, who was unarmed, dodged back into the saloon and got a sawed-off double-barreled shotgun, accosted Smith, and told him to throw up his hands. Smith fired, missing Foley at close range. Smith seemed to be a poor shot, and Foley fared little better since his weapon refused to fire. After Smith sent another bullet wide, Foley demanded that Smith throw up his hands. When Smith refused, Foley beat him to death with the butt of the shotgun, as reported in the California *Tonopah*, on March 9, 1907.

In another instance, in Goldfield, Nevada, a drunken quarrel flared up over the merits of Turkish cigarettes. Charles Clark was thrown out of a saloon by barkeep Edward Sites. Enraged, Clark screamed, "Stand back," and lunged toward Sites, pistol drawn. The first shot missed Sites by six-inches, the rest by more. The shooting led to an unintended casualty, according to historian Sally Zanjini. A prostitute was wounded fatally when a bullet flew through the saloon ceiling. But then, "Nevada shooting was just plain rotten but about on par with most Western shooting," noted an onlooker.

Bristling egos and ready guns erupted in violence and deaths. "Two American graves, with a paper stating that they were both from Johnson County, Arkansas—the name of one Hickey, the other Davis"—greeted traveler David Demarest. "Near this place they quarreled about their cattle. Hickey struck Davis and a fight was the result, in which Hickey called enough and was let up. But no sooner had Davis turned to walk away than he received a stab from Hickey, [and] died in 10 minutes. The murderer was arrested by the order of the emigrants in general, tried and sentenced to be shot. The order was executed. 12 rifles were used, six loaded with ball and six blank. A grave was dug and Hickey was placed near it. At the first fire, he fell and was buried with his neighbor."

In England, in order to claim justifiable self-defense, a person must flee a pernicious dispute, or at least retreat, before resorting to violence. Not so in the United States, where the idea of "no duty to retreat" if threatened was so broadly accepted that it may have contributed to the steep homicide rates in the West.

What drove a man to crime? Arguably, the freedom of the frontier should have given more room to more men, but loose-knit laws and random enforcement were also license for crime. Moreover, many argonauts were rootless, without family or community attachments, in new mining camps without social controls. Homicide generally rose in a population heavy with young men, particularly, wrote historian Charles Stephens, in the "violence prone years before age thirty five. A gold rush acted as a magnet for the kind of men likely to commit violent acts."

Others became rogues and robbers by personal design. Black Bart, otherwise known as Charles E. Bols, was a reclusive mining engineer who abandoned his family and went to work in mines in Idaho, Montana, and California. Unlucky in this pursuit, he decided that finding gold on a Wells Fargo stage was more likely and turned to banditry. Courtesy marked his unique approach. After bowing to the women and occasionally sparing their favorite belongings, he would thank his hosts with a poem left at the scene of each crime, signed "Black Bart, the Po8." Repeated success must have lowered his guard, for one day he dropped a handkerchief with its laundry shop chop mark, as unique to an individual as a thumbprint. The handkerchief led directly to Bols.

✦ ✦ ✦ ✦

VIOLENCE COULD ERUPT from either side of the law. No tin star could shine up a reprobate lawman. Marshals and sheriffs, masters of their territories, were often lawless themselves and quick judges of who should stay and who should go. Turncoat lawman Jim Courtright, a long-haired Civil War scout, became a marshal in Fort Worth, Texas, in 1876. A brooding man who drank too much, he killed two squatters and from then on veered between law and mayhem. He was typical of a type of lawman, beholden to none, as was Marshal George Flat, who saw two men who somehow displeased him come into his town. He sauntered out and, without warning, shot each in the back with a .45. They fell directly in front of a restaurant, and when the diners rushed outside, Flat ignored all inquiries, sending the bodies off to the local boot hill, where a few words were mumbled over them and the matter was ended. The marshal, although exonerated, was reprimanded by removal of his commission. Asked to surrender his star and guns, he replied defiantly, "Come and take 'em." A few nights later, making his rounds, he passed an opening between two buildings. A flash lit the night, and several shots rang out. He was instantly killed, there was no evidence on the scene, and a well-known deputy, who was handily nearby, moved in to handle the details.

Wyatt Earp was another to move between law and outlaw. Elected constable of Lamar, Missouri, in 1870, he was a conscientious lawman until his wife died of typhoid two years later. Earp drifted into the Indian Territory and was soon arrested for stealing horses. In 1874 he joined his brother James in Wichita, Kansas, and worked as a policeman, again proving to be reliable and conscientious. Later he worked first as a policeman, then as an assistant marshal of Dodge City, where he struck up friendships with gamblers Doc Holliday and Bat Masterson. Earp joined his four brothers in Tombstone, Arizona, where brother Virgil was temporary town marshal, was replaced, and then became permanent town marshal after his replacement mysteriously disappeared. Virgil and Wyatt invited their gambling friends Holliday and Masterson, to join them. As lawmen they ruled until opposed by a coalition of small ranchers, led by the Clanton family. A feud developed, challenges and threats flew, and by 1881 the Earps' popularity was in decline. Citizens suspected them of stage robberies. After a shoot-out their affairs declined, even though the Earps were vindicated as acting within the law. Revenge, threats, gunplay, and killings followed the brothers. Wyatt gambled professionally in the mining camps of Nevada and Arizona, and his brother Virgil finally joined him, opening a gambling hall in San Diego in the 1890s. Their behavior veered back and forth between legality and criminality.

✦ ✦ ✦ ✦

HOW MANY MEN met their deaths violently on the frontier? One estimate: approximately 20,000 between 1830 and 1900, including Indians, Chinese, Mexicans, and Americans. In southeastern New Mexico alone, between 1875 and 1881, cattle wars, rustling, and general lawlessness killed more than 200 men, while 400 were listed as having violent deaths in Nevada between 1860 and 1880. A survey of 402 homicides in Nevada between 1846 and 1881, mostly in mining camps, found that gambling disputes and drunken quarrels outnumbered quarrels over women two to one. By 1909, 75 percent of the killings in Goldfield, Nevada, were crimes of passion; women had become part of the violent frontier.

To kill a woman on the frontier was a heinous crime, unthinkable. Yet John Millain murdered the prostitute Julia Bulette of Virginia City, Nevada, by strangling her in her bed. Wearing a black armband he then ghoulishly marched in the funeral procession. Bulette was a compassionate and popular figure. Every man in town turned out in her honor, although their wives slammed down the shades in embarrassment. Millain was caught when he attempted to rob another woman. Bulette's possessions had been pawned and were traced to him. Her death had been at the price of a diamond pin, coral earrings, a jet cross, a long gold guard chain, enameled sleeve buttons, an engraved silver brick, an engraved gold ring, and assorted stockings, capes, handkerchiefs, and gilded lace. Millain was tried and found guilty of murder, but during his confinement the virtuous women of the Comstock pampered him with wines, jellies, and delicacies and pleaded with the court for a change in his sentence to life imprisonment. Despite their intervention, he was escorted to his death by forty special deputy sheriffs armed with Henry rifles, followed by sixty national guardsmen, and swarms of men, women, and children, along with Mexicans, Paiutes, and Chinese. There, in a tranquil natural amphitheater, he prayed, dropped to his knees, and swung to his death on April 24, 1868.

Even outlaws had their parts to play in establishing western civilization.

5

COWBOYS RIDE THE RANGE

❖❖❖

I wonder how many persons ever meant more to me than that horse.
We had a way of communicating with one another.
—*William Timmons*

✦✦

Oh! What a night . . . am in Hel of a fix. . . . My back is Blistered badly.
. . . I had a sick headache bad. . . all our letters have been sent to the dead
letter office. . . . Flies was worse than I ever saw them . . . weather very
Hot . . . Indians saucy . . . one man down with Boils & one with Ague.
. . . Found a human skeleton on the Prairie to day.
—*George Duffield*

WHISTLING AND SPURRING great remudas of cattle along the Chisholm or Goodnight-Loving trails, the western cowboy cut strays, roped dogies, and generally lived out the myth of an offbeat, vivid, and footloose nomad of the plains. Rowdy yet stylish, cowboys flaunted Stetson hats, snappy quirts, rawhide riatas, and pounds of inlaid silver, dandy regalia that belied the grinding tedium of their daily routine: herding, spring bog riding, fence mending, windmill greasing, dogie roping and throwing, cutting cattle from the herd, fence riding, and castrating bulls. So garish was cowboy attire that it almost bordered on self-parody. Cowboy Teddy Blue's sister could hardly tolerate his shiny leather pants and boots; he looked "just like an outlaw." Yet jaunty couture masked everyday efficiency: Chaps protected the rider from nettles and thorns, a bandanna absorbed sweat, and the high heels of fancy boots were made to grip the stirrups and keep him in the saddle. In reality, the cowboy was simply a hired hand who worked hard, earned little, and was often too broke to own his horse. Usually in the employ of huge cattle outfits—vast kingdoms such as Texas's XIT, the Spur, the Matador, and John Chisum or George Littlefield in New Mexico Territory—the cowboys who joined their ranks, like serfs in a European fiefdom, gained legitimacy by association and not much else.

Cowboy roots burrowed deep into California, where Mexican vaqueros had been drovers and herders long before America began its profitable trade in cattle. Vaqueros were skilled herdsman, noted General E. D. Townsend in 1855. Riding through "very hilly and rough" sandstone terrain outside Los Angeles, he surprised a cattle drove scrabbling down the hillside. "I walked behind them to see how the vaqueros managed to drive them over a road . . . impossible for horsemen to pass; but they followed the stray cattle up rocks almost perpendicular and down again, with as much ease as if on open level ground."

Wild cattle pounded through California in the 1840s and 1850s, their ownership, under Mexican law, established by might, not right,

by whoever caught and branded them first. Title was not inherited, and any calves of branded cows were considered fair game. The finders keepers system gave rise to a heady and entrepreneurial spirit, in which sharp eyes prevailed and private herds grew under the ministrations of the herders, whose job it was to brand whatever strays they could catch.

This Mexican tradition continued as unofficial range policy in the West, even during the peak years of the cattle industry from 1866 to 1890. Even the least-lettered cowpoke could pick out a brand, or lack of one, with hawklike accuracy, or read a cow's earmarks—unique notched or slashed ears to identify ownership—as readily as the weather. Hieroglyphics such as "U Bar Lazy J" immediately identified an owner. "The brand is put on the left hip or

shoulder," noted Isaac Lord, "and is easily seen at quite a distance." A running iron—a short bar, poker size—easy to wield and commonly used by rustlers, seared brands into thick cattle hide.

Cattle were collateral or could be used as weapons, as demonstrated by Fine Ernest, a prominent member of the cowman community in New Mexico who was angry at the crowds of squatters settling on his leased land, the Maxwell land grant. Despite improvements—crops were already sowed that year—he demanded that they depart at once. For emphasis, he drove three thousand head of rampaging cattle through their corn and wheat fields. The settlers blasted the cattle with buckshot, a retaliatory move that engaged everyone in a state of raging warfare.

Cowboys were hardworking men who knew the ways and wiles

of animals, whether horses or the cattle they herded. When seeking lost heifers, they intuited a calf's path back to the spot of its last suckling. They checked horses' withers for swelling, which would prevent riding for as long as a week, knew that a horse could rear up and fall back for no reason, identified trouble by the twitches and flare of a horse's nose, and could outwit a belligerent horse that had sucked in air to swell itself up by giving it a quick blow to expel the air, then tightening the cinch. They understood what a horse wanted when it pulled on the bit. Every cowhand expected the steer to tauten the rope suddenly and topple both horse and rider and knew that a stray finger on a saddle horn might be sawed off by the rope.

Work ranged from tending windmills, fixing firebreaks, castrating cattle while fighting off clouds of blowflies, and repairing fences, to line riding, the loneliest duty of all. The line rider had to patrol the boundaries of the ranch, hunt predators, and track stray cattle on trail drives that could be as long as twelve hundred miles and take three to four months. A line rider labored in all weathers, including blizzards, and might be gone for months, wandering through the high country, with only his horse for company.

Master and horse fealty was commonly cemented by sweets. "A convincing way to show friendship was to offer him a little sugar or biscuit. . . . I made a sugar . . . eater out of him in the winter of 1896–1897," said William Timmons of his horse, Buck, who was "gentle . . . never cross with other horses, but . . . wanted his privacy." Carlisle Abbot, journeying through the West in 1851, "picked up" a wild mustang in Nevada. Cowboys cleaved not to wives but to

Unidentified Idaho cowhands relaxing.

Western Colorado cowboys with dead horse, ca. 1900–1910. Photo by Fred Garrison.

horses. Although most cowboys did not own their horses, for those who did, man and beast were inseparable. "A cowboy loves a horse that helps him do his job and perform the impossible things," wrote Timmons, "and Buck did all that. Buck was the best horse I ever threw a leg over. . . . My backbone still aches!"

Dangers abounded on the open range. Cattle could stampede at the flick of a quirt, and often did. One cowboy, John R. Cook, marveled at the sight of a cattle rampage, in which "6000 steers [were] lying down chewing their cuds, when [an angry squatter who had been asked to leave the property] rode along the east side of the corral . . . and threw a big cat over the fence plump on a steer. The ground fairly trembled—the stampede was on." Rails splintered, and fence posts flew, pieces landing two hundred feet distant. The cowhands had to ride for hours to round the cattle up. Even then many of the cows were lost, to become strays for some other outfit to collect later.

Courage and equanimity were foremost in the cowboy's life. When confronting his mortality in the thrust of a bull or the whiz of a bullet, the cowboy would stay tranquil and dispassionate, the better to deal with emergencies. Show sentiment? Never! men exclaimed. This would shame them in the eyes of their cohorts. Oliver Nelson's sidekick Billy confronted a typical scene:

The grass was growing fast, and some of the cattle died from bloat. A man passing said there was no need to lose any, just to stick a knife in and let the wind out and they would get over it.

Billy came in one morning and asked for a butcher knife. . . . Under the bluff close to the creek lay a yearling, swelled up till all four feet were off the ground. Billy walked up, knelt down between its feet, and said, "here's where I save a steer." He drove in the knife, cutting a six-inch hole in its paunch. The whole side blew out; blowed his hat off and he fell over backwards. The calf bawled, got up, walked off about fifty yards and layed down for keeps. Billy went to the creek, washed his face, coat and knife.

Cowboys were constantly put to the test, whether enduring the saddle for days while riding the line or bronco busting, an important part of the cowboy's regimen. Without tame horses, range riding vanished, and without bronco busting, there were no tame horses. But docility was hard won, as cowboy Timmons discovered:

The two buckskins . . . were hard to stay on; I couldn't grip them and had to ride on my spurs. Somebody had told me that if I'd wet the inside of my leggings I could get a better grip and . . . that the broncos wouldn't buck so hard. I decided to give it a try. I went to the water trough and dampened the inside of my leggings; then I got on the horse without my spurs. He lurched forward, arched his back, and put his whole heart into dislodging me. At

Black cowboy in Colorado, ca. 1880s.

every jump I worked up and couldn't get down into the saddle. I went so high that my head bobbed over and struck the bronco between the ears. I went hurtling over his head.

I staggered to my feet and realized that my mouth was bleeding. When my head struck the horse, my lip had been cut by the head-stall buckle and my front teeth knocked loose. The lower teeth came back over my tongue, but I pulled them in place and went to the water trough to wash out my mouth. There I found that my lips had holes in them; the water ran out. I caught my bronco, unsaddled him, and turned him loose.

Idle hours were the cowboy's bane. Too long on the trail, hard worked, and brimming with animal spirits, the bored cowhand, spurs jingling and purse full, could drive a frontier town into bedlam in short order with amusements that were generally at the expense of any outsider, or "dude," who happened through. Initiation was brutal. The dude might be forced to dance, his feet peppered by gunfire, or to suffer a can tied to his coattails under a hail of bullets. Nothing could protect the Englishman on tour when cowboys were in town, while one drummer who ate alone in his hotel room rather than mingle with the residents of a New Mexico town was arrested, clapped in jail, and charged with horse stealing. A mock trial, complete with prosecution, the threat of hanging, and a defense attorney who slapped the drummer repeatedly on his bald head when emphasizing a point, was part of the theater. The drummer was horrified. All proceeded seriously until judge, jury, and witnesses finally "ran screaming with laughter" from the court.

Often danger for the cowboy lay in misadventure, clumsiness, or simply being in the wrong place at the wrong time. One young cowhand described his decline into trouble to his parents in 1887, writing from hiding in Mexico. His partners had sold his thirty-two mustangs and tried to "beat" him out of the money. "I shot both of them," he wrote. "Killed one of them dead and crippled the other. I went up to him and beat his brains out with my Winchester." That said, he went on to describe his new life: "I am doin well, I way [weigh] 169. I am liable to come home any time. You would not [k]now me. I have got my hair painted black and eyebrows." Then he added, "direct your letters to Yellow House Texas, to L. D. McIntire. That is my name in Mexico."

Those who "hung with" outlaws tempted violent deaths, but even peaceable men, such as Elwood Beal, who worked the ranches in Lea County, New Mexico, could be felled by fate. He was struck by lightning and killed, as were three of his four mules, while his wife and young son were spared. John Albert Lawrence began working as a cowboy in 1870 at the age of twenty-four, ran his own cattle in the major cattle drives of the New Mexico Territory, and lived happily as a rancher until all his horses ate locoweed and went crazy or died. Afterward he left New Mexico for Coleman County, Texas, where one hopes he fared better. Shorty (no last name) continued riding

even in his elder years and met his end when he froze to death during a storm in the 1890s.

⁂ ⁂ ⁂ ⁂

THERE WAS NO single cowboy temperament. Some were "ornery" by nature, others peacemakers, but few were outright racists. If they felt prejudice, the generally fluid nature of western society, as well as the absence of institutions that tended to foster discrimination, created a system that allowed blacks greater entry than did eastern society. Cowboys fell less into bias, perhaps because lack of property bred less defensiveness. Black cowboys were mostly ex-slaves from Texas ranches or runaways from Reconstruction in the South. One in seven cowboys was black, and several even became trail bosses, despite discrimination. Two of the most celebrated, Nat Love and Jessie Stahl, became celebrated radio performers and Addison Jones, a cowboy in Lea County, New Mexico, was the only black documented in the county's records. He worked George Littlefield's cattle for many years. Love, known as Deadwood Dick, wrote his reminiscences in 1907, telling readers he "gloried in the danger, and the wild and free life of the plains, the new country I was continually traversing . . . [as] a rough rider."

A cowboy kept himself company however he could. For many, that meant singing in the saddle, filling the night sky with unabashed western laments, folk ditties, and songs from memory, whether gentle, poignant, or raucous. The solitary life drew out a man's poetic nature, cowboys knew, and that flowering had little to do with schooling. Unfettered and unlettered was the cowboy ethos, although in later years, noble British youths, known as remittance men because of their money from home, rode the range, along with educated young Americans with a taste for western life. Saddlebags held Shakespeare, along with guns, grub, and kerchiefs, but cowboys discovered early the difficulty of reading after fourteen-hour days.

A typical cowboy song embellished daily life:

As I was a-walking one morning for pleasure,
I saw a cowpuncher a-riding along
His hat was thrown back and his spurs was a-jingling
And as he approached he was singing this song.

Whoopee, ti-yi-oh, git along, little dogies
It's your misfortune and none of my own. . . .

The song, "Git Along, Little Dogies," lamented trail herding, the travail of the drive west, and particularly the night shift, in which driving rain, slashing lightning, panic-stricken cattle, and unfamiliar terrain, all in the dark, were the worst of all experiences. Trail songs echoed through the night air, lonesome and melodic, twining with the nightly cry of coyotes.

As saddleback poets cowboys fell into hypnotic rhythm, swaying in their saddles, their voices rising like campfire smoke. Just as women traded recipes, so the cowboys traded melodies, adding their own creations to such standbys as "The Chisholm Trail" or "Oh! Susanna." From bordello to rodeo, the cowboy's music thundered out, steady and predictable as drumming hoofbeats. They sang of love, death, big sky, and beyond.

Cowboys were always on the move. He was always leaving town, always bidding farewell—"Goodby, Old Paint, I'm a-Leaving Cheyenne"—always in a state of perpetual leave-taking that created an aura of deep yet romantic instability. Because he seldom married, or married late, foremost in the young cowboy's mind was the idealized woman, a virtuous young girl he might glimpse one day but could seldom, if ever, meet. Moreover, if he dared an encounter, he would soon be discouraged by her parents. Cowboys were notoriously shy with the opposite sex; for some, that seemed part of their charm. Bashful and boyish, they could face down runaways and castrate bulls, but when it came to courtship, they lost courage and became taciturn. To them, decent women were an ideal, elevated to inaccessibility. In fact, the myth of the lonesome cowboy was well founded, because of both his own ineptitude and the high mortality rate of women on the frontier, which in 1859 and 1860 was 22 percent higher than for men in the more settled regions of Dakota, Nebraska, Utah, and Wyoming.

Eyes like the morning star,
Cheek like a rose,
Laura was a pretty girl
God Almighty knows. . . .

Shy or not, the cowboy had to master the social world if he wanted to follow up on romantic hopes. Some tried to dance, even taking lessons. "I was so awkward . . . I couldn't join hands and circle to the left," admitted cowboy Walker Wyman, riding herd in the Texas Panhandle. He quickly gained the support of a Mrs. Winn, the "most friendly and best looking woman" at the dance, to guide him through the paces of a bumpy quadrille. Others diffidently tried to attend school but could never really find the time. Nearly all cowboys found that they could communicate through highjinks and tomfoolery. One eager cowhand, described by ranch hand William Timmons, had a favorite stunt to attract women. He would "catch with his mouth anything thrown across the room," never missing a food projectile, whether peanut, apple, or flying bits of popcorn. When Timmons himself met two likely young girls, his best move was also prankish:

I was scared. I'd never seen two prettier or friendlier girls, but I was scared of my shortcomings. I wouldn't know how to talk or act around them. . . . Mrs. Neurnes, who was always my good friend, thought I was too backward. . . . That evening she said, "Billie, go down to the well and get some frogs from around the old watering trough. Try to find three or four little ones. Tonight, put them between the sheets. They'll be very still until the girls kick the cover loose; then the frogs will hop."

That sounded like a harmless prank. I got the frogs in a can after supper, and while everybody else was out on the porch enjoying the beautiful moon I put the frogs under the bed covers. [When] the girls went to their room [and] the commotion started . . . they all had a big laugh. Finally, it was all blamed on me . . . but we were all soon friends again.

Grooming efforts also signaled women of a man's intent and were occasionally attempted. Timmons described one cowhand's efforts: "Panch Arnett showed the most signs of trying to spruce up for the occasion. His hair had grown so long that unless he kept his hat on, stray locks would flop down in his eyes. At the barn he'd found some old sheep shears, which Billy Connolly kept to trim fetlocks, and he'd trimmed the front of his hair almost even with his head. It was a sort of a bangs appearance. He looked cute, and seemed to have a wonderful time."

The news of an impending dance shot like fire through the ranching community. Amateur musicians and volunteer groups, such as the Long Creek Comet Band of Grant County, Oregon, found their followings between 1890 and 1920. Dances were "attended by all the ranchers, their families, and riders within the radius of forty miles," wrote cowboy Timmons. "Besides my partner, George Runyon, who played the fiddle . . . there were several other musicians in the neighborhood to take their places when they tired. This was fortunate for them, as these dances continued for two nights in succession and did not end until broad daylight." A Mr. George, of Faulkton, South Dakota, recalled: "I danced all night, along with everyone there, because the river had risen too high for us to go home."

After the men had shaken hands all around with their friends and "engaged in general conversation," said Timmons, it was time to do-si-do. "At the first sound of music everyone stampeded for the house, from which all the furniture and beds had been removed and taken to the bunkhouse to make room for the dancers." The affair turned rowdy as "the sounds of music, the raucous voice of the leather-lunged caller, the shuffle of feet, the jingle of spurs, and the whoops of the dancers was positive proof that these laddies and their lassies were having the time of their lives." If women were present, a certain etiquette prevailed. "Although outnumbered at times by six to one, no lady ever refused to dance with a man," wrote W. C. Howard, "providing he was courteous and respectful. Neither would she engage any partner for future dances, this being strictly contrary to the code of the west. Here all men were considered equal. There was no such thing as class distinction and favoritism was not shown to anyone."

In the eyes of the ultra-conservative religious, usually Calvinists, a tuned-up banjo or the fiddle's wail started up more than a dancing set. It also signaled, for many, the moment that a young man might forfeit his religion, given the sinful nature of a mob of dancers who gyrated about to such stylish tunes as "Cripple Creek," "Love Somebody," "Needle's Eye," "Thimble," "We Fish Who Bite," "Who, Where, What," "Dan Tucker," "Grin and Go Foot," and "Good Night." Young men of religious persuasion—those forbidden to dance—were free to attend a party, a lesser evil in which apple peelings, bean trimmings, even a carpet tacking were reason enough to celebrate. Music might prevail at the party, as long as no one played games that called for "skipping over the floor" in a dancelike way, according to historian William Haney. Even more refined was the social, at which genteel young folk whiled away the evening in quiet board games of Flinch or Pit. Religious songs were sung, food was served and supped, and even the purists who maintained that Flinch was too much like cardplaying would settle down to a good time.

↣ ↣ ↢ ↢

LIKE OTHER FRONTIER drifters, the cowboy gravitated to the local saloon on a regular basis, finding in the huge bar-length paintings of classical nudes, poised lyrically against Olympian settings, his sole exposure to "art." On request, the barkeep would "inflate" the painting with a shot of air from a hidden rubber bulb under the bar. As the air stream hit the nude in the vicinity of the painted navel, both the painting and the cowboy would breathe ecstatically. Inevitably, the cowboy after his heated encounter would have to cool off with another round of his favorite drink, perhaps a mule skinner's cocktail, a rough mixture of blackberry brandy and barrel whiskey, local to Colorado, or with the ancestor of the boilermaker, a shot of whiskey followed by a shot of beer. Bartenders would run a cowboy's tab for a month, often accepting saddles, blankets, horses, even acreage in payment.

To spark human interaction, a cowboy might treat the bartender to a round. If, in turn, the cowboy loner was *offered* a drink and then refused, the pregunplay hush that fell over the bar signaled "duck and hide" until the firing was over.

Most saloons were cowboy-friendly. Its walls decked with the pensive heads of moose, antelope, or deer or enlivened by guns, spurs, sombreros, iron cattle brands, riatas, and leatherwork, the saloon comforted the cowboy with memorabilia of his profession. Some liked their saloons rough; a sombrero, dangling overhead, might display a bloodstained bullet hole. Others, apparently, did not. Cowboy Walker Wyman took issue with a saloon in Pierre, North Dakota:

Texas cowboys dancing.

There did not seem to be any loafing place except saloons, so I went into [one]. It was a dirty place lined with loafers sitting on beer kegs. I told the tough-looking bartender I wanted a glass of beer. . . . I tasted the beer. It was warm. . . . I laid a silver dollar on the bar. He looked at me rather hard, said it was $1.60. . . . I wanted to get out of that place so I slid another dollar across the bar. The bartender put it in the till and looked out the window, rather bored. . . . I . . . said, "How about the change?" He looked out into the street, walked slowly to the till and got the change, and laid it on the back of the bar near the back room entrance. I started out pretty mad. He called out, "Get your change." I told him, "Keep it. You need it worse than I do."

Saloons also attracted women, and some became dealers, drifting around the gambling houses, tempting the cowhands to part with their pay while discreetly offering themselves up to an odd bargain called the cowboy wedding. "We married a girl for a week," said cowboy Teddy Blue, explaining how he would treat a woman like a lady, however briefly, presenting her with a symbolic, cheap tin "wedding" ring before the couple retired together for a week or more. At week's finish the honeymoon was over, the cowboy was eyeing the road, and the mock marriage came to an end.

Other liaisons were even briefer. Cattle towns had a number of brothels handy, as described by Walker Wyman: "We first went down by Old Hallie's house and the waiter said we should call on her. We knocked at the door and made a lot of noise to get her up as it was pretty late by that time. She lit a lamp and came to the door dressed in a fur coat over a pair of pants belonging to one of her all night guests. She wanted us to go on as she already had her hands full sleeping with two men." Later a candy vendor approached the group. "He tried to sell me a pretty interesting-looking book filled with pictures of naked women. When I refused to pay $1.50 for it, he was sore as a boil."

Gambling was a challenge, a sport, and a game to the range riders and ranchers. In a life that centered on the roundup and the long drive to market, the quick excitement of monte, faro, and blackjack, the flash of money trading hands, was heady as liquor. In big games, cattle, ranches, and mines were often staked. The most disastrous bet ever waged was the whole territory of New Mexico, signed away by its governor at pistol point. He had foolishly "raised" a Texas gambler who had bet ten thousand head of cattle and his ranch. Ultimately, he decided not to "call" against the territory, and New Mexico remained free. In Virginia City, Nevada, Joe Timberlake, an Arizona rancher, played one-thousand-dollar chips at faro. He lost forty-two thousand dollars in a single spree.

Cowboys entertained themselves in town by playing tricks, sometimes atop their horses. Spurred into saloons and gaming houses by their rowdy and fun-loving riders, horses often had firsthand looks at the card tables and billiard tables as their riders cantered amid the pool tables, then paused to strike up a game. Some cowboys even played a kind of polo while riding on horses. In Montana, according to writer Duncan Emrich, passengers on a Northern Pacific train were startled to see mounted cowboys in the dining car, while in Missoula, cowboy Sam Arthur, about to ride his horse into every

Roundup chuckwagon.

room in a saloon, was stopped by a hail of bullets from the outraged proprietor.

Rodeos were a more conventional showground for the skills of the roving buckaroos. Here a cowboy could test his and his pony's mettle, from roping to running calves. Suited up in flashy regalia, he streaked through the ring, twirling a well-aimed lasso. Fiesta spirit reigned, and cowpunchers from Cheyenne to Durango strutted their abilities in the rodeo ring. The first cited rodeo was a "round up" held

Texas cowboys bathing, ca. 1880s.

in Santa Fe, New Mexico, in 1847. Later rodeos were based on the everyday activities of the cowboy, roping and bronc riding, and only later, after Buffalo Bill Cody took his famous *Wild West* show on the road, beginning in 1883, did local roundups and rodeos feature bull-dogging (steer wrestling) and trick roping and bull riding. Early rodeos took place wherever cattle were being herded and rounded up. Later rodeos offered cash awards and a popular venue for more theatrical entertainment.

✦ ✦ ✦ ✦

THE MYTH OF the cowboy revolved around freedom, wandering, irresponsibility, scrapes with gunslinging, and getaways. To many, said cowboy William Timmons, he was a "typical . . . nuisance, [who] wears queer clothes, shoot[s] off pistols and strange oaths to frighten tenderfeet." Others saw him as a mythic hero, a dusty knight of the plains and prairies, ready to defend or do battle. Capes, hats, horse tricks, and fancy bandannas aside, most cowboys—according to a consensus of former XIT cowhands—saw themselves simply as workingmen, who, as pointed out by Timmons, were "like most other wage earners . . . [who] work . . . in order to live, and not for the joy of the thing he does." A ranch manager of the XIT spread in Texas took a dim view of cowboy caliber. To him, the XIT stood for "honesty, soberness, and no gambling. And the ranch stood squarely against stealing."

Mr. A. L. Matlock
Aug 16 1887

Dear Sir

In answer to your question as to what class of men we have had on the ranch; as a general rule I would say it has been the tailings of Texas cow boys, and they have been a hard lot generally to deal with. There have been but few men join the ranch but what were gamblers, and would further state that we have had some thieves. There has been more or less gambling on the ranch ever since I have been on it, and I can say for a truth that I am the only man on the ranch that has discharged men for gambling. . . . I have got evidence of men selling grain and provisions and putting the money in their pockets, and I discharged all that I had positive evidence against. . . . This class of men have given me a great deal of trouble. . . . We are getting rid of them as fast as possible and trying to get discipline on the ranch it [is] leaving me with a desire to quit the work.

I am respectfully,
B. F. Williams

Indeed, cowboys could be rowdy, frolicsome, uppity, and disrespectful, yet many were "true gentlemen" who hailed from the South, bringing west traditions of chivalry and gentility, often marrying and having families. Despite the popular image of careless living, cowboys were often ambitious and schemed and figured ways to amass money or buy land or stock. Rather than the illiterate and brutish men of myth, some cowboys, such as John Turner Beal, had a craving for culture. Although his cowboy years started at the age of twelve, as an adult Beal hauled back five grand pianos for his and other pioneer families in New Mexico. Whether he played is not known, but he went to extremes to see that music graced his household. Cowboys were known to play bridge as well as to dance. Upon retiring, some cowboys turned completely respectable as sheriffs, tax assessors, and justices of the peace. New Mexico cowboy James Love became, over time, a restaurateur, a pool hall and domino parlor operator, a hotel proprietor, an ice-cream store owner, and an oil field worker after spending many years on the range.

After a generation of riding freely across the open range, by 1860 many cowhands were ready to call the land, or some small part of it, their own. The myth that cowboys loved the outdoors did not always hold true. V. M. Chambers, tired of the "trials" of the range, began to think of what he could do that did not involve the weather, wrote historian Connie Brooks. That often meant acquiring his own little "spread," perhaps a small herd of cattle. Chambers aspired to move from cowboy to cowman and thus to a greater level of economic independence. But to raise cattle successfully, a settler needed from six to ten thousand dollars, hence a grubstake of some kind.

Often the cowboy dream was no more than a 160-acre dryland homestead where he could raise a few milk cows, farm, garden, and raise children, such as that owned by Walker Wyman, who had been financed by his parents in his cattle-raising efforts. "I was now ready to settle down to the life of a rancher and watch the herd grow," he said. "One can pass away a good many hours just watching the calves play and the cows fill themselves with grass."

Close shave on the open range. Photo by Edwin Smith.

6

ARMY LIFE

❖❖❖

I will never give up the ship while there is a pea in the dish.
—*Colonel J. W. Fannin*

❖❖

The duty required of us has been the *most* disagreeable that ever was assigned to any company to perform. . . . We could do nothing [and] have labored under a "big disgust" the whole time.
—*Cave Couts*

❖❖

No one can serve in the cavalry and not feel humiliated by a fall.
—*Elizabeth Custer*

❖❖

A Soldier well Cloathed is worth two Naked ones. . . .
[Clothing] Inspires them with Corage Whereas a Naked man is Cowed and ashamed of himself. . . .—*John Rogers*

FROM THE AMERICAN Revolution on, armies ebbed and flowed across the continent, bringing military men to the frontier's edge to found forts, protect trappers and traders, aid in settlement, and keep Indians at bay. There were also frequent skirmishes and wars to contend with, from the Mexican War of 1846 to the Grattan Massacre at Fort Laramie in 1854. Citizens, immigrants, and travelers made their own rules; there was no lack of flagrant ignoring of federal authority on the western frontier.

Cantonment Leavenworth, built in 1827 to launch the fur trade, was the first in a series, followed by Fort Dearborn near Chicago; Fort Howard, Wisconsin; and other posts in Iowa and Minnesota. By 1850 the U.S. Army had developed a permanent western presence, with garrisons and forts stretched like beads from Council Bluffs to Fort Vancouver. From the ghastly trenches of the Civil War came the rank-and-file men so war-torn they could barely stand, yet unwilling to leave the military at war's end, fearing even worse living conditions away from the forts and garrisons. A typical fort, such as Fort Kearny in Nebraska, contained twenty houses used as barracks and officers' quarters and a post office enclosing a square of about one acre, with twelve six-pounder guns mounted three on each side of the square. "What they were placed there for I could not imagine as they could not fire them off without knocking down the buildings," wrote John D. Young. Equally perplexing was the fort's location, with "no shelter from an enemy no elevation to the ground and

Battery A of First Artillery, combined with the survivors of General Custer's regiment, 1891. Photo by J. C. H. Grabill.

a mile away from the river." A law forbade camping within two miles of the fort, thus securing a safety perimeter. Each fort was an outpost, difficult to reach, and a reminder to each man that he was an ambassador to the wilderness, whether for good or ill.

A soldier's job was to protect traders and settlers, provide skilled labor for major building and distribution projects, negotiate and maintain Indian treaties, and "punish marauders and protect travelers," as Captain Cave Couts said. The latter, he worried, often resulted in soldiers' being forced to protect "lawless banditti of half savages, midnight assassins, horse thieves, negro stealers, house burners, etc. etc. from the just laws of the nation from which they

had fled. . . ." Such commissions were resented. Why help the lawless just because they had crossed the border?

As the military crisscrossed the country, bringing with it garrisons, horses, and guns, it also brought young men into new geographical regions, exposed them to new foods, and acted as a cross-cultural equalizer, throwing together North and South, East and West, Anglo, Asian, and African American. Men of disparate rank were exposed to one another's habits, and ideas were freely traded. Officers routinely recycled old newspapers and magazines for enlisted men to read. White soldiers often served with black, and while an abolitionist might welcome the opportunity, others were

Army Life

loath. Civil War correspondence between Union soldier Jacob Bruner and his wife, Martha, while impeccably neutral, reveals that pay was an incentive for commanding a unit of black soldiers.

Camp Logan La.
April 15th 1863

Martha I seat myself to inform you that I am well and hearty. We are now enjoying the finest kind of weather.

But—now to business. My dear wife perhaps you are aware that the President has decided to arm the negroes in rebeldom. There are now several regiments in course of organization. One or two are being raised in this vicinity—they are to be officered by white men.

I have accepted a First Lieutenant position in one of these colored regiments: my wages will be One hundred and ten dollars and fifty cents per month: or thirteen hundred and twenty six dollars per year! I expect my Commission in a few days.

Millikins Bend Louisiana.
April 20th 1863.
Dear Martha,

. . . I hinted that I intended to go into a negro regiment. Well I have my appointment and have taken the oath of office. I am First Lieutenant in the 9th Louisiana Volunteers of African descent.

My letter of acceptance and oath of office is now perhaps on its way to Washington.

My appointment is directly from the President of the United States.

My wages will be the same as a first Lieut. in the volunteer Service. . . . No doubt some will laugh (at my expense) but I don't regard them and don't ask their friendship or favor.

Officers direct from military academies found military society "so gay and brilliant" that one regiment, the Eighth Infantry, imported Italian musicians to play Mozart in the wilds of Fort Russell, in the Wyoming Territory. At some forts, frequent balls were held, and officers were noted for their pressed white gloves. Yet according to Elizabeth B. Custer, even "gentlemen of cultivation and of the highest honor, and their wives, equally ladies of culture and refinement," were eventually brutalized by the rigors, and realities, of military life. Elizabeth Therese Baird, writing of Wisconsin in 1824, noted that Fort Howard was "more completely separated from civilized life than any military fort of the present day." It was garrisoned by the Fifth Infantry and their wives, and the feeling of isolation must have been great since after several years of garrison life the soldiers turned shaggy and recondite. "They were the most disreputable-looking lot I ever saw," exclaimed Katherine Fougera upon seeing her husband's outfit, which was also Custer's cavalry. "Many wore beards. Their faces were burned to dull reds and browns, and their campaign hats and flannel shirts were utterly ruined with alkali dust."

For young enlisted men, the shock of military life came early. For John Spring, it was "humdrum, everyday life [varied] between drill, fatigue, dress parade and guard duty." Wrote seventeen-year-old John R. Cook, on his swearing-in day in December, 1857:

I was sent into a room . . . to put on my first uniform. There was a near-sighted, cross-eyed fellow in this room who had charge of affairs. There was a long table piled with clothing. It was the worst lot of shoddy stuff that ever came from a factory. I had to take a pair of pants that were many sizes too large. Then we hunted over the pile of pea-jackets and got the smallest one. . . . Then my hat! . . . It was black, high crown, about a four-inch rim, a green cord around it . . . and a large fluffy black feather plume. . . . Shoes came next . . . then came a knapsack and a haversack. The knapsack I loaded up with two suits of underclothes and a fatigue blouse. Then came a pair of dog-hair blankets; and when I strapped the whole outfit on my back I must have looked like Atlas carrying the world.

He was sent to defend the Kansas border against post–Civil War guerrilla raids from Missouri. He also was to bring home his dead brother's effects to an incredulous mother. How could her son have died? she cried. "When she gazed at the gruesome sight of that blood-stained and gashed hat, she stood mutely looking for a moment; then placing both hands over her heart uttered a deep sigh and was staggering backwards."

Observer John D. Young was amazed to find that at Fort Kearny, the "United States Regulars [were] fine appearing men but sadly deficient of clothing. Almost every man was out at the knees or elbows. Even the officers looked shabby. I saw them trying to get gloves on which required a great deal of skill They were full of holes and the fingers would not go out in the right place. . . ."

Army life, however, was less about attire than worth. A man's bravery under fire, his distinction in the field, and his ability to behave beyond the ordinary lent stature and self-confidence. Novice soldiers had no idea of their abilities, but for everyday courage, few acts of valor surpass that of an Irish soldier, McDermott, who was part of a trapped battalion in the Dakotas in 1876. Fellow soldiers lay flattened on a hillside, exposed to Indian gunfire if they dared move. Nearby a creek trickled invitingly, out of reach of the wounded and dying, who were parched and suffering from thirst. When McDermott asked permission to go into the ravine and fill the canteens, his commander, Lieutenant Gibson, saw the danger. "I could not order you to take such a risk," he warned, hoping to avoid a needless death. "But I will take it, sir," replied the man, and snaked through the grass to fill his canteens. Three trips later he was still alive. His unrewarded act of bravery saved the lives of many in his brigade.

"I kept at work and did my duty without shrinking," wrote De Witt Clinton, an officer stationed in New Mexico. "I shall never surrender or retreat," wrote William Barrett Travis, commander of Texas troops at the Alamo on February 24, 1836. "I am besieged by a thousand or more Mexicans under Santa Anna. . . . The enemy has demanded a surrender . . . otherwise, the garrison are to be put to the sword. I have answered the demand with a cannon shot, and our flag still waves proudly from the walls. . . . Victory or death," he concluded, adding the postscript "The Lord is on our side."

Dangers threatened, and to young recruits riding for the first time in the Union army, the western plains were a raw experience in roughing it. "I must be prepared for all kinds of hardships, even to eating mule meat," wrote DeWitt Clinton. When "rations were

exhausted hunger set in," recalled John Spring, who was more fortunate. "We discovered on the borders of a mountain creek a weed called *quelite*. We gathered and cooked a few camp kettles full of it, and found it quite palatable." From sunstroke to ambush, soldiers suffered together, trying to gauge upcoming trials, at times turning to pranks to relieve the stress. When Spring encamped near Gila Bend, Arizona, with a company of regulars, "some of the boys obtained a bow and arrows and . . . [made] a target of the old steward. They wounded him in the most fleshy part of his person." As punishment, "the drum major [prepared] a number of tough, pliant switches from trees growing on the border of the river to administer severe chastisement to the offenders."

⁂ ⁂ ⁂ ⁂

MILITARY MEN HAD much to learn. While some campaigns were effective, others seemed almost comic in their confusion. Henry Washington Carter was "going along without any thoughts of danger, when . . . a man fired off his gun, [crying] 'Indians! Indians!' We thought of course we would be attacked immediately . . . our martial ardor was fully aroused—only to discover that it was a false alarm." De Witt Clinton had a "hand to hand encounter" with an Indian, then "let go my revolver at him until its five barrels were expended and being excited I then threw the pistol at him, in hopes I suppose of giving him a black eye." Equally inept was George Armstrong Custer, a man with a knack for misfires, when he shot his own horse by mistake during his swearing-in ceremony.

Custer, so celebrated that Walt Whitman composed "A Death Song for Custer" in his honor, began his career brilliantly. He lived in style, riding regally in a carriage with a silver harness, pulled by magnificent matched horses with four to six soldiers trailing behind. Impetuous, successful cavalry charges won him distinction. By June 1863, at the age of twenty-three, Custer was the youngest brigadier general in the Union army, leading the Michigan Brigade's headlong charges against Confederate soldiers with the shout "Come on, you Wolverines!"

Custer joined General Winfield Scott Hancock's campaign against the Plains Indians in 1867. Hancock knew little about Indian fighting, and the campaign accomplished nothing more than expending

men and horses. In November 1875 the federal government decided that the days of nontreaty Indians were over. Sitting Bull was informed that he had to report to the reservation by January 31, 1876. Thus began the chain of events that ended in Custer's death during the Sioux War of 1876–77, a massacre in which he and 266 officers, enlisted men, and others of his command, the Seventh U.S. Cavalry, perished at the Little Bighorn. This was argued by many as the most pivotal Indian war in American history, a crushing defeat blamed largely on Custer's disobedience to an order. He had been instructed to march twenty miles southwest before turning north and west. Had he followed orders, the attack would have occurred

a day later, when other military forces were in the vicinity. A survivor, Major ———, described the battle:

We arrived on the bank of the Little Bighorn River and waded to the other side. Here the water was about three feet deep with quicksand and a very strong current. We got to the other side, dismounted, tightened our saddle girths, and then swung into the saddles. . . . When we got to the timber . . . some of the men laid down and others knelt down. . . . We got the skirmish line formed and here the Indians made their first charge. There were 500 of them coming from the direction of the village. They were well mounted and well armed. They tried to cut through our skirmish line. We poured volleys into them, repulsing their charge. . . .

Lt. Hodgson walked up and down along the line, encouraging the men to keep cool and lie low. Finally, when they could not cut through us, they strung out in single file, lying one side of their ponies from us and commenced to circle. They overlapped our skirmish line on the left and were closing in on our rear to complete the circle.

We had orders to fall back to our horses. This was where the first man was shot, Sgt. Miles F. O'Hara. . . . He was a corporal going out on the expedition and was promoted sergeant a few days before his death. We found his head, with the heads of two other men, tied together with wires and suspended from a lodge pole in one of the Indian lodges, with all the hair singed off. . . .

I looked in the rear in the direction of the river and saw the Indians completing the circle riding through the brush. I mentioned it to Captain French. . . . He replied, "Oh, no, those are General Custer's men." Just on the moment one of those Indians fired and Private George Lorentz of my company . . . was shot, the bullet striking him in the back of the neck, coming out of his mouth. He tripped tip forward out of his saddle.

Just then, the Indians fired into us in good shape. . . . Major Reno rode up and said, "any of you men who wish to escape, follow me." The order was given to charge, and away we went up the steep bank charging through the Indians in a solid body, Major Reno being in advance. As we cut through, the fighting was hand to hand, and it was death to anyone who fell from his horse or was wounded and was not able to keep up with the command. . . . The Indians were in great force on all sides of us. In this charge, there were about thirty men killed . . . but we reached the river. Bloody Knife, chief of scouts, also Charlie Reynolds, a white scout, and Isaiah Dorman, Negro interpreter, were killed. Lt. Hodgson was wounded and Lt. Donald McIntosh was killed. McIntosh was a half-breed Cherokee Indian and a brave and faithful officer.

Some . . . dozen men became separated from the command, and hid themselves in the brush or in the woods or under the river embankment, and some of these men told me afterwards that they stood in water up to their necks . . . to keep out of sight of the Indians. . . .

At this point the river was about fifty yards wide . . . with a swift current. Lt. Hodgson asked one of the men to carry him, his horse being shot and he being wounded. A trumpeter of my company, named Charles Fisher, better known as Bounce, told him to hold on to his stirrup and the horses drew [him] across the river. He was shot the second time and killed.

The opposite bank of the river was very steep, and the only way to get up to the bluffs was through a buffalo trail worn at the bank and only wide enough to let one man pass through at a time. Before we crossed the river, the fighting was desperate, and at close quarters. In many instances, the soldiers would fire the revolvers right into the breast of the Indians and after their pistols were emptied, some were seen to throw their revolvers away and grab their carbines. . . . The Indians were about ten to one of us.

In scaling the bluffs, Dr. James DeWolf, a contract surgeon on the expedition, was killed. Also Sgt. Clair, and more. Their bodies with a number of others laid under cover of our guns, so the Indians did not get a chance to scalp them. After we gained the bluffs, we could look back and could see them stripping and scalping our men and mutilating their bodies in a horrible manner. The prairie was all afire.

I counted as many as thirty arrows shot into one man's body and left there. It appears that some of the Indians sat on their horses and used their lances. . . . We could not tell who many of the men were. If their uniforms had been left on we probably could. Their bodies were scattered over the battlefield probably one and one half miles square. . . . In burying of the last of the men, we came to a gravel knoll, and here we found the body of General Custer. He was shot in two places, one bullet striking him in the right side of his face. . . . The general was not scalped.

I served through the Civil War and saw many hard sights on the battlefield, but never saw such a sight as I saw there. . . .

War with Mexico produced countless opportunities for American troops to support one another in bravery, even at risk of their lives. When Colonel J. W. Fannin left Goliad with 450 men on

Unidentified army men surveying Indian encampment, ca. 1889.

March 19, 1836, he was hounded by Mexican troops under General José de Urrea, resulting in many Texans left wounded and dying. The body of U.S. soldiers refused to abandon their fallen compatriots, so all the men surrendered. Urrea promised to send them back to the United States but instead chose to kill them in one of the war's worst massacres. Recalled a survivor, John C. Duval: "On the morning of the 27th of March, a Mexican officer came to us and ordered us to get ready for a march. He told us we were to be liberated on parole. . . . About half a mile above town, a halt was made. . . . I heard a heavy firing of musketry in the directions taken by the other two divisions. 'Boys! They are going to shoot us!' and at the same instant I heard the clicking of musketlocks all along the Mexican line. I turned to look, and as I did so, the Mexicans fired upon us, killing probably one hundred out of one hundred and fifty men in the division." Duval was knocked over when a man fell on him. After rising, he fled toward the river. When a Mexican tried to bayonet him, he was saved by a Texan "coming from another direction, [who] ran between us, and the bayonet was driven through his body." Selfless act or accident, the action saved Duval's life.

✦   ✦   ✦

A TRAGIC CAMPAIGN was recorded by Captain Sam Walker of the Texas Rangers, who, in pursuing Santa Anna's troops across the Rio Grande, kept a meticulous journal of the chase, his own capture, and his near death. The men were captured, he believed, because Sam Houston had starved them for so long "they had become reckless & careless." When the Rangers invaded a small Mexican town, "the men were hungry & no grass for their horses and . . . that many of the men . . . commenced plundering by taking such things as was necessary to their actual wants. . . . Pillage had commenced and it was difficult to check it immediately. . . . [It] was ascertained that some of the men had taken articles that they were not entitled to by the rules of war. . . . The captains . . . were all ordered to see that all property . . . should be delivered up to the Quarter master . . . and then delivered to the Alcalde of the town." Each soldier pledged himself "not to molest any private property and be submissive to orders."

After, the Texas Rangers tracked the Mexican Army deeper into its homeland, where steep ravines and dry escarpment hid any trace of water or food. Again the men were getting desperate. Walker wrote:

Some of our men found water about a mile & a half from camp. We . . . proceeded to kill the fattest and best of our horses & mules & jerk the meat for our subsistence and cut up the saddle flaps to make sandals to protect our feet from the rock & thorns. The scene here was awfully grand, so much so that language cannot fully describe it. It presented a map of destruction and a set of men reduced to the necessity of eating mules & horse flesh apparently in fine spirits & willing to endure any hardships & make any sacrifice to regain their liberty.

Days passed. The desperate men were "scattered for several miles over the valley with their blankets spread on the thorn bushes to protect them from the sun. The groans of the men were now distressing . . . some of them had been drinking their urine several days. Some of them eating or chewing nigrohead & prickley pear to raise the moisture in their mouths while others were scratching up the cold dirt & gravel from the shade of the bushes and applying it to their breast & stomachs to cool their fevers." Finally, they decided that survival meant surrender. "We had only one musket between us and we throwed that away and walked into camp."

Chained and tied, the prisoners were marched deep into Mexico. When they arrived at Salado, they heard the "melancholy intelligence" that every tenth man was to be shot as both punishment and economy, since food was scarce for either army. "We at once determined to bear it like men & soldiers," Walker wrote. "Our fate was decided by drawing beans from a covered mug. A white bean signified exemption from the execution, a black bean Death. Seventeen men drew black beans, and they all died with more than usual firmness. The groans of the murdered ceased, [the Mexicans] having shot some of them 10 or 15 times and that in the most brutal manner, shooting their heads and faces instead of . . . through the heart as . . . requested."

Walker and the few survivors finally escaped, and the bravery and support shown among the men, whites and blacks, have lived on in popular tales.

A MILITARY CAMPAIGN against the Mormons, June 1857, was also a learning experience. According to John Young Nelson:

Our expedition consisted of some two thousand soldiers and over two hundred waggons, each waggon drawn by six mules . . . . The non-combatants [broke] in the mules, more than one-half of which had never before been in harness. This was done by the waggon masters—taking them on to the prairie, there filling the waggons with sand, starting off for fifteen or twenty miles full gallop, pulling up short, forming a corral, getting out their dinner, eating, jumping up, and starting off home again. In this way the mules, after a few lessons, *became* quite tractable and gentle. . . . At times there was more sport than we wanted, for a whole train of teams would stampede and tear off madly, upsetting and smashing waggons, and killing mules, whilst some of the leaders would break away from the harness and run for miles before they could be recovered.

Traveling cross-country with huge numbers of wagons and men proved a tiresome business. "At some of the larger streams we had to give in, and sit down and wait until the waters had subsided," Nelson recalled. The Platte River was so swollen that crossing was impossible, so they finally caulked the wagon boxes tight, harnessed twenty-four mules to each wagon, and floated over. Another danger was gunpowder. How would it survive heat and shocks?

On lowering the wagons down a mountainside one of the zinc ammunition boxes . . . jolted, [and] exploded one of the cartridges. The case contained over a thousand [rounds], and these went popping off, one after the other, until all were expended. The shots were flying out in all directions, amidst yells, shrieks, and execrations. The waggon-master had the presence of mind to gallop his team out into the prairie, whilst the entire outfit made for the best cover it could find. The driver, who was wonderfully plucky, kept his team well in hand and never moved, knowing all the time he was sitting on a magazine which might blow him to

pieces at any moment. When it was all over . . . the strain had been so great on the poor fellow's nerves that he went mad. He was called the Lightning Torpedo Man after that, [and] although he subsequently recovered he was always more or less silly.

In the West rigid rules of warfare relaxed slightly with the influx of green enlistees, men who knew nothing of military ways and were wanderers, ex-traders, or scouts down on their luck, in need of jobs. The quality of commanders was also in decline, thought Henry Washington Carter, who saw his "respected Chief, Col. Gardner . . . dining out when some man . . . insulted him in some way. The Col. [threw] a leg of chicken at him. The other man replied by throwing a plate at the Colonel. Pistols were then drawn and some shooting was done," but apparently neither was seriously hurt.

John Young Nelson recalled the discouragement of a group of Union soldiers near Fort McPherson on the Platte River after an Indian-hunting platoon had returned empty-handed. Feelings against their commander, Colonel Brown, ran high, even mutinous. "A resolution was passed by the officers that his orders should not be carried out." This seemed indecisive; the men wanted more action. Several officers then placed a ten-pound shell under the colonel's bed and laid a train of powder from it to a far distance. The fuse failed to ignite, "and the next morning the Colonel was just as frisky as ever." At dawn tents and wagons were readied, but "much to the Colonel's surprise, the troops refused to move. The artillery, who were Southerners, were ordered to fire upon the men; but the entire command was of one opinion, and the artillerists were told that if they fired a shot they would be seized and blown to pieces from the mouths of their own guns. They thought better of it, and caved in." Discontent deepened into mutiny. The poorly dressed men, their feet and hands frostbitten, were weak and starving. When they finally straggled back to camp, there was open rebellion. The oblivious colonel was startled by their rancor; they were equally startled when he issued an invitation to a private soldier to "lick him" if he could. The moment he "received a resounding beating," all grievances vanished. The men welcomed the colonel back, and however briefly, all was well.

Some commanders were so shameless that even the army eventually took notice and tried to get rid of them. "My regiment . . .

bought out a Major for $23,000, to get him out of the army—he being very disagreeable," wrote James Ross Larkin, riding with the army on the Santa Fe Trail. Cave Couts, on command in California, wrote of an "unpleasant" military experience in his diary, dated 1846. A literate and fairly keen observer, he offered a glimpse into a regiment trapped under reprobate command. What to do?

An unpleasant assignment in Arkansas. The duty required of us has been the *most* disagreeable that ever was assigned to any company to perform. . . . Protecting a lawless banditti of half savages,

midnight assassins, horse thieves, negro stealers, house burners, etc. etc. from the just laws of the nation from which they had fled, settled or scattered themselves along the state line. . . . We could do nothing. Gen. A. gave the orders and Capt. B. was satisfied to please *him*, and has taken no responsibility on his own shoulders. We have labored under a "big disgust" the whole time.

Sat Sept 3 1846
Our Commandant has had a "glorious time" for several days. To exercise authority, without reason or common sense, drink

Army Life

101

whiskey with Mr. Rayson & molest the half of his command . . . is to him, all that is required of a commanding officer of such an expedition. Charges are bound to be preferred against him upon our arrival in California, even if his conduct in future should be *just and impartial* he has already done too much.

Thursday Oct. 5th Just out of the mountains, since leaving Encino. . . . The route is passable with wagon using the men for mules. . . . It might justly be considered a *miracle* that we made our way through, under the circumstances. Our commanding officer *drunk* nearly *all the while* and interfering with everyone's business, giving the men whiskey by the bucketful from 7 o'clock until encamping, never looking an inch beyond the end of his nose, whilst on marched down the canada, though urged to hurry out, lest he should be caught by a rain, and from the torrents (which we could see frequently occurred) that would rush from the mountains down the ravine, and [drown] our whole train.

Sunday Oct. 22. Arrived at Ft. Tubac, a small presidio, to day. Yesterday and today, the Maj. has been worse than I have yet seen him, able to set on his horse this morning at 8 o'clock and no more! Came to me last night, tight of course, and insisted on my letting a horse of my company run a race, which he and Evan had made, I refused notwithstanding all his entreaties, and he seemed to think quite hard of it.

Few records document the private, sexual lives of soldiers. Army movements were usually followed by a phalanx of laundrywomen, a euphemism for concubines and cohorts, as well as by actual laundry providers supported by handouts and military largess. "A lady with ladylike manners and small feet and hands applied to be laundress to our company," wrote John Spring, stationed in Arizona. "I do not know how much washing she performed, if any. I only know that she had frequent visits from the more decent men of the company during all hours of the day and evening." Deeply resented by army wives, the laundresses offered their laundry services with grim endurance, elbowing their way through crowds of Indian women ganged up around the fort's perimeter. Given the daily proximity near crowds of women, soldiers fell easily into dalliance. This behavior eventually led in 1876 to the edicts of the Banning Committee that outlined rules about immorality at frontier military posts, made public by a rumored liaison between Custer and the Indian woman Monasetah. Officers were commanded to maintain strict moral standards and give up their Indian women, while enlisted men were less restricted.

Garrison soldiers, shy or rowdy, often had idealized notions of women. Although there were bountiful camp followers, there was a dearth of "proper" women at military bases, leaving most men with skewed memories of "true womanhood," usually an image of women as saintly, remote, and angelic. The lack of practical courting experience prompted fantastic versions of "true" femininity, and occasionally, starved chivalry turned to eager excess. In one case, Major Marcus Reno was so smitten by the beautiful young daughter of a commanding officer that, unable to approach her in real life, he hovered outside her window at night; she was simply too unattainable. His ardor was unacceptable, and he was called a Peeping Tom and was stopped only by a court-martial.

If sexual liaisons occurred between men, they were less documented. Who would write of them? One interesting story, however, was recorded by Katherine Gibson Fougera, who accompanied her husband on Custer's forays into the Dakota frontier in the 1870s. At the garrison was a "tall, thin Mexican woman" who was the "superlaundress" of the encampment and the wife of Sergeant Nash. Mysteriously she always wore a veil, part of Latin coquetry, no doubt! Skilled at laundering delicate clothes, she was the favorite of the officers' wives, who brought her baskets of fine silks and linens to clean. A talented cook, she stirred and patted tamales into mouthwatering morsels and offered her culinary services to all. Also a careful midwife, she "handled babies not only with efficiency but with marked tenderness as well." When asked why she had no children, Mrs. Nash would draw her veil even closer and sigh deeply: "Ah . . . it is not given to us all to be mothers."

Indeed not. When Mrs. Nash suddenly died, this regimental paragon of laundry, birthing, and kitchen skills turned out to be . . . a man! Indignation turned to hysteria as women recalled the intimacy of childbirth, the confidences, the firmness of her touch. Mrs.

Nash had been a political fugitive who escaped across the Mexican border. Sergeant Nash, who had been stationed in the area, suddenly appeared with a "bride." Nash as a husband automatically gained the advantages of a married soldier, with more freedom, better food, and individual quarters. The fugitive "wife" learned to cook, and Nash, "goaded by greed and his appetite," according to Fougera, settled down to married life. But perhaps Nash also used the deception to maintain an inadmissible relationship.

Others fared less happily, finding in the fruits of military life an unrewarded and often needy old age. Stephen F. Austin clearly understood the hardships that he had suffered for the sake of Texas. "I have no house, not a roof in all Texas, that I can call my own. . . . I make my home where the business of the country calls me. . . . I have no farm, no cotton plantation, no income, no money, no comforts. I have spent the prime of my life and worn out my constitution in trying to colonize this country. . . . All my wealth is prospective and contingent upon the events of the future. . . . I am still in debt for the expenses of my trip to Mexico in 1833, 1834 and 1835. My health and strength and time have gone in the service of Texas, and I am therefore not ashamed of my present poverty."

Some officers, however, made quite snug fortunes. Indian campaigner Captain Clary had invested family money in land speculation and thrived. Captain Randolph B. Marcy was unusual in being an infantryman who ranked among the elite engineers through sheer merit and who also earned money from his popular books on the West. Less fortunate financially was Captain Martin Scott, "the great shot," who distrusted speculation. Since he bought cautiously and made some money, Scott jestingly claimed that he "became rich honestly." G. H. Bumgardner wrote to Uriah Oblinger, who was trying to collect a pension from the military and having difficulty, "Everyone who served for 3 years or more should have a large service pension." Oblinger had asked Bumgardner to testify to his medical problems. Bumgardner seemed uneasy with the request. "I know that you suffered from piles & catarrh more or less all the time but all the testimony I could give would be general . . . as for fainting spells I do not remember them now." Oblinger also asked C. S. Bishop to testify before a military board on his medical debility. "I will do what I can for you," wrote Bishop. "[But] I never treated you for anything excepting those spells of fainting. [Did] you ever have Rhumatis?" Bishop agreed to appear in Oblinger's behalf in exchange for "Notary fees . . . RR fare and dinner."

By the 1890s, and the end of the frontier, the army had accomplished its goals. Indian tribes had been defeated, and the West had been explored, settled, and snugly integrated into the nation. Many soldiers had deserted its ranks, but even more had devoted most of their adult lives to the country's service, earning a private's salary of thirteen dollars a month and a lifetime's worth of adventure, heartache, and some understanding.

Part 3

SETTLIN' IN

❖

7

HOME ON THE RANGE

❧

A man without house, home or family is not a citizen anywhere, in the real sense of the word.
—*Henry Brokmeyer*

✷

Having conquered Kansas, he knows well there are no worse worlds. . . .—*Carl Becker*

✷

Breaking sod was a slow and expensive process. . . . John Darymple broke five thousand acres a year in spite of hardships.
—*John Bartu*

✷

The mule is a singular animal. Every spring it has to be broken to work, as if it never before had known what it was to be harnessed.
—*William G. Johnston*

IN THE WEST the prairies seemed so endless that one lonely settler, awed by the distance he'd come, tied a handkerchief to a wagon wheel to count out its revolutions. Czech emigrant Frank Sikyt marked the miles from Missouri to Nebraska at a pace of twenty miles a day. With only a "compass and a gallon of whisky," he reached Nebraska in "pretty good" spirits. Near Hay Springs, Nebraska, early settlers left a path across the plains littered with rag-tied weeds, marking the trail back to civilization. Weeds, roots, stumps, and rocky outcroppings defined the distance to and from a homesteader's claim, often a spot so rugged that the steely-rooted bunchgrass lay tangled as a pelt, refusing to be cleared from the fields. Plow teeth would snarl and mat with the wiry roots, to be combed off by hand, piled at the edge of the field, then hauled away to be burned.

The homesteading farmer "has a heap of little fixens to study out, and a great deal of projecting to do, as well as hard work," wrote Illinois diarist James Haines, commenting on the steep and inescapable costs of farming. First, a man must make his way west, bringing along his entire family—a high enough expense. To equip an eighty-acre western farm, without the cost of land, he needed an outlay of at least a thousand dollars, not to mention the shelter and feeding of his family through the long period between planting and harvest. Once land was acquired, he had to clear, furrow, plant, and fence it, then buy or borrow draft animals, livestock, seed, and tools. On

Family in dugout in Oklahoma, ca. 1885.

forestland, timber was often cleared by cutting, or "girdling" a tree, allowing it to stand for four to six years, then toppling the dried hulk to be cut or burned, leaving its root base thrust like metal straps deep into the ground. This was effective for heavily treed areas or homestead land that could be left for several years before planting crops, and it kept the cost of clearing timbered land at from five to twenty dollars per acre.

Sod had to be broken and crumbled, easier, perhaps, than clearing timber, but exhausting. If the field was properly turned, the prairie farmer could usually clear 80 to 160 acres in two to four years. Breaking sod was a slow and expensive process, taking place in June and July on the high plains; professional sodbusters were hired as a day labor force. In the first year, when there was no profit in the land and no seeding, many homesteaders made money by picking up buffalo bones to sell at six dollars a ton.

"An intelligent, prudent man, with five hundred pounds in his pocket, may rely on finding that sum sufficient to start him successfully on 320-acres of land," wrote one traveler. Other estimates, taken from broadsides and advertisements of the day, cited up to five thousand dollars cash. So difficult was farming that over time everything fell into disrepair: harrow, plow, scythe, and more. Following the great boom of the eighties, central Dakota, western Nebraska, and Kansas were scarred with broken patches that turned quickly to sod and weeds, caved-in wells, and crumbled walls of abandoned shanties. Economic reverses reigned. Farm ownership was often a morass of disputed land titles, accumulated mortgages, and failed crops. Seldom did a letter reach home without the mention of financial or personal woe. "You said if there was anything special we wanted . . . well here it is," wrote Nebraska homesteader Uriah Oblinger to his sister. "A yoke of cattle, a wagon, a cow, a well, an orchard full of fruit, a good house & barn a crib full of corn 6 big fat hogs, and a house full of Furniture [and] send by express." Farm life often seemed a chain of endless attrition.

"Products of the farm were very cheap," wrote James H. Rinehart of Iowa. "The usual price for corn was from ten to twelve and a half cents per bushel, and in some instances it dropped as low as eight cents. Nice dressed hogs sold for $1.50 to $2.00 per hundred, and at one time as low as $1.25. The usual price for eggs was from three to five cents per dozen in summer, and from seven to eight cents during the winter. Farm labor was 50 cents by the day, or $10 by the month."

Despite such rigors, observed British traveler James Hall, "men were drawn to settle down in regions where there was complete freedom of choice; where, map in hand, one can roam through beautiful nature for hundreds of miles in order to select land and its cover of woods and meadows according to one's own desires." Fifty houses sprang up in sixty days in Lawrence, Kansas, in 1855. To file a claim, the homesteader needed a cabin that was at least twelve square feet. A man might "stake off" a tract, then throw down a perimeter of logs to prove that building was in process. Some would simply scatter around logs, then, after proving ownership, take them home again. A shingle driven into the ground, inscribed with the homestead name, also served as a claim, as well as a more casual marker, a rock placed at each of the future four corners of the house, with a split stick holding a tiny bit of window glass in the center. After camping out within his imaginary walls for several weeks, the claimant could swear that he lived in a house with a roof and a glass window and thus buy a fine tract of land for sixty to eighty cents an acre. Too easy! Many believed the government's breezy ways were too tolerant and encouraged failure.

Yet for many, home-building efforts were sincere. "I am now located in a log cabin constructed by amateurs," said J. M. Booth, one

Unidentified homesteader, ca. 1915.

of many men who learned about building by doing it. Men of good heart and family instincts doggedly persevered, building their broods one-room shacks, twelve by fourteen feet square, ashamed that there was nothing else to offer. Yet lime-slaked walls could turn bright and cozy, and with luck, a man could be proud of his family's "real little home." "If one cabin is not sufficient, another is added until the whole family is accommodated; and thus the homestead of a sub-

stantial farmer often resembles a little village," noted James Hall. All a man, and his family, needed was a minimum shack and at least ten acres under cultivation.

Families in Nebraska, the Dakotas, and Kansas often burrowed in sod houses, like gophers. Men hewed the thick dirt into bricks, then layered them into walls around a single large room, sometimes with a cellar or storeroom on the side. On a dirt roof, pieces of sod one foot by two feet were layered over rough planks. Clay was lathered on top, filling the cracks and rainproofing the room—just barely. J. M. Booth remarked that if the homesteader was thirsty at night, "he has only to turn over onto his back and keep his mouth open" to be satisfied with rainwater. Plus, he could always tell what the weather was without opening the door to see because of the roof's "being of an airy openwork style." Typically, a room brimmed with beds, none of them privately partitioned off, but made "private like" by a crown of pinned-up cotton sheets, said Caroline Kirkland. A large chest functioned as the family wardrobe, often draped with "the go-to-meeting hats and bonnets, frocks and pantaloons of a goodly number of all sizes." For decoration, the wall might sport "large broadside sheets, caravan show bills . . . a few iron spoons, a small comb, and sundry other articles." James H. Rinehart recalled: "There was an attic where most of the larger children could be stored at night and three or four of the smaller ones slept in the trundle bed." Outside were stables and chicken houses, where tall air vents poked like straws ten feet over the roofs, allowing the animals to breathe through a blanket of winter snow.

Sod walls were porous and nonsupportive. In one case, reported by the *Minneapolis* (Kansas) *Messenger*, in 1867, "Sam White's cattle broke out and one of the steers weighing about sixteen hundred pounds wandered onto the roof of the Woody family's dugout. When directly over the bed occupied by Mr. and Mrs. Woody the steer broke through, falling across the head board of the bed. Mr. Woody finally got the steer off the bed and looked after the injuries of his wife and child. This is a great country, where cattle . . . fall in on people while they are asleep."

Family life was a collection of weed brooms, newspapered walls, flour sack underwear, and cow chip fires. Children struggled to carry water, slept on straw tick mattresses, and were slathered in cow manure poultices. Women twisted hay for the fire, carded their own wool, knitted pyramids of mittens and socks, and resigned themselves to always being hard up.

Frontier farmers dressed nearly alike. During the summer, each wore a hat of plaited rye, oats, or wheat straw and a shirtlike garment that dangled outside his pants, called a jumper or, in some localities, a wamus. His farming uniform might be of thick duck or denim or, if he owned sheep, homespun wool. Summer invited lighter wear, pants of cotton, flax, or tow linen cloth, all in the simplest, plainest style. Dress pants were styled from heavy grain sacks costing fifty cents apiece. "Comfort and utility absolutely controlled material, make and fit of all male garments, whether for summer or winter, hot or cold weather, home or wear abroad," wrote observer James Hall. In the summer, bare, calloused toes scuffled through the bunchgrass, hoping not to cross paths with a venomous reptile. The family footgear was saved for dress-up occasions, but it was hardly unusual to see a barefoot man dancing. Lacking winter socks, men wrapped rags around their feet and muffled their boots in gunnysacks to keep their feet from freezing.

↦ ↦ ↤ ↤

A FARMER LEARNED how to judge the soil, make and use organic fertilizer, break stone, calcine lime, and cull the best wood for buildings, furniture, field implements, fences, and firewood. He had no need of a carpenter and ideally turned to a cabinetmaker or mason only for the finer work. To farm successfully, a man would have to transform a forest into arable land; till fields for grain; sow a garden; raise tobacco, cotton, hemp, flax, and other products; breed cattle and foal horses; market hogs and cattle; shear sheep; butcher beef; stitch together his own shoes; and draw maple sugar. As a hunter he would have to process animal skins as skillfully as the best of tanners. For the hardworking farmer, each year his holdings would increase by a quarter section, more land would be fenced, more crops cultivated, more buildings added, more improvements made in the home, and his livestock would burgeon. The more he learned, the better became his family's prospects.

"So far we are doing well," wrote Czech settler Vavrin Stritecky. "And if God, the Lord of all the earth, will give us (continued) good health, we will do better here than in Europe. It was very difficult for me 10 months ago when I parted with my dear homeland, but in that short time a person forgets, as they say—out of sight, out of mind—and we are growing accustomed to this wild America and we want to make a new homeland for ourselves here."

"We lived on an eighty-acre farm," wrote cowboy Oliver Nelson. "Flat, black, sticky land, poor crops, it was fenced with rails, worm

fashion, cross-staked and ridered. We had no barbed wire then, but a fellow was advertising a number 8 wire to be stretched and then clinched [with] three point barbs. It was no good. The barbs would get loose and slip." Barbed wire was patented in 1874 by Joseph F. Glidden of De Kalb, Illinois, and the twisted, spiked wire was first used at the Frying Pan Ranch, in Amarillo, Texas. After its success, the prairie homesteader as able to control his holdings.

As a Dakota settler Nelson observed many European immigrants claiming homestead lands, including John Bartu, who emigrated from Bohemia to Wisconsin at the age of fifty-four:

He left Wisconsin in the fall of 1885 and headed for Dakota Territory, filing on a section of land. He purchased lumber in Bismarck and constructed a house about 16 by 16, consisting of only one room. This shack had only one door leading outside and two windows. He bought a cook stove, for the dual purpose of cooking food and heating the room. Wood for fuel was obtained from nearby Beaver creek.

In May, 1886, the mother arrived with 5 children. They had sold their personal property: their horses, cows, machinery and furniture, and brought with them only their clothing, bedding, some kitchen utensils and crockery. Mr. Bartu sent a man with a team and wagon to fetch them to their new home.

They lived in the small shack only during the summer, and that fall, with the help of a neighbor, they built a larger home about 14′ x 24′ of sod. This house contained two rooms and a storm shed. A curtain or light drapery hung in the doorway between the 2 rooms. They had a door opening into the shed and another to the outside, but both doors were homemade. Each room had 2 windows. Mr. Barbour showed them how to lay the sod, grass side down. Every other layer was laid at right angles crosswise, to the preceding one. Openings for doors and windows were left small enough so they could be trimmed to fit. The roof was of lumber, which John Jr. hauled from Bismarck . . . the inside of the house was plastered with a clay and straw mixture.

When a house was done, no farm was considered workable without a well, usually hand dug in a risky operation that sank pipes more than a hundred feet directly down to tap water. Steam-powered well-drilling equipment was prohibitively expensive but, when used, would chew out a deeper shaft, right down to the good table water below. Montana farmer Josiah Rhoton siphoned water 210 feet to reach his livestock, while Lawrence Frizzell, on his homestead south of Fort Rock, drilled three wells, also over 200 feet deep. Windmills, flighty as seagulls, were recognized as a brilliant means of harnessing wind power to suck up well water for farming and domestic use.

⁺ ⁺ ⁺ ⁺

IMMIGRANT FARMERS HAD much to learn in the West. In Europe they had tended their birthing cows as tenderly as midwives, while in America, wrote Vavrin Stritecky, "It is really peculiar how resilient the livestock is," each cow giving birth entirely alone. Such loneliness was a strong theme for the Stritecky family, surrounded by non-Czech neighbors, cut off by language and habit from community, friends, and relatives from the homeland. "Hardly anyone writes to us," Stritecky, unsettled by the silence from his home, said in a letter home. "I am sending you [a picture of] our farm," he told his relatives. "Only it's a photograph taken when the trees had already lost their leaves, so it's rather sad. And it was cold that day, even the pigs aren't outside and the cattle grazed somewhere else, so they aren't visible."

⁺ ⁺ ⁺ ⁺

FOR MEN, THE calendar gave as much variety as a farmer might expect. Seasons bloomed into a riot of spring planting before collapsing into a drowsy routine of summer harrowing and fall harvesting, a cycle interrupted only by brief jaunts to the store, the

mill, and the tavern, with time off to cast for lake perch or hunt game. Summer crops grew silent and lush, yet a man, straining to listen, might hear the sound of corn quietly growing. "The leaves . . . unroll . . . until the entire leaf is free·except the stem, which still adheres to the stock. It is the rupture of this part . . . that produces the particular 'clisp' sound, heard on all sides on a still July night in a corn field," said Henry Brokmeyer. During corn cutting, men would "blade and top" the heavy ears, pulling the tassel tops into a rough bundle, then cutting the corn by hand for shucking. During fall and early winter, all hands were busy, stripping the corn husks. At winter's first chill, the wary farmer would grind up a three-month supply of feed and pack the haymow for the hungry animals, haul coal near the house, nail heavy paper around the walls for insulation, then buttress the paper with manure, piled against the walls to keep out the cold. Since the manure froze brick hard, there was usually no odor. In winter, men built and repaired fences on good days or hauled in wood, since the frozen ground made it easy to transport. On rainy days, wheat was threshed in the barn.

Settler John Darymple of South Dakota broke five thousand acres one year, using six hundred head of horses to pull 130 binders in the same field. Harrowing the fields came just before broadcast seeding in the spring. "Get up at 3 am to feed horses," he wrote. "At 4 o clock the rest of the family would rise. Then the horses were harnessed to get ready for the fields. The women would cook breakfast, and everyone eat, and after, the men would go into the field as soon as it was daylight and work all day until dark."

John Bartu hitched four horses to a heavy canvas binder to harvest grain. A shocker rode alongside the binder and bundled the wheat. Each thatch landed not in a heap but in a firm bundle to withstand strong winds. Each thatch was also slightly spread out at the bottom so air could waft through the wheat and keep it dry. Bundles were laid, heads inward, in overlapping circles: the artful skill of grain stacking. In Oregon, wigwams of retted flax dotted the dry fields, where flax was reserved for domestic use. As late as 1838 nearly every farmer in the northern United States grew a small plot of flax for his family's clothing needs. In the crop cycle, oats were harvested first because they ripened first, and barley and wheat came after. Oat and barley shocks trembled with kernels; no man left a barley field without a prickly skin of barley "beard" coating his clothing and piercing through cloth, skin, and equilibrium. The bright yellow stubble of a well-shocked field, aglow with reflected sunlight, delighted the farmer. Wheat bundles were tossed high, and profits happily tallied.

By 1887 modern machines could thresh seven hundred bushels in four hours or nearly fifteen hundred bushels a day. By 1897 the threshing machine capacity had nearly doubled. Threshing the old way called for a wheel with spokes, harnessed to five horses that trudged around in a circle, turning a wheel connected to a drive shaft, which ran the threshing machine. Occasionally, threshing party workers, disgruntled by low pay, might pitch forks into the threshing machine or secretly slip rocks into the grain bundles, breaking the feeder arms and teeth and causing costly delays while repair parts were sought. At times fires burst out in the straw, fanned either by wind or by mischief. Labor organizers were often responsible, and if one slipped into the local harvesting and damaged a thresher, locals would have to decide his fate. "Chase him off!" neighbors of settler Barbara Levorson in North Dakota cried when an organizer slipped into the local harvesting and damaged the thresher. "No," others

Rounding up the sheep, California, ca. 1915.

said. He would only slip back later to stir up excitement. Better to watch him carefully. After threshing, farmers collaborated to haul their grain to town, usually traveling together with their wagons for safety. Grain was weighed by buyers who were often dishonest in their calculations.

Festivities sprang up as naturally as rye grass in sod, rollicking through remote outposts from Missouri to the Pacific Northwest. Men might whoop, howl, and "likker up," or constrain themselves into genteel escorts for wives, mothers, and sweethearts. Either way, the blessings of nature and fellowship were enjoyed at county fairs, logrollings, barns, bees, and picnics. When men sat in a circle and husked ears of corn, it signaled not only the promptings of a neighborhood frolic, a husking bee, but the beginnings of the country's most distinctive cooperative effort, the harvest ritual, enlivened by corn liquor, clouds of tobacco smoke, and vigorous sociability. Huddled around a sliding pyramid of corn, men and women stripped and shucked the golden ears, hands flying, laboring over a tedious task, brightened considerably by the good-natured synchrony of the group. Could any man husk alone? The bee drew society together, lightening the labor and adding flair to the workaday world. Usually festivities started at moonrise, when the silver orb bathed light upon a "long ridge about four feet high" of golden corn, according to a Green County, Indiana, chronicler. Two young men were elected captains, and teams "set to husking with all their might, each making as much noise as he possibly could."

These male-dominated events might quickly turn brutal. "I have never seen more anxious rivalry or a fiercer struggle," wrote Daniel Drake, with men trying to outwit, outwork, and finally trick their competition. While fingers flew, feet surreptitiously pushed corn to the opponent's side, redistributing the load. Quart after quart of rum, whiskey, or hard cider was downed as the "green quart . . . bottle" was passed around. Tipsy and belligerent, men fought, shoved,

and challenged one another until sleep or stupor finally settled in around midnight.

Men thrived on logrollings, timber-clearing festivals, and sugar bees, in which they probed trees for sap to turn into syrup. There were even "dunging frolics," where fields were cooperatively slathered with manure. But nothing unified male strength and cooperative spirit like a barn building, a house raising, a prairie dog poisoning, or a shrubbing (the cutting away of small timber), tricky, skill-demanding efforts in which an "air of genuine risk as well as masculine display of strength hung over the[ir] united efforts," according to historian Jack Larkin. In a house-raising party, men struggled to push up a rough-sided two-story wall with long poles, arms trem-

bling and muscles strained, each became an intimate part of his neighbor's life, as friendships were sealed, whiskey was traded, and stories were told. Some men, whooping with laughter, demonstrated daring by leaping down from the towering barn frame, landing splayed and bruised at the feet of their awed companions. Another frontier day, enlivened by corn liquor and deep economic need.

Holidays called up rounds of festivity, enlivened by rowdy and rude horseplay—jostling, wrestling, and intense drinking side by side. "This being Xmas we were obliged to indulge the men with a holy day for which they had hoarded up their ration of whiskey," wrote settler William Dunbar. "The consequence was a great deal of frolick." Inebriation led to competition, as men stood chest to chest, pushing to outdo one another in muscle-bulging displays. For men, holiday festivities soared with the sound of dynamite, exploded with anvils or whole barrels of explosives, blasted on the hillside.

Settlers found other opportunities for fun. Midwestern winters saw steamy livestock races on the frozen lakes as huge, frisking horses pulled light cutters, the riders muffled in fur, sleigh bells jingling, while skiing, coasting, sledding, and laughter lessened, for a moment, the grim reality of a family's life. Often the older men had lived out their dreams of independence in their new home, and any kind of warmth, gaiety, or "jollification" was an encouragement that all was well and they had not failed.

Buffoonery, jokes, and pranks warned away despair; any event was a time to laugh. A North Dakota farm cook, tired of his labors, "took old bread and crackers and poured rancid fat over them" and kept them frying on the stove. "Soon black smoke poured out of the stovepipe and a horrible smell hung around the cooker," according to observer Ole Dovre. The chef, meanwhile, leaned against the doorway, enjoying the furor he'd created. Surprise parties were a favorite with all. Revelers would ride off to someone's claim shack or shanty with sandwiches and cake. "Once in a while the hostess would have a jar of pickles . . . and that was surely a treat," wrote Minnie Slack McCaughey.

All-male festivities were common, from the womanless dances of the mountain men to a "pioneer party, for males only," hosted by Dr. Daniel Drake in Ohio. William McGuffey remembered the splendor of Drake's mansion, "Buckeye Hall . . . with a large stone jar in which was inserted a buckeye tree in leaf, which reached to the ceiling. The mouth of the jar was covered round the tree with moss. Ranged round the jar were small shells of pumpkins, filled with earth, in each of which was set a young buckeye branch. . . . In the other room, on a table, were two large buckeye bowls, one filled with popped corn, the other with apples. . . . The company for some time amused themselves with the contents of the bowls, after making acquaintance with fellow natives." The party was launched when the host entered with a "huge buckeye bowl of sangaree made from native wine, in which were floating several gourds. A bumper was then drunk to Our Pioneer Fathers, and other sentiments followed."

Disputes flared up yet could also be patched up. "Denton . . . was the only man in the neighborhood with whom I had any personal trouble," wrote Kansas Sheriff John Cook. "And that was caused by his hogs and my fence, his hogs not being allowed to run at large by law, and my fence not being hog-tight." After their dispute, the men "drifted" apart. In Montgomery County, Kansas, a Mr. Heaton took up a claim. Leaving his wife, goods, and lumber, Heaton started for a sawmill, about four days' journey, for more lumber. His absence was an opportunity for a "covetous" land grabber, Soapier, to ride up and order Mrs. Heaton off the land. The next day Soaper returned with a party of men and moved away all the Heaton possessions—except for Mrs. Heaton, who "stood in the door of her tent with a Smith & Wesson revolver in her hand, and refused to budge." After the men left, she rode into town and reported the incident to Sheriff John R. Cook, who gathered up ten settlers who "mounted and galloped across that six miles of virgin prairie, laughing and joking like a lot of schoolboys out for a lark, Mrs. Heaton riding . . . the lead, her Smith & Wesson hanging . . . around her waist." Soaper had breached two codes: the sanctity of womanhood and that of private property. Perhaps he believed that a third code, that of squatters' rights, would prevail. Usually a would-be settler could take any unoccupied piece of the public domain, up to 160 acres, if he wanted, and squat. But not in this case. Said Cook: "The moral law of every frontier settlement is held inviolate and will brook no interference. The presence of Mrs. Heaton meant that the land was occupied." "It was a dirty, cowardly deed for you and your gang to come here and hector and threaten just one lone woman that only weighs eighty-nine pounds," one man cried out. Soapier rode away, threatening to "settle it in the courts." Two weeks later, wrote Cook, "we were all arrested at our homes . . . served with warrants. . . . Any one of us could have resisted . . . but . . . we were law-abiding citizens." The men hired a lawyer, Bishop W. Perkins, who "pitched in and handled a vocabulary of words that took us all by surprise. He juggled words and phrases in such rapid succession that he completely spellbound his hearers. He [painted] a word picture of frail little Mrs. Heaton, alone on a desolate prairie, about to be devoured by human wolves." The case was thrown out, yet one more "legal farce" that Cook had seen during the early settlement of southeastern Kansas.

It was also a victory against squatters, a migratory and shiftless

Apple harvest, ca. 1900.

type that lived without labor, moving about, staking numerous claims, then selling them. The squatter could simply be an idler, briefly claiming someone else's land, or a professional, who would stake, claim, sell, and vacate repeatedly, gaining control of valuable mill sites, fords, and lush cropland, then inducing a real farmer to buy. "A pair of boots . . . would have secured the right to a tolerably good lot," noted J. Ross Browne of Bodie Valley, California. "The

squatters near Ft. Leavenworth (Arkansas) have to take out tents and pitch them in order to claim their farms," wrote De Witt Clinton. "They bring two or three mattresses with them and their families stay all night and in the morning put back to Misouri where they live, leaving their tents standing to keep off other emigrants. These men do not intend settling the land but only do this to gain property. Real settlers are very scarce."

Yet hospitality and generosity were the true homestead ethic. If a fire burned a man's hay, a neighbor sent over a load. If a man's crop failed, neighbors pooled a few bushels to tide him over. If he fell ill, they helped him sow the next year's crop. At evening time, the back porch drew men from near and far, to clean their Colts, shine their muzzle-loaders, spin tales of hunting, dogs, and crops, and brag about local game kills, usually quail, prairie chickens, ducks, geese, and deer. When John D. Young "camped at sunset within a few rods of a Kansas farmer's house," it was only hospitable to pay a visit. Simple pleasures ensued: "We purchased . . . some warm biscuits and fresh milk and had a supper fit for a king. In the evening the farmer invited us to his house. There was to be a singing school there that night. We had a very merry time of it. There was a good many young folks present. We sang some songs together and then a rivalry started between Illinois and Kansas to see which could sing the best songs and in the best style. After a few hours of merry strife we acknowledged the supremacy of the Kansas girls."

On the farm, curiosity and generosity both burned brightly, and a farmer frequently nudged his plow to a halt and hung over the nearest fence to chat if a stranger, or a neighbor, happened by. "Now set you down" was the inevitable command, and no stranger departed hungry.

Rural life was a lending library of borrowed boots, reapers, plows, pots, crocks, bags of flour, spices, recipes, even books. "Not only are all kitchen utensils as much your neighbors as your own, but bedsteads, beds, blankets, sheets travel from house to house," wrote Britisher Caroline Kirkland. "Sieves . . . and churns run about as if they had legs . . . and my husband [has been asked] for his shaving apparatus and his pantaloons." Inveterate borrowers knew that "making do" usually meant following a neighbor home from the mill and clustering near him with tin cups outthrust, until nearly all his flour had disappeared. Sundries and foods eventually trickled back, but what about grinders, ovens, horse collars, shovels, hayracks, implements, and tools? Hospitality ruled the farming frontier; "doin'" for a stranger was the basis of humanity itself.

To some, borrowing verged on banditry, and the phrase " 'Cause you got plenty" stood as reason enough for any request, no matter how farcical. One Michigan man lent a neighbor his martingale, which then journeyed to "four dwellings, two miles apart, having been lent from one to another, without a word to the original proprietor, who waited impatiently to commence a journey." A familiar phrase with an ominous ring was "Are you going to use your horse *today*?" Nebraska homesteader Uriah Oblinger was one who chose not to beg or to borrow. "My boots are full of holes & cant wear socks in them," he wrote. "I will try and get a new pair when I sell my flax. . . . I carried my pumpkins on my back as I have to be a pack horse now a days, but I am living in hopes of a team some day."

Hope was the mainstay of rural life, sometime fulfilled, perhaps defeated, but offered from one to another as readily as horses were borrowed, plows were shared, and men cooperated together to build, burn, hew, and harvest. "Every time I go over my claim I like it better," added Oblinger, ever hopeful despite repeated hardships. "I am determined to make it a nice home."

8

FRONTIER HARDSHIPS, DIRE STRAITS

❖

I will say . . . that whenever a fellow gets bad lost, the way home is just the way he don't think it is. This rule will hit nine times out of ten.
—*Davy Crockett*

✦

I wrote a letter home by the last mail and the rats carried it off the same night. I wil try to be in better luck this time.
—*Andrew Phelps*

✦

Only those who had backbone and faith . . . and those who couldn't leave, remained.—*Jean Saville, Dakota settler*

✦

There were five parties of us and we all camped together. A worse played out set you never saw . . . my feet were dabbling in a brook all night and my 20 lbs. of mackinaw blankets were soaked, the rain came through our badly put up tents—we could [not] get enough ground to stretch them and we were soaking wet as usual. . . . To sum it up we worked harder for four days than many men work in a lifetime and were never dry for one second but I wouldn't have missed it for any thing and am going up that river if it takes all winter.
—*Robert Fitzhugh Hunter*

✦

Until 1895 the whole history of [Kansas] was a series of disasters, and always something new, extreme, bizarre, until the name Kansas became a . . . synonym for the impossible and the ridiculous, inviting laughter . . . jest and hilarity.—*Carl Becker*

T HE WEST SUFFERED from no lack of grim misfortune. While American homestead policy flung the West as wide open as a barn door, the results were often judged a failure, evidenced by the abandoned claim shacks that dotted the prairies. Crops proved paltry and income scant. Men died, women turned inward, and children grew stunted, both emotionally and physically. Yet doggedly, as if propelled by some magical breath of spirit and regeneration, many settlers struggled on, hardy founders of families to come. Instead of fleeing, these pioneers dug in. Battered but indomitable, they considered themselves better for doing so. Why?

"[Disaster] always furnishes an ample harvest of the marvellous to those whose want of intellect disables them from gathering amusement from other sources," said British traveler James Hall, whose typical European disdain for all things American reduced the perils and pitfalls of the American West into anecdote and tall tale and little else. He abhorred the voracity of the muscular fall mosquito, an insect "so dissipated" and so given to loathsome habits—"frolicking all night and sleeping all day"—that he deemed riding through Shawnee Town on the Ohio River a dangerous malarial escapade. He would "gallop through town as fast as possible . . . [figuring] that if he should [escape] falling into the hands of the *natives* he still [might] have his joints racked with the ague, and all the blood in his veins sucked out by the musquitoes."

At times the frontier seemed like a potentially fatal obstacle course. The men who dreamed of manifest destiny, the unfettered conquest of land for their own means and pursuits, could also be felled by it. Mayhem, death, dismemberment, and despair seemed to reign. "I have been very unfortunate," wrote one immigrant. "I've cut myself four or five times; I cut my hand in the summer whilst mowing . . . I cut my foot very bad four weeks ago, it's not well yet. I cut two of my toes off; Mr. Silcog sewed them on again: they seem to be getting on well considering the time." When asked if it might not be safer back in Corley, Ireland, he recoiled. "If I was to cut my right leg off I should not think of returning to Corley again. . . . I could do better here with one leg than in Corley with two."

Mishaps mounted with every mile, and even the earth proved hazardous, as men discovered when they tried to plow, harrow, or dig wells. After burrowing straight down like a gopher, the man at the well bottom had to strain his eyes upward, scanning for heavy objects hurtling down. Also fatal was suffocation or gas inhalation; both victim and rescuers could smother at the bottom of a well, as did "Raymond Duchapalay of Fort Rock . . . [who] got gassed and killed. He fell off the bucket and they felt the bucket lighten and knew something had happened." In Wolf, Montana, a group of settlers on a high, flat plateau south of town had their own brush with a well bottom, which luckily ended humorously. "They dug down to the rope's end, then got a drill and went down to 325 feet, where they quit. While they were digging, a hen fell in and hit the digger on the head. It killed the hen and damaged the man; help went down and tied him to the bucket, and they drew him out but he was groggy for a few days ([t]hey had chicken for dinner)."

More often danger bred disaster, as when "the faint moan of a dying man" was heard by an English settler, Caroline Kirkland: A falling tree had crushed a man harvesting honey. Woodcutters lived

Ephriam Swain Finch showing how he killed grasshoppers. Photo by Solomon Butcher.

precarious lives as well. "The woodsman is continually subject to accidents of the most appalling kind," said Kirkland. "In cutting down the supporting tree, the first felled is almost certain to slide or to rebound in a way which baffles all calculation, and accidents are frightfully frequent."

Wild animals prowled at night, a danger to camping men. Rinehart family lore tells of an unnamed man from a family from Tennessee: "One of the Matlocks . . . was once attacked at night by a panther while he lay asleep near his campfire. His weapons were not in reach, and finally, after a very hard tussle, the panther was forced into the fire and held there until it burned to death. When Matlock's companions appeared on the scene shortly after the struggle,

Ed McDaniel carries fresh water to his cabin near Nome, Alaska, 1902.
Photo by Wilfred McDaniel.

they found him torn and bruised from head to foot and so badly burned they had to carry him home in a sheet. For a while he seemed almost dead, but he afterwards recovered fully from his wounds."

Weather was another uncontrollable force. Huge fronts swept in with Old Testament vengeance. Storm winds would rip and tear and shout and rend like crazed creatures, bashing headlong into houses, barns, and sand hills, dimming lights and stripping trees. The wind could sound like a shrieking sky devil, until every head ached from the strain of listening.

Blinding sandstorms howled up and down the midwestern and western desert reaches, stripping soil and collapsing houses, barns, and fences. Men had to dig their families out, and animals might suffocate in the dense, whirling grit. Wrote emigrant Samuel Emlen to his sister, Mary D. Emlen, on January 10, 1876:

Dear Sis . . .

On Sunday we had one of California's greatest drawbacks, a sand storm. The wind blew incessantly and terribly, it was impossible . . . to stand in it let alone navigate against it. The sand and gravel flew through the air as thick as the snow, bringing the blind and bruising . . . as it struck you hard. The plains were green with grass and the flowers had begun to bloom. Now they are as bare as they were when I first came here, hardly a spear of grass left standing. . . . Roofs were blown off nearly all the buildings in the neighborhood. Many of the buildings themselves blew down. Fences carried for nigh on ten miles and things generally scattered to the corners of the earth. Two men here stepped outside the door their hats flew from their heads and over the plains with lightning speed. One of the men was foolish enough to start after his and impelled by the wind he fairly flew for about five minutes, after it. But the wind and sand storm blinded him and he gave it up. And then came the tug of war. Returning he put his coat over his head and step-by-step retraced backwards. He was nearly an hour retracing and was almost over come when he reached the house. Neither of the hands have been heard of. . . . The sheepmen, on the plains, are in a terrible way. The sheep were scattered . . . in all directions and mixed up terribly. Many of them have not been found yet, one man whose camp was just below here lost his whole band, twenty five hundred. Had his house and everything in it blown away. But has recovered most of his sheep since.

Sacramento was struck by a storm when Israel Lord was riding through. "Considerable damage was done in the city last night by the wind and rain. . . . The new Catholic church, which was almost enclosed was blown from its foundation . . . and much damaged. . . . A large unfinished house on J street was blown down." Worse, "the air is like a furnace and the heavens like heated brass."

Whirlwinds and twisters raged throughout the plains during turbulent summers. In the Dakotas, on August 20, 1887, as funnels touched down, then whipped back into the sky, settlers barely had time to find shelter before the lightning flashed. Settler Martin Diehl lived in a hastily built house without a foundation. While walling up the cellar with his young son, he splashed into a puddle and grasped a pole for support. Lightning sizzled down the chimney and through the floor and struck him with a report like a gunshot. His wife, Isabella, caring for a sick child, rushed out and saw her son standing as if dazed, rubbing his ears and making strange sounds. Her husband was obviously dead. She sent the boy to summon a neighbor, and when the boy arrived, dazed, at Lou Mabbott's house, he could only repeat, over and over, "Diehl, Diehl."

Jean Saville of North Dakota saw a tornado "tear the hay stacks apart and the next morning the bundles were strewn everywhere, many of them wound around five acres of trees near the house. It also wrecked the machine shed." In 1892 a cyclone wrecked the Methodist church in Saville's town. He had the ride of his life, reporting: "Our house lifted at one end and all the furniture rolled or slid to the other end. It was dropped with no damage except to our nervous system."

Blizzards raged, and harsh winters blasted the settlers, deceiving them with mild days, then unleashing sudden whiteouts, catching out those who had left the safety of home and barns and headed for town. Faces froze, fingers stiffened, and toes crackled. Sheep sank into the maelstrom, to be lost until spring. Houses and barns were guide wired together as men, blinded by snow blankets, thick as velvet, felt their way along. A determined blizzard could whip drifts over the tops of trees, erasing every landmark. The wind "left a smooth, straight bank so high that we could see only the sky from the west windows," wrote one North Dakota settler. Near-frozen cattle huddled under the drifts, thin spirals of steam marking the spot where they stood, dark and stiff as icicles.

When a blizzard trapped a schoolteacher and her pupils in a South Dakota schoolhouse all night, there was scarcely enough coal to keep the potbelly stove fired. The nearest settler, Neal Larson, together with his hired man, fought through the storm to bring coal and a kettle of hot soup to the trapped pupils. The men unraveled a ball of twine, according to historian Ragna Mellom Severson, tying one end to Larson's doorknob. By following the twine backward, they were able to thread their way home. And when a North Dakota blizzard buried the sod stable of Ole Farber, word went out, mobilizing the men in a twenty-mile radius. They set out on skis across the bar-

Flooded Kansas town, 1881.

Crossing the Cannonball River, North Dakota, ca. 1900s.

ren snowfields, between snow-covered trees, to reach the buried farm. "The sod stable was entirely buried," wrote Barbara Levorson. "The men shoveled wide steps in the hard packed snow down to the stable door. They could not bring the animals out, so they had to carry water in pails down to them. Then they uncovered part of one of the haystacks and with a big hay knife they sliced down through the hard packed hay just as we would cut a layer of cake if we wanted a piece of the top layer. . . . It took several men many hours to do the necessary chores." After, they were given steaming hot coffee and a huge breakfast.

Oliver Nelson lived through the winter of 1885, a mild season that suddenly broke apart during January like fragile china, killing herds of cattle and decimating the stockmen. "All the draws heading east or west along the Canadian [River] filled with snow. The cattle drifted before the wind into these traps, and others behind them

pushed them in further. Then the snow covered them. Some died within two hours after the storm struck. Ten days later they were still standing packed and frozen stiff, only the tips of their horns showing above the drifts. They stood that way till the snow melted away."

Death reached out randomly, felling one man "who had frozen to death a few miles west of the city," reported J. B. Clack, of Abilene, Texas, who presided over the inquest. "He was sitting with his back braced against a mesquite tree in plain view from the road. It was evident that the man had frozen to death unconscious of the fact that he was freezing; for he held a pipe in one hand, and a match in the other as if he had intended to light the pipe and smoke while resting. However there were indications that he might have attempted to kindle a fire. . . . The man was a stranger in our part of the country."

A sudden furious storm struck Iowa farmer Helge Anderson and his wife, Thora Tweeton, one night, when they were in the barn doing chores. His bedridden mother lay in the house, and the fire was low. How to get back before she froze? The couple held hands and lowered their heads but were immediately blinded by dense snow. They fell to their knees and crept along like wolves, edging toward the house.

In the Midwest, winters were so powerful that towns, homesteads, and railroad tracks might disappear under drifts of snow, making food delivery as well as communication impossible. As supplies dwindled, a handful of wheat, ground in a small coffee grinder, might supply one family with food for a month.

Nor could hailstorms be ignored. Henry Washington Carter recalled one of the "most striking events" of his trip:

We hadn't stopped for the night very long before the sky was overcast with heavy black clouds and frequent flashes of lightning . . . by and by we had a terrific storm of hail and sleet, hail stones as big as pigeons eggs—the wind and hail were incessant and resistless for nearly an hour. Tho we had thick skulls some of us, yet we couldn't stand it—so we lay down under the wagons. The cattle were perfectly panic struck and broke madly from the coral and were soon driven by the storm out of sight. . . . As soon as our feelings would permit and the weather abated we came out, and looked round. It was a good thought that we had the wagons to shelter us and that they were so heavily loaded; in fact we . . . owed a debt of gratitude . . . in all probability our bacon . . . saved us.

No winter closed without rain and flood. Journals are filled with descriptions of rampaging rivers, cresting waves, and creeks turned suddenly into rivers. "A huge wall of water, carrying trees and driftwood, came tearing down Valley creek, sweeping the brand new customs house into the bay," wrote Mary Hanifry of Port Angeles, Washington, in 1863. "Also lost in the flood was the Victor Smith home with all its outbuildings. Mrs. Smith managed to save herself and her small children, but the deputy collector and inspector, W. B. Goodell and Captain J. W. Anderson, were killed by falling chimney bricks." Another flash flood was recalled by Henry Washington Carter:

Last year it rained up the creek . . . and the water came down in a ten-foot [wall]. I'd taken a bath and was dressing. Another boy was at the south window reading. All at once he looked up the valley, and called out, look at the water! I said, "likely it's a mirage; watch that tree and see if it moves past it." Soon the boy said, "It's to the tree! *It's over the tree, run!*" I jumped out the door, run 150 yards east and up the hill. It caught the other fellow and washed him . . . against the corral, but I got him out. We never seen the house again; it was scattered all down the creek. We picked up what pieces we could find.

"An upswept wave of water, 8-ft. high," engulfed a canyon in which two families were traveling, horrifying onlooker J. Ross Browne. Had the men been more experienced, they might have interpreted the frenzied behavior of the horses minutes beforehand, but too late, "the wagon was capsized and dashed to pieces among the rocks. The screams of the women and children rose high above the wild roar of the flood, 'Oh, father! Father! Save me!' echoed down the rocky canyon." Wrote Browne: "[I]n less than a minute nothing was left to mark the tragedy. Women, children, wagon, horses, all had disappeared . . . carried away like feathers. Prodigious boulders of solid stone, six or seven feet in diameter . . . had been

rolled for miles through the canyon." Only mutilated human remains drifted downstream.

"Sacramento was all under water," gold seeker David Demarest lamented. "From two to eight feet, except a part of J Street on the levee. . . . Three days later, a boat came up with our lost men. After they left us they travelled on through the water, sometimes knee

Tornado in Kansas town, 1884.

deep, at other waist and neck deep, and sometimes they had swimming to do. That first night the only dry place they could find was a large tree, in the crotch of which they made a fire, and each roosted on a limb. The next morning after searching some time, they found but one way to go without swimming . . . and they arrived more dead than alive."

Water—too much or too little? Drought bedeviled western travelers, from Nevada's Humboldt Sink, where "powdery alkali dust rose in thick clouds" and what water there was was so strong in alkali "it was like drinking lye," to the California-Mexico border, where the desert extended from Chihuahua north. A small party of traders headed toward Santa Fe in spring 1821 on a commercial expedi-

tion. They sought a shorter road, but their enterprise failed, according to the English novelist Frederick Marryat. "There is not a drop of water in this horrible region, which extends even to the Cimarron River, and in this desert they had to suffer the pangs of thirst. They were reduced to the necessity of killing their dogs and bleeding their mules to moisten their parched lips. None of them perished; but, quite dispirited, they changed their direction and turned back to the nearest point of the river Arkansas, where they were at least certain to find water."

Henry Washington Carter and his party, struggling along an Indian trail through arid mountains, were already parched and weakened when they "broke all [the] gourds and lost all their water. We were now all getting excessively thirsty. The little water in my canteen was soon exhausted, and we were soon sucking pebbles to keep up moisture in our mouths, others sucked their knife handles as if they were sticks of candy for the same purpose, and fatigue was added to our thirst as we proceeded. Several had sore feet and were ill. . . . Several declared they could not go much further. About four o clock . . . 3 in our party gave up and threw themselves under a tree—they could go no farther."

They eventually found the Gila River—fortunately before anyone died of thirst. Yet parched men could hardly resist swimming in a stream after a hot day of travel, a temptation that could end badly. In another incident, David Demarest wrote, "At evening several men went in swimming. While there one of the party called for help and appeared to be sinking. Our Backus a good swimmer went to his aid. They both sank for a time, but Backus again raised to the surface alone and with the help of others reached the man much exhausted, but failed to save his friend. The man's named Bradshaw. . . . Tried all evening to find the body by dragging the river . . . but all failed."

➳   ➳   ⤝   ⤝

FIRE, MANY TIMES caused by drought, could devastate farms and ranches. "A low, sullen roar, like distant Niagara, announced the onset of a prairie blaze," commented farmer James Haines on the incessant Illinois fires sparked by sun-bleached prairie grass and high winds. "Flame, light, motion and sound combined to make a spectacle and scene. . . . Billowy, swaying clouds of black smoke, lifting skyward, would suddenly explode into flame, lighting the whole landscape."

"A fire might go on for weeks unless stopped," wrote Oliver Nelson, thus prompting a local firefighting technique:

Fire in daytime is too hot to handle, so they would fight it at night. They would drive out a bunch of old cows and bring along two wagons with several barrels of water. When they got to the fire, they would shoot a cow, cut its head off, and split the body in halves; take one of the halves and fasten a wire ten feet long to the hind foot and another to the fore foot, a long rope to each wire, and a saddle horse to each rope, then drag the half carcass

along the blaze, flesh side down, one boy riding the burned-off side, the other ahead of the fire. Right behind it came the other half, rigged up the same way. Then several men would follow on foot with wet gunny sacks to beat out what was left. They worked this way in two directions, one wagon following each outfit. A fresh cow was killed every two miles. That way they could put out about fifteen miles in a night, but it wasn't fun.

In the face of disaster neighbors pitched in to help. "In the fall of 1896 our barn and three large haystacks adjoining it burned to the ground, started by a match in the hands of a four year old," recalled Ragna Mellom Severson. "He had found a match under the hired man's bed and lit a handful of hay near the barn. The fire was unquenchable. A wooden water tank nearby was empty. Kind neighbors for miles around housed our animals and donated hay, and a new barn was built the next spring during a surprise Shingling Bee."

Fire, always likely to flare up, scorched the North Dakota hamlet of Temvik until quenched by the town's volunteer bucket brigade. Merchants rushed with extinguishers, women pumped water, and everyone loaded up with barrels of water. "The blaze was extinguished . . . before too much damage was done."

➳   ➳   ⤝   ⤝

FIRE WASN'T THE only threat to a man's property. In Illinois an old settler could not afford to register all the property he had claimed and was forced to leave 180 fallow acres unclaimed and exposed to claim jumpers. Jumping was a popular pastime in the West, and the settler tried desperately to secure the hundred dollars needed to register his coveted tract. Then rumor came to him that a neighbor, a "good old Quaker friend, Dr. Griffith," had "entered the claim away from him." Wrote his neighbor James Haines: "He [found] the offender and charged him with the great wrong. 'Yes,' Dr. Griffith replied. 'I have entered thy favorite one hundred eighty of timber because thee said thee could not get the money, and I feared somebody else would enter it away from thee. But, friend Martin, I entered it in thy name, and it is thine now forever not mine. . . . And whenever thee gets a hundred dollars thee can give it to me. There will be no interest to pay. The land is thine.' "

OF ALL THE hardships, hunger was the most pervasive. Often men were lost or separated from their main parties, and climbed rocky terrain or walked long distances without food. Without provisions, they boiled bluebirds, blackbirds, and bleached buffalo bones for nutrition. Boot leather soup, once a jest along the trail, at times became a desperate possibility as men neared starvation. Edible tubers were scavenged. Men crunched grasshoppers and stripped saplings to suck out the juice. Rice was often boiled in brass kettles rimmed with verdigris, which the cooks "stirred in," thus contaminating what little food was left. Gold seekers in the California foothills might survive for weeks with tiny bags of tea and scraps of beef or bread. Wrote Henry Washington Carter, traveling through Death Valley:

> It was thought expedient to bury some of our provisions under a Hill, expecting to get them again on our return that way some days after. We halted half a day for this purpose and interred a considerable quantity of bread and bacon under a hill that could be seen a long way over the plains and we thought we should have no difficulty in finding it again. . . . [W]e attempted to strike the spot where our provisions were buried but all in vain[;] we couldn't find the hill. In this dilemma it was thought best to steer our course for Fort Thorn, about 10 miles from this point, and we went straight for it: there we got some provisions and the Col. decided to try and strike the point where the provisions were buried, and this was successful. We found the hill and dug up our buried treasure.

"There was not in the whole crowd a piece of cracker as large as my thumb nail," wrote gold miner Carlisle Abbot. "For with the aid of a little warm water from our canteens all of the crackers had been eaten as we trudged along." As the days passed, Abbot and his fellow travelers "began to get dizzy," often stumbling and falling. Finally, one man proposed drawing straws "to determine whose horse shall be killed for food." Abbot lost, and his horse, Old Pomp, was chosen to die. "Poor old Pomp . . . so we might suck the mar-

row from his fleshless bones, and boil for food the hide that covered them! This gave me the blues, and that night I could not sleep. . . . I am ashamed to say that I wept myself to sleep. . . ." Abbot mourned, but luck was with the horse; someone unexpectedly shot a deer, and the company had provisions enough to last until civilization.

Hunger strained the network of Samaritan travelers who shared supplies, but none expected that rats would preempt humans in the struggle for food. "Every morning one may see . . . bags cut or eaten, or torn into with holes from two to eight inches long and from a few ounces to several pounds [of flour] pulled out and scattered about each one of them," wrote Israel Lord. The [rats] eat, drink, cut or tear their way through every thing but brick walls."

Even the best fed could be scurvy-stricken after a winter's worth of canned goods, curling up in agony from the body's lack of vitamin C. "We never had fresh vegetables," wrote Klondike resident Michael MacGowan. "Men's . . . teeth fell out, they bled and had fierce pains. Many of them died and . . . corpses stretched frozen on the tops of cabins—left there in frost until the thaw came when they would be buried." He added: "I went to the hind end of the wagon, opened the mess box, got some bread, took a spoon and dived into the apple-sauce. Eating out of the brass kettle from one side, I ate several large spoonfuls of it with my bread, then poured a quart cup full of water out of the keg, drank about half of it; then dived into the apple sauce again. . . . I had not gone far until a strange sickening feeling came over me. The sun was shining down and the heat radiating in front of me. I was getting dizzy headed and squeamish in my stomach. . . . Sick? Yes, unto death." He "was soon relieved" of all the poisoned applesauce with a salt-water emetic. "The fact was, I had been verdigris-poisoned from the brass kettle, and for several days I was an invalid without any appetite. And fifteen years elapsed before I could eat applesauce again."

The gruesome travails of the ill-fated Donner party stretched the imaginations of all who heard it: desertion, starvation, death, and the resorting of some to cannibalism among the ill-fated families of George and Jacob Donner, James F. Reed, and William Greaves, all of whom had left Missouri for California late in the season and were caught in the High Sierra during early-winter snows. Horses stumbled, cattle sank into drifts, and children were too frozen to go on.

They found several cabins, hoping to weather out the worst of the storms and continue when possible. "Each family built some kind of house, and killed all their cattles, as they could not live, the ground being covered with snow," wrote survivor John Breen. On the forty-second day of their captivity women and children were gnawing hides, as well as the flesh of the unfortunate dead, to stay alive. Wrote survivor Patrick Breen:

Wednesday 10th.
Milt Elliot died last night at Murphys shanty about 9 o'clock. . . . They have nothing to eat [there] but hides all are entirely out of meat but with God's help Spring will soon smile upon us.

Friday 26th
Froze hard last night. Today blowing briskly. . . . Mrs. Murphy said here yesterday that she thought she would commence on Milt & eat him. I doubt that she had done so yet it is distressing. The Donnors told the California folks that they commenced to eat the dead people 4 days ago.

After forty-two days a group of the men decided to escape over the summit and seek help. "They took a small share of provisions expecting to get to the Sacramento Valley, but . . . a heavy storm began the day after they left . . . which lasted several days, and as not one of them had ever been in such a place before . . . most of the party was lost. A curious feature was that the women stood the hardship better than the men. I believe none of the women of their party died," wrote John Breen.

The first rescue party found a scattering of survivors so weak they were almost dead.

⤞ ⤞ ⤝ ⤝

NO LESS STARTLING were Indian attacks, witnessed by John D. Young, hiking with "fifty able-bodied men" to Colorado in search of gold. Passing quietly through Cheyenne country, they were nervous about a single circling Indian, probably a spy. When nothing happened, they relaxed their guard. "We grew careless. . . . We had our dinner cooked and were sitting down on the grass to enjoy it com-

First mission building at Running Antelope's Village, Grand River, South Dakota, 1885.

fortably when all at once like an electric shock came the alarming cry of Indians we saw multitudes of warriors pouring down towards us fast as their horses could gallop from all directions It seemed as if the very hills sprang suddenly to life. . . . There we stood fifty men opposed to more than a thousand of those wild devils the 'Comanche' of Kansas." The Indians circled but did not attack. After hours the travelers decided to cautiously line up their wagons and leave. The Indians "pressed very closely on to" them, but did not attack, pretending at times to wish to sell them buffalo robes and moccasins. Whenever guns were waved, "the Indians scampered off like a lot of frightened sheep."

So much heartache, so many obstacles—no wonder the "blues" were common, driving wives mad and men to gaze fixedly at the horizon, wondering if life had meaning. "One week from today I shall be 27!" thought Edward Fitch as he watched the clouds march-

Unidentified black farmers.

husband of Emily Hawley Gillespie, of Iowa, suffered a periodic despondency that drove him to the barn with a rope "to hang himself." Each time he was stopped by his children, who fetched him back to the house. When not obsessed with his own suicide, he accused his wife of plotting his murder. "You mean to kill me!" he would shout, and for emphasis, would secretly poison her prized chickens with salt—perhaps to watch something, if not himself, die. The husband of Ann Grench was so consumed with dark moods that, said a friend, "It would be better for her to stay with him only [occasionally], during Lent, for instance."

Grief unsettled men's minds, as in the case of "poor Theophile la Chappelle . . . a member of the legislature, a bright and intellectual young man. . . . He became insane soon after [his sister's death] and spent the remainder of his life at the Hospital for the Insane, near Madison," wrote Elizabeth Therese Baird. Playwright Charles Hale Hoyt was overwhelmed by lunatic grief at the death of his wife and committed to a sanitarium in July 1900. Later he was released on petition by his friends and placed under medical care until his death.

⤝　⤝　⤝

MONEY, OR THE lack of it, could mark a man's success or failure in the New World. No hardship struck as deeply or more wrecked a man's perception of himself than financial disaster, as seen in the thin wrists, hollow eyes, and ragged clothes of their loved ones. Some men, discouraged and beaten, simply picked up and left. Others struggled on, trying to patch together livelihoods. Some failed from poor luck, some from ignorance, some, even, from overgenerosity, allowing customers open accounts. "I gave the store the once-over. There were too many things to look after there. Many of the customers said, 'Charge it,' " admitted one store owner. "It was too complicated for me."

Pulled down by unbelievable financial tangles, men faced disputed land titles, accumulated mortgages, failed businesses, and the unexpected deaths of investors. Economic reverses were rampant, and letters home were shadowed by the constant need for money. People were sought, and judged, for their connections to the well-to-do.

"Here my last dollar ran out," wrote David Demarest of his jour-

ing by overhead. "Such an old man I am, with a wife and family to take care of." He felt used up, "his sheet . . . about full." No wonder so many "fill our insane asylums . . ." wrote author Hamlin Garland. For Benjamin Alfred Wetherill, sequestered in his Alamo ranch in the foothills of New Mexico, "the winters [brought on] a serious case of the blues for the reason that often we were snowed in." The

ney in 1849 and 1850 from New York to the California mines. "Our intention was to go to deer Creek, but the state in which our finances were made us decide to accept the offer of a teamster." For a young man, zesty, footloose, and self-reliant, running short was simply an invitation to adventure. Change course and work elsewhere? Simply another of life's adventures.

Henry Washington Carter, also young and footloose, was less ebullient about poverty. "I had been unemployed for some time, dollars were getting scarce, there was something wrong in the exchequer, there was a tightness in the chest," he wrote. "I had heard about a certain ubiquitous wolf that haunts sometimes the doors of very deserving people, I began to understand what people mean when they talk about 'coming out at the little end of the horn.'" He continued: "Many a fellow traveller from the Keystone state had quite an assortment of boxes; in fact we were all traveling in a style rather above our means. Young [Carter's partner] and I had little consultation of the state of our finances and we ascertained that all our dollars might be counted on our fingers. The other young men with us were rustics from Ohio and I expect they were as poor as ourselves. We all went to the tavern hungry and hopeful. We had our supper and went to our beds or rather mattresses, for we all slept on mattresses in one large room."

Debt stalked many, including the dashing army hero George Armstrong Custer, who died owing nearly thirteen thousand dollars. He had signed a note to a Wall Street broker, engaged in a wild stock speculation based on borrowed money, and lost, victim to the American myth of failure and recoup, in which a man could start over time

and time again with every hope—and chance—of finally succeeding. He could turn failure around, as did Erskine Greer, as noted in a Bancroft interview:

obtained a tract of land close to Sacramento and by years of patient labor and intelligence made money and improved his place to a degree higher than any farm in Sacramento. During the flood of 1860 he lost everything he had which included 130 cattle and 30 horses, all fine stock. He began again on a ranch and he then was employed to secure the right of way for building. In 1869 he opened a hotel in Sac and was in that business for four years. He then bought 640 acres of land and had 6000 in the bank but it proved to be in an unhealthy district and before he left it his family had been sick, etc. and when he did leave he was again "broke." He then opened a grocery store in Sac and was marvelously successful for a period of 5 years. He then opened a wholesale house but it proved a bad venture and he left the business without a dollar. He could not remain in Sacramento so hurried to the country and bought his present place for 100 per acre.

Wrote the interviewer: "It is safe to say there is not a neater or better kept farm in this country in the state." Hardship was inherently western and American, and it plagued men relentlessly throughout their lives. Suffering produced a fixed western character, one that embraced cooperation, when necessary, but that could thrive alone, by whatever raw means possible, and even be thankful for it.

Part 4

The Marryin' Kind

❖

Alaskan Hills

Photo on previous page: Alaskan hills, near Nome, Alaska. Lottie Renny, Wilfred McDaniel, and sled dogs enjoy a Sunday outing and view of the Bering Sea, 1905. Photo by E. McDaniel.

9

BACHELORS, DANDIES, AND CITY MEN

He was just an old bachelor, and he just come and went as he pleased.
—*Ila Bowman Powell*

❧❧

With all his tidy housekeeping and capability in his own kitchen Peter M'Quirk was not at all effeminate . . . but a voluntary recluse, who had his own views on life and his own reasons for his bachelorhood.
—*Peter Burns*

❧❧

I'm getting tired of sleeping with bachelors. . . . I would rather sleep with one woman than 2 men anytime.
—*Uriah W. Oblinger*

To some, the pleasures of courtship came too late. Love failed to bloom, or fear overrode desire, leaving in its wake a safe, though occasionally nervous, unmarried man, the bachelor. His role in frontier society was well defined, embracing ubiquitous uncles, cranky argonauts, and shy, dusty cowpokes so reverent—and reticent—when confronting a female presence they seemed frozen to the spot. The prairies were huge and isolated, and without wife or family, the bachelor might languish alone—or with other bachelors. "Its a queer sort of life we lead," wrote miner Carlisle Abbot. "Back breaking work all day; doing our own cooking and washing; no amusements except a friendly game of euchre and an occasional trip to town, [where] there is nothing worth while, except the gambling saloons and the Mexican girls at the fandango house. We long for the company of decent women."

The scarcity of women was particularly evident during dances. Square dances were then in vogue, and it was difficult to fill two or three sets with mixed partners. Men drafted to be women as dance partners sported handkerchiefs, knotted around the upper arms to reveal their "lady" status. A reward of twenty-five cents per female was often offered in the hope of finding women, but the money was seldom paid out. "This is a lonely place for single men," wrote Nebraska settler Uriah Oblinger. "There are a number of single men [of] bachelor age & nearly all have a bird in view as soon as they can get a cage ready."

Whether bachelor or married, frontier men maintained a complicated relationship with women. Some, such as J. M. Booth, were conversationally disrespectful toward and cavalier about women as when he confided to a friend via letter that his physical needs would be satisfied "if there were any senoritas to be had." Others, such as C. H. Giller, writing from Iowa Hill, California, in 1857, simply wanted to wed and were not particular who. "I could have got Darty without any trouble," Giller complained to his friend L. P Griswold,

"but if I cannot get her I shall pitch in for that ere grass widow at Edgards & if I cannot get either I will come back here & take one of these digger squaws." But most men were chivalrous, thanks to arrivals from the South after the Civil War whose gentlemanly codes of behavior eventually were adopted as western traits. "There was nothing more precious than a woman's honor," noted French critic Alexis de Tocqueville, surprised at the relatively esteemed position of American women compared with that of Europeans. "A seat for the lady! Get up for this lady" heralded the entrance of a woman on a Colorado train. British traveler Isabella Bird was impressed by the American men who leaped to their feet, while an English traveler refused, protesting, "I've paid for my seat and I mean to keep it." He was booted out the door amid a "chorus of groans and hisses."

Single men depended upon women. Who else could fix rips and bake bread? Henry Brokmeyer was fascinated by the nearly wordless solution found by an elderly bachelor, Mr. Olff, and his niece, who had reached a companionate accord. "He seems to cling to his niece with all the tenacity of his peculiar nature . . . she brings him meals to his room and is attentive to his every want. They have many characteristics in common—have less use for language than any persons I ever met."

"Batching it" did not come easy for either of two Norwegian men in North Dakota, both called Ole. Often the worst aspect of their lot was sleeping, according to J. M. Booth, writing from Muddy Spring, California, in 1850. "There are six of us living in the shanty and we have three beds—[thus] two to a bed. Rive is my bed fellow—it was rather awkward at first as I was continually in fear of making a mistake, or that my bedfellow might do so, at first I used to sleep in a pair of strong corduroys, but have now gained sufficient confidence to dispense with them."

Dining out in Yellowstone Valley, Tonka, Montana, ca. 1880.

Wilfred A. McDaniel, 1874–1954.
Photo by Andrew P. Hill Studio, ca. 1905.

Man being tattooed. Photo by Stellman.

Unidentified couples at Spearfish Falls, Dakota, June 20, 1890. Photo by J. C. H. Grabill.

Even worse, recounted diarist Barbara Levorson, was the lack of fresh meat to eat, which led them to consider rodents. The rubbery, round badger abounded locally, and they had little trouble capturing and killing one. They carefully skinned it and cooked up its better parts. Well boiled or not, it was unchewable. It merely stuck to their teeth. Disgusted and disappointed and citing "the lack of a woman's touch," they never tried again. "We are going to have a Christmas dinner & expect to have four kinds of meat, which I expect wil be sheap, lam, ram & mutton & for desert onions smothered in cream. If I only had a wife here to doe my cooking, washing & mending then I would be *punkins*," complained gold miner George McKnight, from Columbia, California, in 1851 to his brother John in New York.

The bachelor meal lacked variety, especially when the bachelor was working in the field. "Helge Anderson would cook up a large kettle of oatmeal in the morning, eat some of it then; at noon he would eat some more of it, and if there was some left in the evening he would finish it for supper," wrote Levorson. The bachelor longed for a dinner invitation and would go to any extreme to sit down in an actual family setting. When cowboy William Timmons visited a ranching family, the Rays, he grew misty-eyed over the idea of home, family, and a well-set table:

> Everything looked so nice. There was a table full of good things to eat. I hadn't had a bite since breakfast, and I had traveled sixty miles since then. Yet my appetite was poor. There was a beautiful tablecloth and napkins, and I kept using my napkin so much Donald said, "oh he's trying to twist his whiskers—and he hasn't got any whiskers to twist."
>
> What a relief it was to get downtown to the hotel and, the next day, get a haircut, clean shave, good bath, and a new pair of riding pants to replace the travel weary ones I had. Never again did I wear blue ducks or an old wool shirt to town, and my boots were always blacked and shining when I rode in. I got a razor of my own. . . . But I was still scared of girls.

Such fear would have been reciprocal had "girls" the chance to see how a lone man lived. In the mining areas a bachelor shack was identified by the stacks of rusting tin cans outside, thrown helter-skelter

Unidentified men fighting, ca. 1915.

Ed and Jessie McDaniel in tundra cotton grass, near Nome, Alaska, 1905.
Photo by Wilfred McDaniel.

Jack Johnson with his white wife, 1911.

Interior of Raymond's drugstore, Lawrence, Kansas, ca. 1880s.

as soon as the tomatoes were dribbled out. Cramped for space, dingy, and often riddled with spiders and rats, the "bachelor cabin," as described by Oliver Nelson, would not tempt romance.

A board with four shelves was a double bunk, pullman style, with poles for springs and hay for feathers; apt to have seam squirrels (lice) but no bedbugs. In the northeast corner was a cupboard with four shelves; here were tin plates and cups and iron handled knives and forks, four sixteen-inch ovens, and a fry pan. Between the two doors was a 12-foot table, with boxes around it for chairs.

There was a fireplace with a stick chimney, and an iron hook hanging in the center to hang a four-gallon coffee pot on; a coffee-grinder was nailed to the side of the fireplace, and below the grinder was a shelf for a three-gallon sour dough jar. Under the window in the west was a box desk to hold extra pistols, tobacco, or anything the boys didn't want to drag around. Then we had a gun rack in the southwest corner, and half a dozen guns.

Such grim and limited surroundings also impaired romantic correspondence. Who could read or write with ease when, like J. M.

Booth, he used "a crooked table the boards of which are split not sawn out," with "the chimney being the only window in the shanty"? He complained: "We get into the fireplace to read, but as yet we have got no accommodations there for writing." Worse, he added, "my paper is blowing about and my fingers are half frozen."

If unable to connect socially, men like James Ross Larkin, adventuring along the Santa Fe Trail, could always fall back on memories of Mother. Any reference to the matriarch tapped deep bachelor response. Wrote Larkin: "Jan 18, 1857 Sunday. Read the Letter written to me by my mother & put in the Bible she presented to me. It is a valuable letter, containing excellent advice such as a mother can give."

Nor was Mother far from the mind of Carlisle Abbot, a traveler in the goldfields of California. "Another letter from home and I received a box of things that mother made and sent. . . . Down in the corner of the box was a Bible. She said she knew I had the one she gave me when I came away, but maybe I had thumbed it until it was worn out. I would not tell her for a thousand dollars that I had not opened it for six months. . . . Pard [his partner, John Anderson] was as soft as I was over the letters and the box and his eyes filled with tears, although he tried to disguise it by furiously blowing his nose."

The situation was no better in the cities. Thousands of single men milled about the streets of San Francisco during the gold boom years of the 1850s, the normal years of courtship, marriage, and family rearing cast aside for adventure and the chance of fortune. Restless roamers without immediate family had only solitary pastimes, save for the occasional naggings of their panning partners or escapes at local saloons. Thus the occasional sight of a decent woman, or a toddler, threw them into states of profound longing. Gold miner T. A. Barry described how, upon seeing children, men crowded about, "asking permission to kiss them, to shake hands with them, to give them gold specimens . . . or a little gold dust to make them rings, [and followed] them along, as if fascinated by the sight of their child faces and voices." Cowboy William Timmons found himself tongue-tied by the sight of "two beautiful daughters, Eleanor and Agnes, fourteen and eighteen," who surprised him in their father's barn one day. "These girls looked so clean and so nice in pretty spring dresses that I was scared of them. They were friendly and perfectly at ease,

Unidentified couple kissing, ca. 1870.

Bachelors,

Dandies, and

City Men

141

telling me that supper was just ready and inviting me in to eat with the family."

Many men were bachelors by choice, sleek, urban sorts who lived in the gold boom cities where money was plentiful, luxuries were rampant, and investments could net from 8 to 150 percent. In the western cities a man of modest wealth in the East might transform himself: dress stylishly in the latest New York fashions, drive a plush carriage, be groomed to a sheen, and heed the call of worldly pleasures. Gaiety and drink beckoned, and the tinkle of pianos invited men into saloons and poker clubs, although all too often men could quickly slide from decency into the rootless world of the dandy. Harriet Levy, a young San Francisco girl, spotted "a line of mashers" standing "three deep," who slouched in front of a cigar store on Market Street. "They were 'dressy men,'" she wrote, "dandies young and old who stood facing the street, smoking long cigars, or picking their teeth with quill toothpicks." What respectable girl could take them seriously?

Cities offered young bachelors glamour, a faster pace of life, and tantalizing glimpses of worldliness and sophistication—even in the West. Income and social mobility marked the men who migrated to St. Louis, Denver, and San Francisco, among others, and stirred up a sense of abandon. From trolley cars to touring cars, mechanized travel minimized distances, expedited far-flung, and often unchaperoned, courtships, and gave young men a sense of independence. Free to take in moving picture houses, nickelodeon parlors, and restaurants with velvet-draped private booths, the young men of the western cities perceived themselves as racy glitterati, at home in the world of change. Cultured society had high expectations for gentlemen. They should be educated, well dressed, and frankly professional and should model themselves upon worthy men. Poets were particularly

No. 2370. Happy Hours in Camp. C. and B. & M. Engineers Corps and Visitors Photo. and copyright by Graybill, Deadwood, Dak. '89.

Happy hours in camp. C and B & M Engineers Corps and visitors, 1889. Photo by J. C. H. Grabill, Dakota.

Officers dancing in officers' quarters, Fort Bridger, Wyoming.

in fashion and, transported by inspiration, labored over verses in the style of Sir Walter Scott, no matter how imitative. Or they quoted the poet directly, claiming authorship. Few were immune to poetry's pull. There included Dr. Daniel Drake, who turned lyrical at the mere notion of the frontier, particularly the untamed regions of backwoods Kentucky, where, he mused, "if the movements of a solitary tree in the midst of the tempest are beautiful, the struggles of the forest are sublime." The Illinois circuit judge James Hall founded a literary magazine, the *Western Souvenier,* announcing to the world, "O! A new Souvenier is come out of the West." The gentleman poet, "[b]y mingling the grace of diction with attractive subjects," hoped to succeed in a world where cattle and cowboys might roam the streets, but where westerners struggled to achieve cosmopolitan standards in the drawing rooms, churches, and social clubs.

As diarists many men confessed freely to the privacy of the page. Thomas Edward Watson of San Francisco, naturally romantic and sensitive, had to maintain the male traits of assertiveness and ambition. Only in his diary did he admit to reading and writing great quantities of verse. Men, he also knew, were judged on their clever, graceful words, and he himself, he believed, had attained a highly poetic level. Admitted Carlisle Abbot: "I now write more in this diary than when I started it and saying things I would not care to have anybody read. I think I will burn it up soon, although I like to go over it and see how it all happened."

THE GOLD BOOM carved out a growing social scene on the West Coast, drawing together the highly unsophisticated—men who had never seen an orange or a lemon, never tasted oysters, or read Shakespeare—with sleek bachelors, who might make social calls from gathered calling cards, "get tight and Run the hurdy gurdies til Midnight," dine on late-night oyster dinners with friends, treat themselves to dancing lessons, and generally plunge into the social whirl.

Then, as now, sex was on men's minds. The line superintendent for the Oregon Stage Company demanded in 1862 that the following "delinquency" be reported: the "names of drivers allowing females to ride on the Box," part of a courting inducement offered by the dashing drivers of the overland stages. In 1808, William Thomas Prestwood of Illinois boasted that he "would have two mistresses in twelve months," which his diary accounts reveal. He noted his level of sexual experience with several women over the years, bragging often about "bedding," "carousing," and "thumping," yet on May 14, 1820, the "blessed body" of Celia Clark brought an end to Prestwood's bachelorhood, although not his roguish ways.

Bachelors, like knights errant, swept into the homes and lives of marriageable girls, "calling" on them at a rate that could occupy every day of the week. A girl's family would announce its address and visiting time only to find the porch filled with unknown young men, gloves and calling cards in hand, ready to be fed and fussed over under the guise of prospective marriage. In reality, such calls were a bachelor's mealtime in which dining was enjoyed without obligation, as he sampled his way from door to door. By late in the century hungry young men were no longer as welcome as they had been.

There were those men who were dedicated to single life. Some turned to the safety of married women, particularly socialites whose husbands were away or disdained dancing, and escorted them around town. Others tired of standing at moral attention and added snippy antifemale rhetoric to a litany of allegations already in effect against Chinese, Indians, and blacks. "I have always maintained," wrote J. Ross Browne, "that the constant interference, the despotic sway, the exactions and caprices of the female sex ought no longer to be tol-

Unidentified man reading a letter.

erated. And it is with a glow of pride and triumph that I introduce this striking example of the ability of man to live in a state of perfect exemption from all these trial and tribulations." Bret Harte in one of his California missives, added "The ladies are comparatively inferior . . . throughout the state."

Men reluctant to wed could always wait to find the "right one." Nineteenth-century life had ample room for all kinds. The bachelor fulfilled an important social role in the West, spending money liberally and acting as kindly uncle, interested companion, or bon vivant around town.

10

UPSTART WOMEN, MARRIED MEN

❖

You must not repine. You must be chearful and happy
[for my fate] is interwoven with yours. . . .
—*John Coalter*

❖

You know you must have a wife, but you must not make a mistake,
either. You musn't get one of them fly-up-the-creeks.
That wouldn't do at all—
—*Jochen Hanse-Peter*

❖

To the lovely ladies, once our superiors, now our equals.
—*Anonymous lawmaker*

❖

Those pioneer women! They did more than their part. The frontier was
fine for men and dogs, but hell on horses and women.
—*William Timmons*

YOUNG MEN, FRONTIER bound and delighted to shake free from society's tyranny of opinion, fled the formal world of long courtships, arranged matches, and inherited lands and hurried toward the goldfields or to claim homestead lands, while women developed their own sudden and seemingly inexplicable interests, including voting, contraception, and cheap, easily won divorces. Both were rudderless exiles on the frontier, adrift in an unfamiliar world of loose social restraints.

Men found in this restless new society an ideal climate for escape. They could head for California by packtrain, stagecoach, or overland wagon, leaving children, debts, work, and spouses behind. Under the old English common law, to desert a wife, even a common-law wife, was no crime, nor could a legally wed spouse be imprisoned for debts under the terms of the U.S. Constitution. Men could dodge their debts to faraway families without legal constraints, and many did.

Such freedoms were not lost on women, who generally were left at home, with children, unable to vote or own property, but still depended upon to keep the family farm running. Mostly they were highly competent in the business of keeping afloat, since frontier living often combined the work of men and women into "whatever had to be done." Daniel Drake recalled the chores that he and his sister had to do: "Liz was taught [milking] . . . as early as possible, see-

Unidentified Iowa couple, 1870. Photo by J. B. Carpenter.

ows of fallen soldiers inherited land, money, and family possessions and became a new force in American society, one to be reckoned with.

Women's competence must have perplexed men, who often believed, as did the historian Hubert Howe Bancroft, that they were childlike beings, easily bewildered, with brains too small for complex thought, and hearts so tremulous and overbrimming that they could scarcely function. Only a man could provide them safety and satisfy their needs. Wrote Bancroft: "Give her a home, with bread and babies; love her, treat her kindly, give her all the rights she desires, even the defiling right of suffrage if she can enjoy it, and she will be your sweetest, loveliest, purest, and most devoted companion and slave. But life-long application, involving life-long self denial, involving constant pressure on the brain, constant tension of the sinews, is not for women, but for male philosophers or—fools."

Whether single or married, frontier men maintained a complicated relationship with women, who believed the men were peculiar and knew they were sentimental, although most men would do anything to hide that fact. A man's concept of womanhood, having been shaped and romanticized in the life of his mother, was equally obscure. "I want you to cook, wash, iron, scrub, bake, make & mend and do a great many things to numerous to mention," confided Uriah Oblinger to his wife, Mattie, writing after many months of separation. Women were often alone, having been deserted by drunken husbands or, worse, mated with brutish husbands who sired numerous children without any means of caring for them. Even earnest, hardworking men scarcely had the energy for family life. "It angered [the educator William McGuffey] when he returned home from his wanderings to find [his mother] slaving in the bare farmhouse without comforts or leisure . . . [while] his father, [who] worked uncomplainingly in the fields or barn . . . at night sat snoring in the chimney corner, too dog-tired to read or engage in edifying conversation."

The debt to motherhood was great; few could ignore it. Young McGuffey, a brilliant backwoods youth, unable to afford school, recalled his mother's praying out loud in the dark one night, asking

ing that it was held by the whole neighborhood to be quite too girlish for a boy to milk; and mother, quite as much as myself, would have been mortified if any neighboring boy or man had caught me at it."

Gender roles were redefined during the Civil War as the wid-

God to find a way for her son to study for the ministry. Something, some presence, stirred in the darkness, and hoofbeats sounded as a lurking stranger galloped away. The next day at breakfast the family was interrupted by a pale, somber man, a minister starting an academy in Greersburg, Pennsylvania, who had overheard her prayer in the dark and, divinely inspired, offered William a scholarship. No wonder motherhood equaled sainthood in the adult male mind and imbued women with saintliness.

Chivalrous treatment of women, common in the South, had journeyed west after the Civil War, imported by legions of ex-soldiers whose old-fashioned manners toward women and benevolence toward children were taken up as the popular standard. Examples abound, from David Maynard, who traveled to Puget Sound and found that "it was good, after the weeks on the trail, to relax in a house with windproof walls, to listen to rain on the cedar shakes . . . to eat white bread and fresh vegetables, [and] to talk to Catherine Broshears, who was beautiful or even to her sister-in-law Elizabeth Simmons, who was not." Chivalry ranged from a shy offering of assistance through the mud or brambles to the daring rescue of the daughter of a Spanish governor of New Mexico from captivity by an

Unidentified family, ca. 1860s.

Indian tribe by a young fur trapper, James O. Pattie. Her gratitude overflowed at his selfless behavior, while he was bashful as a medieval knight: "Not attaching any merit to the act I had performed, and considering it merely as a duty, I did not know how to meet her acknowledgements, and was embarrassed."

High-minded men might die to defend women in need, but chivalry verged on infantalization. Men governed society, and the careful watch they kept over the female sex, guarding against any deviation, could only prove stifling. The struggle between the sexes was voiced by Nancy Stoner, writing to her son in May 1879 upon the birth of his daughter, Hope: "My son . . . when [your daughter] grows older teach her not to fear men, as a great many mothers do, but teach her to make men fear her." Difficult work, indeed, and men struggled to maintain control.

Feminine idealism tempered the moral dynamics of the frontier, and middle-class women gradually began to organize reform movements against the pastimes of gambling, drinking, and more. As civilizers they moved steadily to right the rocking boat of male morality and proved a threat to many men.

But not to all. Miner Carlisle Abbot became enraptured with "a French woman, Marie," whose assertive ways were European and interesting. He wrote: "I never liked another woman as well. She is straight, and I think I am willing to marry her. She will make me a truer and more agreeable companion than some little, sniffling, narrow-minded Puritan brought up on Calvinistic doctrine and mince pie, predestined to dyspepsia and doctrinal doubting." Abbot had been struck by love, which propelled him along the courtship path toward marriage.

The story of how men married is as old as time and has its counterpart in how women married, also of historic note. But all romance began with courtship before ending in the final, nuptial stage, and courtship could not take place without willing partners. Men who longed to marry were faced with a grim truth, a severe lack of women. Throughout the West there were seven men to every woman, and in remote Idaho, a "Spinster's Paradise," there were 16,584 bachelors to 1,426 single women, according to a survey taken by the *Ladies' Home Journal* in March 1899. So desperate were some men they took to advertising, and mail-order marriages became an established means of commerce for entrepreneurs such as Asa Mercer. In 1866 a steamship carrying one hundred single women, called by the press "a Hegira of Spinsters" and a "Cargo of Females," each having paid $200 for a seventeen-week voyage designed to end the great male shortage in the East and the lack of women in the West, sailed from New York to Seattle. Mercer appealed to "high minded" women for the task, a "passel of genuine ladies" to make "suitable wives of good moral character," who would, he hoped, marry the bachelors awaiting them. An older applicant, Mrs. Chase, was told midway in the journey to pay Mercer an additional $250 and that "she would probably get a husband as soon as she reached Seattle." Mrs. Chase, incensed at the additional charge, replied, "Mr. Mercer, if I can find a man with white hairs, his pockets well-lined with gold, one foot in the grave and the other just ready to go in I might get married." Both men and women were free to reject their so-called mates, and one happy result of Mercer's passage was his own choice: He fell in love with one of the passengers, was soundly rejected, then accepted by another, whom he wed upon reaching Seattle.

Another mail-order romance ended up well, as noted in the *Devil's Lake Daily Journal* of North Dakota on May 8, 1912:

> About a year and a half ago, John Bartley, a prosperous farmer . . . advertised in some rural paper for a wife with which to share his prosperity. . . . The ad found its way to Mcintosh, Minn., where Mrs. C. E. Davis, who is devoted to her granddaughter, Margery . . . answered the ad without consulting the young lady. When the gentleman's answer came, it not only pleased her, but met with the approval of Miss Davis and immediately a lively correspondence sprung up. This continued a year and [soon] . . . the date was set. The young lady accompanied by Mrs. Davis reached Lakota last evening. It was agreed beforehand that . . . each should wear a bouquet of flowers. . . . Mr. Bartley was at the depot with a large number of friends. It was a case of complete satisfaction and they lost no time in coming to the county seat to secure the license.
>
> He has showered the bride with gifts.

Lack of women affected every community, but for newly arrived Jewish men on the Pacific coast, the scarcity of women was acute. Where to find suitable brides? Many men sent back to European hometowns, and when the women did arrive, the marriages made were particularly secure. In fact divorce was rare in California Jewish families, although, by one account, in Indiana "twenty-nine Jewesses . . . were anxious to get rid of the ties which bound them to the men for whom they had no further use when their money was gone."

Couple on a bridge, ca. 1890s. Photo by Lillybridge.

A wedding was entertainment for all, and one union in 1856 drew German settlers for a hundred miles around, noted the brother-in-law of W. C. Howard, a neighbor of the groom: "One table dispensed tea and coffee, one beer, and still another whisky, gin and brandy. In the other room, tables had been arranged for card playing, and here I found the minister playing 'Ramms.' . . . And thus the afternoon passed; with gossip for old age; playing at hazard for middle age, dancing for youth, early man and womanhood; with ball and bat, hide and seek, walk around, blind man's bluff for early youth and childhood. None was forgotten, none was absent; the whole of life, as it is, was present."

Another wedding, held underground in a puncheon and sod

Unidentified couple married, 1908. Photo by Mary Elizabeth Wheeler.

and gave rise to "great festivity," wrote Noah Smithwick. After the wedding supper, the puncheon floor was cleared; the logs were split and hewn smooth on the flat side, ideal for the "shuffle," the "double shuffle," and to "cut the pigeon wing." Most of the young men were shod in moccasins, not shoes, and the soft leather snagged and caught; they could barely keep time to the capering tunes. The fiddle music was joined by a black man who "scraped on a cotton hoe with a case knife," and a clevis and pin player who plinked and wheedled along to "strengthen the orchestra," using a metal pin used to yoke oxen or horses. Some men were shoeless, so the dancers exchanged footgear, one "dancing a turn," then passing his shoes to the next in line.

Marriage might transform a man—even during the ceremony itself. John Thornburn of St. Louis, writing in 1889, married a high-born Scottish woman he'd met on a trip to Europe. Utterly swayed by her beauty, he wrote of their union:

> I followed behind my [bride] whose long blond lace veil [hung] over her head just so much that I could catch a glimpse of those deep black eyes, that cut me once to the Quick.
>
> What . . . was my feelings at this Critical Moment to be ready to Answer to the Questions Put by the Minister?
>
> Why, I just put my Eyes on a Figure of the Burssells Carpet on the Floor as he went on with his Questions Just pictureing in my mind how many Movements the Shuttle that Wove the Carpet made.
>
> [I] finish the Figure in the carpet.
>
> [Then] the awfull sound came—join hands. . . .
>
> And then—I pronounce you Man & Wife.
>
> Oh—Just to think what next came for me to do, was to give a Good Kiss to my Bride.
>
> Lord what a Kiss it was
>
> Such a kiss.
>
> In the effort I drew Such a Breath, it busted my Waiste Coat in the effort, and the Bride's cheek became of such a rosy red hugh that I thought I had bit her. . . .
>
> So all over. Went and sit down on sofa—our two dear selves were so elated in our Happy Feelings that we . . . just filled the

dugout in a town in Kansas, was presided over by the Reverend Rowland: "There was no floor, and a sheet had been stretched across one corner of the room. The bride and groom were stationed behind this, evidently under the impression it would not be proper to appear until time for the ceremony, but they were in such close quarters and the sheet was so short it put one in mind of an ostrich when it tries to hide by sticking its head in the sand." After the ceremony the bridegroom took the Reverend Rowland aside and asked him to "accept some potatoes in payment for performing the ceremony. He readily accepted and returned home."

When Nicholas McNutt married Jesse Cartwright's daughter, it was the first wedding to take place in Stephen Austin's colony of Texas, home of the "Old Three Hundred," the first families of Texas,

sofa. Our dear hearts . . . expanded so wide we *filled the Sofa.* Me thought to myself—I was [like] a Noble Turkey, as they strut and swell out their Breast, as proud as Proud Could be. . . .

Stranger, go and follow me [in marriage] & then you can feel for your self.

But it must be True Love, or you cant swell out as I did.

"Other men may have as sweet, attractive and loveable wives as mine but [it] cannot seem possible," swooned newlywed Frank Cushing, "married almost a year and . . . happy beyond all expectations." Perhaps, he admitted, "other women were more beautiful . . . more brilliant in natural intellectual endowments, more learned in . . . the acquisition of facts," but the "womanly beauty" of his wife held sway. However, manhood demanded some restraint lest he seem chained to the skirts of his wife, so he confided in a friend his "true" and revised vision of marriage, angelic wife or not. "The illusion [of the honeymoon] rarely outlasts the first six months [and] at the end of a year, I think a man has a very settled and well-grounded conviction with regard to the results of his matrimonial venture." Uriah Oblinger missed his wife, Mattie, so much he wrote to her frequently. "I expect you think I am a little foolish for commencing as a lover might commence but I cannot help it; it is simply my feelings put on paper for your perusal."

✤ ✦ ✦ ✦

GIVEN THE NUMBER of men in the West, there was little that could be called typical behavior. The range was broad as all imagination, and often couples of different races, habits, and backgrounds were bonded.

For those who would marry only from their own backgrounds, it was sometimes better to choose a wife before heading West. Abraham Luckenbach, a Moravian missionary to the Delaware Indians on the White River, was a single man, which meant that he either had to "become a benedict" and live celibate or find a wife. Electing to marry, he shuffled through the names of every eligible young Moravian woman near Bethlehem, Pennsylvania, with Anna Maria Rank, of Lititz, being selected. The marriage was performed shortly before Luckenbach's departure: "[O]n the fifteenth day of October, 1800,

Happy couple, North Dakota, ca. 1880. Photo by Fiske.

John Peter Kluge, with his newly wedded wife and Abraham Luckenbach, [also married] set forth."

Part of life's lesson in the wilderness was tolerance, particularly when it came to coexistence with the Native Americans. In the mountain schoolroom, men who were generally ignorant, steeped with prejudice, and spoiling for trouble learned, over time, that existence often meant dependence, most particularly upon Indian women, who comforted and cooked for them, bore their children, and served as a connection to family members who knew the prime trapping areas, who were skilled hunters, and who often would do the white man's trapping for him in winter.

"Squaw men" married or lived with Indian women—at least during the winter. In some cases they completely embraced Indian culture and left the security of forts to live with their wives' people, ironically often facing cultural discrimination from the Indians. One trapper in the Pacific Northwest gave himself so completely to native life he was seen as a slave, fit only to cut wood and haul water.

Often love blossomed, followed by chivalry and devotion. Love's languishing knew no place, race, or obstacle when Andrew Garcia first spied the Pend d'Oreille Indians' In-who-lise, or "Susie." He knew it was no casual affair. Taking in her sturdy build of "150 pounds," he saw her as his bride. "I told her that I would marry her and put a ring on her finger, a thing that very few of them got those days from a white man." Another backwoodsman, John Young Nelson, an adopted member of Black Elk's tribe of Paiutes, was given a new bride:

> I got up and began untying my presents. . . . I turned to her and said:
>
> "These are all for you. Do what you please with them."
>
> She was simply thunderstruck, and, opening her eyes as wide as saucers, said: "For me? What shall I do with them?"
>
> "Anything you please," I repeated. "They are all yours. I like you as much as those presents represent."
>
> When I returned in about two hours I found my squaw had taken me literally at my word, and given everything away. Not one of the articles I had brought was left.
>
> I thought to myself, this is a good beginning. Whatever your other failings may be, no one can accuse you of want of generosity.

John Wesley Prowers, working as an Indian agent, stopped along the Santa Fe Trail at Bent's Fort to have an ox shod and was struck by the shy glance of an Indian princess, Amache Ochinee, daughter of a subchief of the Southern Cheyennes. Irresistibly drawn, he stayed on at the fort, gazing at her longingly, then finally found the heart to speak. In 1861 he and Amache were married in a Cheyenne and Christian ceremony and settled on his cattle ranch in Colorado. In contrast with the general spirit of infidelity and abandonment of trapper alliances with Indian women, the Prowers match was resolute testimony to a deep and abiding love. They lived happily in a fourteen-room adobe house with their nine children. Prowers prospered in the cattle business and also served as a translator and inter-

mediary between the U.S. government and the Cheyennes. "Father was always exceptionally good to mother's people," recalled his daughter Mary. "They all loved and honored him. The Cheyenne were always welcome at the ranch."

When the Kansas Pacific Railroad built a branch through Las Animas, Colorado, a war party of three hundred Cheyennes came out to protest. Heavily armed, they lined the hillside outside town. They knew that the railroad meant more settlers, and they planned to attack. Prowers bravely rode out and discouraged them. He offered them gifts, killed many cattle, and feasted them all night long. He died at the age of forty-six, a successful man whose vision helped build southern Colorado.

Men could cozy up to married life as snugly as women, and countless numbers did. "Home, with me, was always delightful," wrote Ethan Allen Crawford. To be clamored over by "half a dozen little ones come and rest themselves upon me, all of them having good reason and proper shapes, was a blessing." James Tullock ached for his cabin in the Washington Territory, which his wife, Annie, had gaily surrounded with seventy-five vigorous breeds of ever-blooming roses. "We took pride in our home," he wrote. "We dreamed of what we would make of it in years to come." Cleric Isaac Owen, writing to his wife, Elizabeth, in 1851 from California, told her he missed her company. "I feel homeless. What would home be without your smiles?" She was equally despondent, and in correspondence he failed to lighten her spirits. Finally he tried another tack, food. "Cheer up," he wrote, "and try to get fat by my return."

Marriage could prompt deep joy and the richness of companionship. Of the men who did write, many recalled companionate affection. Among them was Jochen Hanse-Peter, who "caught his wife in his arms and carried her bodily up the bank, as if she were a mere baby. She fairly screamed with delight, but was startled for a moment by the voice of her son, calling from our fishing place." Clearly their affection ran deep. While Hanse-Peter was on a hunting expedition with friends, she even surprised him in camp, bringing out a basket of ladylike accoutrements to grace the hunters' rugged backwoods fare of squirrel ragout, canvasback ducks, and crispy watercress salad. As she artfully arranged table linen, goblets, and glasses, Jochen fretted at the "elaborate, not to say extravagant eating appa-

Charles Lemmon and Susan Hall at desk, ca. 1900.

ratus" in their "humble, primitive enclosure." "What's all this for? What does it mean, wifey mine?" he asked. "To keep you fellows from turning barbarians—husband mine!" she replied.

And so continued the good-natured struggle between feminine wants and the rowdy frontier lives of men whose natural inclinations often were to hunt, fish, ramble, and wrestle and to whom the wilderness was one vast, ongoing invitation to play.

In fact what every married man had to face was the finality of his youth and the acceptance of family responsibility. "Getting married meant something practical then," wrote Illinois settler James Haines. "A log cabin soon followed on a claim made by the husband. Corn

bread, hominy, wild game, bacon, eggs and butter were the main articles of living, all cooked and served by the new wife. No hired girls, no boarding house life. Husband and wife both joined at once in bread win[n]ing. . . . Health and happiness, crowned with parentage and frequent use of the sugar trough cradle made a virtuous, happy home." Early mating and almost universal marriage propelled the frontier population into a frenzy of growth.

Love prospered with cooperation between husband and wife, essential in a frontier setting and hearteningly common. Elizabeth Power Huston, a young Dakota girl, recalled her father's mindfulness, particularly one summer when the family had raised more corn

than it could sell. "Father brought in an arm load of corn-on-the-cob one day, and put some of it in the stove to burn. It made a fine hot fire and was so clean. But Mother began to cry. Between sobs she said, 'I just can't stand to see food burned. Maybe someone needs it.' Father stood awhile, thoughtfully, then said, 'If that is the way you feel we just won't burn anymore.'"

On another occasion, "when Pa hauled turkeys to town for Ma, he would usually have to borrow money from her. He would say, 'I'll pay you back when I sell my grain.' Ma would tell about the loan and say, 'I know he never will though.' I don't think he did repay her very often," said Huston. "Ma [just] had more income than he did."

Loving support and cooperation formed the fabric of many a frontier existence, including that of the eminent historian of California's settlement Hubert Howe Bancroft. "I . . . was growing somewhat old for a young wife," he wrote, "and I had no fancy for taking an old one. The risk on both sides I felt to be great." To this scholarly recluse, the idea of a demanding wife high-stepping about in fine silks was deeply disturbing. He wished companionship without gossip, intrigue, exertion, and trouble. He admitted:

A happy marriage doubles the resources and completes the being which otherwise fails in the fullest development of its intuitions and yearnings. . . . I was so constituted by nature that I could not endure domestic infelicity. . . . I had a world within me whose good-will I could command so long as I was at peace with myself. . . . My home must be to me heaven or hell. There was no room in my head for discord, nor in my heart for bitterness. . . . Nothing so quickly dissipated my ideas, and spoiled a day for me, as domestic disturbances. . . . Often I had been counselled to marry; but whom should I marry?

Bancroft's desires took shape in the modest form of Matilda Coley Griffin, a young woman from a literary New England family, whose calm, loving, and undemanding presence made him "content . . . nay, very happy." They married in 1876 and lived quietly thereafter.

✦ ✦ ✦ ✦

WHEN A WIFE supported her husband's endeavors, tranquillity smoothed their lives, and domestic bliss reigned. "I have been married now almost a year and I have not only been as happy as I expected but happy beyond all expectations," wrote the rhapsodic businessman Frank Cushing. "I underestimated the power of one woman . . . to charm and fascinate me." General John Fremont and his wife were seen as a model couple, thanks to her supportive efforts. According to Bancroft, she was "very animated and shrewdly talkative and thoroughly engrossed in her husband's schemes, assisting him now, as she had done for twenty years, by planning and writing for him." In the Levy home in San Francisco, the patriarch of the household might "bring his fist down upon the table" and "tap three times upon the table with one finger, his signal of concern," but it was Mrs. Levy whose expression would determine the outcome. "Her face veered away from him slowly and rested at her angle of accusation."

Marriage brought satisfaction to some, sorrow to others, and even then the retelling was highly subjective. Some men simply did not know about women, and marriage scarcely helped. A dim curtain fell between them, on one side the wife waiting, and on the other, a confused and often resentful partner. Nancy Stoner answered her son's query about how to make his wife happy with advice on how to spend their Sundays. "Take your wife who needs recreation & go to church and if you are deprived of that get some

Unidentified California mining family.

good reading from the bible, or . . . seat your selves in your own little home and make each other happy." In addition, "after your dinner is over *write* to your own dear mother who is ever longing to hear from you and yours."

Strong women sparked fiery feuds, and anger often drove married partners to escalating levels of violence. The disgruntled wife of J. Dayton Thorpe called him a "damned old fool," struck and beat him more than a hundred times, lobbed scissors at him, brandished a revolver, and eventually ran away from home, claiming she "had no use for . . . a child that looked so much like its father." According to historian Glenda Riley, Thorpe finally sued his wife, Abbie, for divorce in 1895 on the ground of verbal and physical abuse, the first time a man did so in the country. According to him, his wife regularly called him a "damned old fool" and a "damn son of a bitch" and demanded that he "go to hell" when he asked her a civil question. Yet when his wife appeared in court, she revealed his "improper attentions" to a hired woman, later his mistress, and that he had squandered the three thousand dollars she had brought to the marriage.

Domestic violence was a final testament to lives gone awry, and such unhappiness often brought divorce to the rural setting. By 1890, wrote Riley, "the rate of divorces in the West grew far more rapidly than did its married population."

In 1890 divorce was still a stigma but was too common to be a social disaster. Some states were notorious divorce "resorts" or at least reported as such in sensational newspaper accounts, such as the *Guthrie* (Oklahoma) *Daily Leader* in 1892. Such resorts, or meccas, included Arizona, California, Colorado, Idaho, Illinois, Kansas, Montana, Nevada, Wyoming, and Oklahoma, the last with an unheard-of brief—ninety-day—residency before one spouse could notify the other simply by announcing the impending divorce in an Oklahoma newspaper rather than actually serve divorce papers. In 1896, said Riley, the *Philadelphia* (Oklahoma) *Record* accused the territorial courts of granting "mail order" divorces, with neither party living in the state or even appearing in Oklahoma. Shortly after, the U.S. Congress mandated a one-year residency requirement, although divorce rates in the country continued to soar, as shown by U.S. Department of Commerce and Labor statistics between 1867 and 1906. Apparently, the states least stratified by class had the most liberal divorce laws, attracting people of all backgrounds, including, according to Riley, a black man, Aaron Jordan, who divorced his wife, Sarah, because she refused to move to Oklahoma with him in 1893.

Desertion was also common and was increasingly used as ground for divorce. Wanted posters for wayward husbands were common. Domestic discord also resulted in suicide and murder. Emigrant Lorena Hays, writing in the 1850s, described the funeral of a Mrs. Lyons, supposedly murdered on the Fourth of July "by her husband, who was drinking, [and who] probably choked her to death, then, to hide his crime, hung her in the well and called it suicide. He is in jail awaiting his trial." Jack Sheridan of Nevada used a bread knife to kill his spouse, stabbing her repeatedly in the back. A skeleton found in a shallow grave near the Idaho Territory's Owyhee Mountains turned out to be the wife of a local settler, with a "bullet hole in the center of her forehead." The husband had long since departed. Grisly remains testified to the raging hostility and exasperation that often flared up between a couple, often getting the better of one or the other. Such "family affairs" might be shrugged aside by exasperated onlookers; no one wanted to interfere with a man's "right" or "property."

Although wife beating might incur a minimal fine, to Indiana farmer John Grannis, reveling in the freedom of the Colorado gold mines, the scant fifteen dollars was little deterrent. A diary entry, dated New Year's Day 1863, shows his easygoing nonchalance. "Herded the cattle as usual. Had some words with Mrs. Grannis & spatted her on the mouth." Grannis's failure as a miner had turned him mean and disconsolate, and he picked quarrels with his wife. His temper grew blacker, and the "spatting" more frequent. Having left him once, she repeatedly fled to a neighbor. Grannis, a God-fearing man who poured over Scripture nightly, was sure she had become a "free love" harlot. Their eleven-year marriage had run its course; the wife from Indiana had been "spatted" too often. She offered to watch her neighbor's son in exchange for room and board. When the neighbor left for Idaho and the goldfields, she went along. Grannis followed, now mourning, "never again can I lay my head beside my wife and enjoy happiness." She had "played him false," and he was tortured by it. Informed that she would divorce him, he was shocked and took her subsequent marriage as the last insult before his final resignation. "I bought me an outfit to cook for myself," the true mark of the single man.

In another case of domestic mayhem, in 1854 John Vedder, an uneducated, uncouth loudmouth who paraded about heavily armed, married the teenage Lucinda Bohall, in Sacramento, California. To Lucinda fell the woman's tasks—cleaning, sewing, and cooking—while John, outlining the parameters of their married life, informed her that he would stay out at night, deny her costly care if she were ill, and "stomp" her if she gave him any trouble, according to Lucinda. Accused of being abusive, he railed that "she has the G-d d—-est tongue," according to historian Ruth Mather. Spunky herself, Lucinda revealed she had helped make Vedder angry. "We both had tempers and never agreed," she admitted. "We lived very unhappily." When not flogging her, Vedder would throw her onto her wedding trunk and demand that she pack up and leave, taking their "feeble" daughter with her.

Vedder's attacks increased, especially since he was losing at gambling. He even hired a spy to watch her. Some days pedestrians slowed as they heard her pleading for help. Other times they heard her call out, "you d——d whore house pimp," followed by the sound of scuffling and cries. "I am afraid of my husband," she explained. "I want protection."

Chivalry appeared in the form of Marshal Henry Plummer, who helped Lucinda obtain divorce papers and scheduled a stage ride out of town. Blind with anger, Vedder imagined that she was in love with Plummer, whom she scarcely knew. Knowing that her stage left at 2:00 A.M. and that police were in the house to protect her, he crept up the back steps, charged into the house with a pistol, and fired at Plummer. Unscathed, Plummer fired back and killed Vedder, who died in his wife's arms.

An ambitious young prosecutor trying Plummer for murder discovered that Lucinda had cohabited with another man before her marriage to John. Suddenly her virtue vanished, and sympathy arose for her husband.

The marshal was sentenced to ten years in San Quentin. By court order, Lucinda still had custody of her child and "had the right to keep [it] unless [her father-in-law] could prove she had a bad character." The father-in-law kidnapped the child and gained custody, on the basis of Lucinda's "new" disrepute. He denied her visitation rights unless he could sleep at her house and be "somewhat intimate with her."

Colorado woman sitting with portrait of husband.

Eventually Plummer's innocence was upheld by a signed petition. When her child died, Lucinda retired from sight, despairing at her designation as an unfaithful wife, an unfit mother, and a godless woman by men who themselves frequented whorehouses or owned brothels. For Lucinda, her tongue was her downfall.

Men determined a woman's character and standing. "What it is they lack . . . I hardly know," wrote Hubert Howe Bancroft. "We long for the company of decent women," said miner Carlisle Abbott, who was quick to distinguish them from "ladies of doubtful reputation." A husband was reluctantly charged with assault after several attempts to deter his wife from using rouge and powder. Once he blacked her face with boot polish. On another occasion "he painted her face and neck with green enamel, and then spent two and a half hours removing it with petrol," according to the *San Francisco Call* of October 23, 1910.

Loyalty came easily for some but was unthinkable for others. A man might simply drift away to follow his fancy, leaving an anxious wife with little recourse but to advertise for him in the newspaper, pleading for word of her wayward spouse. Such women were not widowed, divorced, or supported, turning them into grass widows, with muddied reputations and limited remarriage options.

Newspapers relished scandal, particularly bigamy, making Doc Maynard, a leading citizen of Seattle, a newsworthy man, his story reported in various publications, including the *Olympic*. Maynard fell in love with a widow while on a wagon train west, moved in with her, and then married her. They took nightly strolls, arm in arm, down the streets of Seattle. On several occasions they were joined by his legitimate wife, who had arrived for a surprise visit. Doc was a fair-minded man and, once he had recovered his composure, proposed that he take care of them both, at least financially. Another bigamist, George D. Collins of Sacramento, was sentenced to fourteen years in prison by a judge who was amazed at his effrontery: "I cannot understand how it is possible for a man to marry a woman and then bring her sister into his home and raise a family by her and introduce her in the presence of his true wife."

Some peccadilloes seemed minor, others as insidious and cautionary as those of William Thomas Prestwood, whose diary describes his life as a married man and the father of six boys and one girl who could not remain faithful to his wife. A compulsive womanizer, Prestwood revealed the most heedless side of the male persona. Callous and willful, he resumed relations with his wife soon after childbearing. He also had a long-term mistress and other sexual encounters.

Not all men kept journals, and in those written, many were guarded in their descriptions of intimacy. Of all the points of view, perhaps the one that best speaks for conjugal bliss is in the words of George W. Riley in December 1880: "It is a fact that ever aparent to me that during all of the quarter of a century that has past in my Married life The greatest good that this world has afoarded me has ben my Ever True and faithfull Wife to Stande by and helpe and encourage doing all in her power to make every thing pleasant to all around. May God Bless hur guide and direct and keep and save us all is my earnist & sincere prayer."

Likewise black women should be sheltered and protected, said the Reverend C. Ransom Jael, addressing the IBW Club in Chicago:

And now, men, the thing that we must do is to protect this woman-hood. . . . There is one thing that the Negroes of this country want to learn and that is to respect its womanhood, not to accost them too familiarly upon the streets; but with all dignity and honor; and then when their women are molested they should learn to defend them. Why my brethren in many of the cities of this Union colored men this very day, I am sure, and every day, walk the streets with their women, their wives, their sweet-hearts upon their arms and permit blackguards and ruffians to throw insults at them as they walk in their company. Is it not true? And . . . it often happens that [when] men see it is a colored woman on the street cars, on the streets and elsewhere that they may approach them with a familiarity that is not decent. Our men must . . . not permit it and our women should conduct themselves with such dignity and propriety as not to invite insult.

I am a minister of the gospel and a man of peace; but the day that any man insults one of mine, I shall resent it with emphasis. And this is one of the lessons, if our womanhood is to be elevated, that men must learn, that womanhood has protectors and defenders. Another duty that we owe to our women is to support them as far possible; take them not into the struggle for winning of bread, but give them that opportunity, as far as it is in your power, for the development of those higher graces and qualities which are peculiar to the sex by supporting them properly in the home.

We have got some lessons to learn. Mark my words to night, brothers! Our womanhood can never shine in all the beauty and dignity and glory which is in store for it until it has our protection.

Marriage in the West proved hardy, despite desertion and divorce. Men found, after many setbacks, a western economy verging on prosperity, thus offering long-term encouragement to struggling families. Although patriarchal bonds were strongly in place, women's growing independence caused men to offer more support. The West, with its dedication to individualism and the pursuit of happiness, offered opportunity to men and women alike, and from this came mutual support and respect. Lacking that, women felt more free to roam. "My husband's got to make himself agreeable to me if he can," stated Louise Palmer of Virginia City, Nevada. "If he don't, there's plenty will." Yet ultimately the success of any marriage, East or West, had to do with the belief that if there's enough love, it can surmount any difficulty.

11

BELOVED HUSBANDS, FAITHFUL FATHERS

Father believed strongly in circuses—
he said they were very educational.
—*Nellie Tichenor McGraw*

❧

My father did not want me to learn a trade, because he considered the
work was hard, and many of them [trades] . . . dangerous.
—*George Conklin*

❧

[T]he greatest good that this world has afoarded me has ben my Ever
True and faithfull Wife to Stande by and helpe and encourage doing all in
her power to make every thing pleasant to all around.
—*George W. Riley*

❧

In this time we had two sons, and I found I was better at increasing my
family than my fortune.—*Davy Crockett*

FAMILY FEALTY FILLED the journals and diaries of America's pioneers. Most fathers viewed their children as small adults, whom they might befriend, enjoy, and work, even if in a limited capacity. The paternal role often mirrored democracy itself: independent, headstrong, with few to help. In the West children would look to a father for guidance and support, but in reality they all were "growing up together." After the custom of English parents, the children's mother instructed them in religion and ethics, while the father kept a sharp eye on behavior. Westward expansion had broadened the notion of fatherhood, as well as that of being a husband, with results that were often a surprise. J. B. Hoss of Pendleton, Oregon, recalled a father who "believed in discipline with a capital D, and when he wanted to whip me he grabbed the first thing handy." But then, the son admitted, "he probably meant well" despite the "heavy hand and a quick-trigger temper." The father of Jane Rooker Breeden cautioned her "to play for game, not for gain," when she filled in for missing members of his card club. Jane learned to play an excellent game of whist while remembering her father's rule. John Ellis, the father of Lewis Rinehart, lived to see his wife massacred by Indians and his younger children tomahawked. Yet he was a model to his son. "He was quite a reader, and could repeat nearly the entire New Testament from memory." He also taught Sunday school in his neighborhood, "which was quite a new thing at that time."

What made a man a good husband and loving father? The frontier may have contributed danger and hardship, but the character of a man was uniquely his own, independent of setting, often reflecting an intense degree of tenderness and affection. When the wife of Silent Platt sickened and died six weeks after he had left for the goldfields, for a week he "was out of his mind and . . . half a dozen times he went down to the wharf, fully determined to jump off and end his misery," recalled his friend Carlisle Abbot. "Then the memory of his little girl came to him and held him back. After the first acute agony was over he realized that he still had something to live for, and resolving to devote himself to the baby he sold his mules, for which he got four hundred dollars, sent three hundred to the grandmother and started for the mountains. . . . The child was healthy, well taken care of, and he was in hopes in a year or so to bring her and her grandmother to California. He had neither inclination nor desire to see the States again."

Fathers had much to protect their children from. When young Mollie Sheehan, enrolled in school in Virginia City, Nevada, witnessed her first lynching, she was horrified by "the bodies of five men with ropes around their necks hung limp from a roof beam." She "trembled so" that she could scarcely run home. Worse, she had recognized one of the limp forms as Deputy Jack Gallagher, "a tall and dark and striking-looking" man, often a guest at her home. Earlier that year she had witnessed the hanging of Joseph Alfred Slade, who cried out, while strangling, "[F]or God's sake, let me see my dear, beloved wife!" Despite the popularity of lynchings in the West—they were often viewed by the entire family, seen as moral entertainment and sideshow—Mollie's father believed in the innocence of childhood and tried to shield her. He insisted that she could not attend the events, no matter what other children were doing.

The idea of holding children's interests first was new and difficult for many to accept. De Witt Clinton noted that the commander of his post, "about 55 years of age . . . and with two children," was educating them himself. "He is rather too indulgent," wrote Clinton, "and makes these children his equals." Henry Slack, a carpenter and millwright from Brown, North Dakota, often sacrificed his sense of family to late nights out, to which he gravitated naturally. He had a "fine voice, could play many musical instruments," and told well the

Family, possibly mixed race, Ukiah, California, ca. 1880s.

many interesting stories collected in his travels. After work, his friends would urge him, "Come on, Henry. Just one song. Just one story. Just one more drink." When his brother wrote from Wabasha, Minnesota, in 1867, urging Henry's family to resettle there, Henry's wife hoped he would have fewer "friends." She prayed for tranquillity, for his full attention to the family, for fewer nights out. At the

"20ᵗʰ Century Madonna," 1901. Photo by H. Seberuce.

On the happiest occasions a man's sense of well-being was reflected in a peaceful domesticity, in which his authority lent stability to the frontier household. What could satisfy more than the life of Martin Murphy, Sr., a California settler, "surrounded by his children, prospered, living in patriarchal abundance, with his flocks and herds, his lands and his numerous household." His house was "the stopping place for all travelers on the highway [and] he was known for hospitality cordially extended to wayfarers," wrote historian Hubert Howe Bancroft.

The skills a man brought along he could pass along, but the unfamiliar was always daunting. He could turn to his children for help or his wife for guidance, seeking succor from them when possible, but ultimately, as every father knew, he was on his own. "A son might inherit a strong frame, willing hands, and an honest and eager heart," explained a Kentuckian, "but the most valuable requisite for any man, self-reliance, was inherited, or by necessity acquired by all." A wise father knew when to pass on responsibility to a child, at least for a while. T. D. Edwards, traveling to Oregon, recalled spotting a wagon that had suddenly pulled away from the rest of the train. "Just then father instructed us to drive on. . . . He and mother went to the lone wagon where they remained for about five hours and during those fleeting precious hours I was captain of the advance fraction of our train, with all the rights, powers and privileges appertaining thereto, and as was customary for one holding that important office I rode on ahead to select a camping place." Hours later his father returned, announcing that a fourteenth member had been added to the party, and the young T. D. was relieved of his duty.

In Abraham Lincoln's letter to his son's teacher, a father outlines the path to a son's maturity.

He will have to learn, I know, that all men are not just, all are not true, but teach him also that for every scoundrel there is a hero, that for every selfish politician there is dedicated leader. Teach him for every enemy there is a friend.

It will take time I know, but teach him if you can that a dollar earned is of far more value than five found, teach him to lose and to enjoy winning. Steer him away from envy, if you can teach him the secret of quiet laughter, teach him if you can the wonder of

beginning Henry cobbled and farmed, and the children "gathered acorns to roast and grind for coffee and played in the woods, wild and frisky as animals." On Sundays they dressed in cloth suits, "little Scotch caps made from scraps left from their suits . . . [and] shoes that Henry had made." When a saloon opened nearby—"Minnesota people liked Henry's music, too"—his popularity soared, and his pattern of being gone at night slowly reestablished itself.

books. But also give him quiet time to ponder the eternal mystery of birds in the sky, bees in the sun and flowers on a green hillside. In school teach him its far more honorable to fail than to cheat. Teach him to have faith in his own ideas even if everyone tells him they are wrong. To be gentle with gentle people and tough with tough.

Try to give my son the strength not to follow the crowd when everyone is getting on the bandwagon. To listen to all men but teach him also to filter all he hears on a screen of truth and take only the good that comes through, teach him if you can how to laugh when he is sad and there is no shame in tears.

Teach him to scoff at cynics and to beware of too much sweetness. Teach him to sell his brawn and brain to the highest bidder but never to put a price tag on his heart and soul. Teach him to close his ears to a howling mob and to stand and fight. Treat him gently but do not cuddle him because only the test of fire makes fine steel, let him have the courage to be, let him have the patience to be brave. Teach him always to have sublime faith in himself because then he'll always have sublime faith in mankind.

That's a big order, but see what you can do because he's a fine little fellow.

Advice came from fathers of all kinds, including the profligate young planter from North Carolina William Thomas Prestwood, whose lessons for his sons included an awkward sexual admonition, direct from the corrupted heart of a jaunty and unapologetic womanizer, with conquests in his own neighborhood numerous enough to fill fifteen volumes of a journal.

"Advice to My Sons"

6 November 1822
The desire of my soul is that my son should be a man and not a child all his life
My son before you do an act consider our Savior's Golden rule, viz "Do so you would be done by." Never do anything that would wound your conscience or you would be ashamed of afterwards.

Father pushing baby in carriage, ca. 1900s.

27 November 1822

My son, learn music, but do not be a pedant with it.

1 January 1823

Above all things, my sons, do not SEDUCE innocent girls

5 January 1823

My sons, court not popularity but always rise by your virtue & merit

20 March 1823

My dear sons, learn eloquence; not barely what you say, but the proper manner of speaking.

Men sought to educate their sons, but those who had left home for the goldfields in California were thwarted by distance and the slow, erratic progress of the mails. Long letters home, often arriving six months later, requested children to behave, obey their mothers, split logs, save seeds, and keep the door latches closed, as well as told them what books to read. Long-distance fathering, parenting by pony express, was logistically impossible. Nebraska homesteader Uriah Oblinger worried about his daughter in a letter home: "I have received all the . . . letters you sent me You ask if I get tired of reading of my baby's little antics of course I do not. Only try and not let her get at anything naughty or unbecoming for bless her dear little life I would not like to have her become saucy or impudent I want her to be a real little lady . . . & then she will be an honor to us and an ornament to our home & also to society . . . how I would love to have a play with my dear child I think it would do me some good."

Education was foremost in most fathers' minds, aspired to by the thoughtful and paid for with the last of a man's income—at least in the case of a Dr. William A. Lindsay, who had unfortunately "lost some *Six thousand dollars*" as the result of a bad partnership. Gone were the results of "many years of professional labor and the strictest economy." Although now perched in precarious straits, Lindsay and his wife still "expended freely for the Education of [their] children, Eleanora, Dewitt Clinton, Wm. Washington Irving and Edwin Smith Blackstone."

Another so motivated was Edmund Booth, who had left his family to work in the California gold mines. From the "diggings" in Sonora, he wrote to his son in the Midwest on September 28, 1851:

My Dear Son,

For the first time I write to you directly and hope you will write to me as often as your Mother does. I wish you to write just as you would talk if I were at home and we were together. You can tell me many things such as how our friends and neighbors are . . . how the crops of corn, wheat, potatoes, etc., turn out. . . .

I send a dollar to Harriet and a ten-dollar piece to get you "Bancroft's History of the United States." It is by far the best of its kind. Bancroft is yet alive and is personally known to me. . . .

You are growing into manhood and will have your part to act on the stage of life. Every man can be useful to his race as [the famous authors] have been. You may or may not be as useful as they. It will depend on yourself. But whatever you may be or do, be ready to do the best. . . . When you are in trouble do not despair. Evil is never lasting. Good remains forever and there is always hope. Be a good boy and you are almost certain to be a good man. . . .

Affectionately,
Your father

Sonora, March, 1853

Dear Boy,

Tomorrow I send you a Chinese book, and also another book entitled "Crayon Armies" of men who have made themselves; who are distinguished as public speakers and writers; and who mostly speak and write for the present and the future. . . . The work is racy and lifelike. Among the characters you will find Horace Greeley, whose paper, the New York Tribune, will probably reach you with this or soon after. It appears that the rate is $4 for two years' subscription. I sent for it last August and will send for it tomorrow.

I hope you will read the paper habitually—not merely the news, but also the books, sketches and lectures. It is important that you should acquire knowledge not only of words and ability to use them, but also of ideas—These are to be learned not all in a day or in a year, but as we use honey, little by little. . . .

Be a good boy, as your mother says you are, and I am glad of it. Write me and try to do as well as you can.

The father's role was to educate his children and act as their moral guide. "I was often at my wits' end to invent stories and explanations to account for my lack of knowledge when questioned about school matters by my father," wrote George Conklin. "But, as he was rather credulous . . . I was much more successful than was to be expected." Still, his father gave him good advice. "'You think you are working for me when you are going to school, but some day you will find out that you were working for yourself and wish you had done more.' I have lived to find out that he was right."

For some, wisdom was imparted through example, repetition, and explanation. In a North Dakota Norwegian community, wrote settler Barbara Levorson, rules were to be obeyed. So when some children "poked around" in the belongings of a hired man whose things had been left in storage with the family for a year, adults were quick to respond. "Uncle . . . looked at . . . me. His eyes were as cold as ice when he asked if we had taken anything out of the chest. 'No' we replied, 'we had not.' His icy eyes swept [us]. And he [said] what was in the chest belonged to the owner of the chest and was neither to be pryed into or talked about."

⤞ ⤞ ⤝ ⤝

MEN MIGHT DISCUSS finances, livelihood, friends, geography, and climate, but seldom did they reflect on their own emotions or behavior, particularly when it came to their own charity, kindness, or benevolence. Often these moments of grace were recorded by others, such as young Nellie McGraw, daughter of a prominent Pacific coast attorney who, in her eyes, was the model of a father. He took the family swimming, picnicking, and to any circus that came to town. Although busy at his work, he knew his wife was even more burdened by their thirteen children; she scarcely ever "got away from home." Wrote Nellie: "Father arranged for her to go to the matinee on Saturdays . . . on the understanding that she was not to

Man and daughter milking, ca. 1870s.

take any of the children. She followed this custom for several years . . . it gave her a change of scene and she got a great deal of pleasure out of it." One day he took them sailing.

We walked along the [Sausalito] pier where there were a number of row boats. I don't know whether Father had ever rowed a boat—but he was suddenly seized with the desire to take us for a row on the bay. We must have been a pleasing sight in our dainty starched dresses. . . . The pier was high above the water and the boat had to be lowered by pulleys to walk down a flight of stairs to board it. For some reason Father preferred to stand by and oversee the launching. As the boat descended I noticed that I could see the water through the bottom but being totally ignorant about boats I said nothing. We all boarded it and settled our flounces and prepared for a fine adventure—and we had it. Father valiantly manned the oars and as we advanced away from land, somebody said "my feet are wet," but as Father made no response we did not mention the fact again until the water was up to our shoe tops. Then Father awakened from the dream of his youth and began to yell for help. We were a good ways out. Father's muscles were in good shape. He waved his oars in the air and yelled to us "start to bail," I said, "we haven't anything to bail with." He yelled, "Get something, use your hats!" Off came our pretty new hats and we bailed—Meanwhile Father kept yelling and waving an oar, but it was probably the frantic work of us children that attracted someone on the pier. Anyway two men rowed out to us and took us aboard and towed our boat in. Father's comments were not pleasant, but he saved the worst until he found the man who had rented him the boat. As the episode was over and father was leading his bedraggled daughters from the pier, I remarked: "I saw a hole in the boat when they were letting it down." His wrath rose afresh: "Why didn't you say so," he yelled, and I meekly answered: "I thought that was the way boats were made."

Elizabeth Power Huston's father was a hardscrabble farmer. In summers he cut and bundled hay, stacking it high. During icy winters he hauled in great armloads of hay to twist into logs and burn.

He taught his children to roll up their sleeves to save the cloth from fraying. "Of course our arms were badly scratched but father kissed the scratches and made them well which was much easier than for mother to have to mend frayed sleeves," wrote Elizabeth.

For Ragna Mellom Severson, "Toys were few and far between," in Deuel County, South Dakota, in 1889. "I recall my joy when Father brought me a curly white lamb on wheels from a large town he visited." In San Francisco, Harriet Levy's father "slept in his heavy red flannel shirt and drawers. . . . Sitting up in bed . . . he looked like an early American statesman. In the early morning," she recorded, "I peeped into the room to see if he were alone. I sat at the foot of his bed and we, Father and I, talked of plays and actors—talked until Mother's voice sharply reminded us of the late hour." He also fed every wanderer who stopped by the back door of their home. "No hungry man should leave his door unfed, he declared," and Harriet's mother agreed.

Montana ranch wife Mary Gibson took notice of how a man could add joy to his family's life despite isolation or harsh circumstances. She recalled her husband's frequent attempts to brighten up her days at their remote outpost. "Phil often took us for drives around the surrounding valley, occasionally stopping at Mattie Castner's hotel at Belt for an excellent chicken dinner. . . . We had jolly times together, roaming over the ranch and climbing the hills."

Part 5

AMAZING GRACE

Photo on previous page: Reverend "Brother Van" Van Orsdel, a genial and outspoken Methodist minister in Montana. Photo by Fullerton.

12

MEN OF FAITH

❖

Perhaps we don't see all. The blessing may be on the other side of the
bush, but it is around somewhere, depend upon it.
—*Jochen Hanse-Peter*

❖

Their appears to bee a good deel of grumbling in camps. . . . Some
wants to go on, and others wants to not travil on the Sabbath; I am
one of the last number.—*A. B. Crawford*

❖

Where were the ministers? An echo answers, PROSPECTING!
—*Israel Lord*

❖

I thank God for the safe survival of strict religious training; and I thank
him most of all for emancipation from it.
—*Hubert Howe Bancroft*

❖

Now if ever wrestle, preach, pray, cry aloud, stamp with ye foot, smite
with both hands, wake saints, sinners, seekers, preachers also.
The Lord help us, we are going downstream.
—*Bishop Francis Asbury*

FROM THE OUTSET, America's destiny was mingled with the
ministry, as men of the cloth scrambled west to save souls,
found missions, and, through pulpit, prayer, and the ubiquitous reach of Sunday school, unleash Divine Providence on the
rowdy unchurched of the American frontier. The West's population
cried out for guidance, so religious leaders believed, and clergy of all
kinds hurried to heed the cry. They're "thick as toads in a puddle,"
sniped Israel Lord, who counted "sixteen or more regular preachers,
besides exhorters, on the South Fork in the distance of ten miles."
In his opinion, the Sierra of California was ripe for revival, and he
applauded all promoters of moral reform.

Despite clerical efforts amid the population, "great wickedness
did break forth," said Lord. In fact the West rollicked with vice and
disorder, since frontier men were hard-drinking sorts, often "well
sizzled," he claimed—and worse. Typical was the sleepy hamlet of
Granville, Ohio, where Lord stopped briefly on his way west. There
young men fell into every manner of debauchery, from lechery to
insobriety, and "Satan's bulwarks" seemed "very Strong." "Born in
sin" was the cry that fell on children's ears; "brought forth in iniq-
uity!" the refrain.

Dozens of denominations sent forth emissaries both to chastise
and to cherish. "Aside from a rather large number of Jews, all inhab-
itants of the United States confess to be Christians," wrote a German
settler, Gottfried Duden, "but in very different ways. In my neigh-

Preacher with wagon. Photo by Stellman.

borhood there are Lutherans, Catholics, Presbyterians, Episco-palians, Methodists, Baptists, and Swedenborgians. Where there is no building for church service, private homes are opened during the hours of worship."

Stump preachers and tent revivalists roamed the countryside, converting countless numbers, unsettling others, praying in tongues and leaving whole populations in a spirit of religious turmoil. Empiric preachers might sneak a look at the almanac to predict an eclipse, then claim heavenly power and biblical authority for their success. One Methodist circuit rider made use of a highly charged thunderstorm, according to revivalist Lorenzo Dow Stephens, whose circuit ranged from Ohio to Canada : "One evening when T. Dewey was exhorting, a flash of forked lightning pierced the air and

rolling thunder seemed to shake the house. Some screeched out for mercy; some jumped out at the windows, and others ran out at the door. From this night on thirteen of the youth resolved together to pursue religion, let their companions do as they would."

Nature's handiwork was ecumenical, also assisting Catholic efforts. "An almost continual earthquake . . . lasted from the night of the 15–16 of December [1812] until now, February 19," recalled Dom Urban Guillet, a Catholic priest passing through Mexican California. "It helped much to bring people back [to their religion]."

So offbeat were some of the "sons of thunder," a popular expression for evangelists, that exhortations, tears, tongues, and paeans of praise worked against them, shocking and repulsing even the faithful. For others, their mere presence prompted a flurry of "the shakes," a physical quaking of the entire body; men and women shook like Jell-O in a demonstration of religious zeal so powerful that in the early realms of frontier Ohio, actual shaking posts were erected so people could hitch themselves up to them for support until the trembling receded. Evangelists were the holy harbingers of "the shakes" and were feared, often shunned, and particularly avoided as dinner guests. Wrote Stephens: "[When] I preached in Pittstown . . . it caused a great deal of talk. Some said I was CRAZY; others that I was possessed of the devil; some said one thing and thought another. Many [came] out to hear the strange man, and would go away cursing and swearing, saying that I was saucy and deserved knocking down. . . . Many were offended at my plainness both of dress, expressions, and way of address in conversations . . . so that the country seemed to be in an uproar . . . and I was mostly known by the name crazy Dow."

Also viewed askance was "Crazy" Bob Martin, the first representative of the Methodist Church, South, ever seen in Colusa County, California, in 1857. Wrote H. C. Bailey:

In the fall of 1856 a strange character made his advent among the ranchers living along the west bank of the Sacramento. He was of medium height, and very spare, with black eyes and sallow skin. Dressed in black broadcloth, worn slick and shining, and so large that it hung loosely on his figure; a white shirt, an exceedingly rare article in those days, much soiled, he wore a battered

stovepipe hat and a queer, old-fashioned cloak for an overcoat. Mounted upon a small mule, he carried his belongings in a large pair of saddle-bags.

His actions were peculiar. The first time I ever saw him was at a neighbor's house. He was drying his outfit, singing, praying and shouting alternately, according to his humor. My neighbor, Hoy . . . a mischievous fellow, had directed Martin to cross Sycamore Slough, about 100 feet wide and eight or ten feet deep, telling him it was all right.

The result was that he, the mule, saddlebags and cloak all were submerged and he or no one else ever knew how they got out. He was praising the Lord for his deliverance and praying for the fellow who sent him in.

His zeal and harmlessness so impressed us that we began to take an interest in him and were glad to see him when he made his monthly rounds. He took all our jokes and sly fun so kindly and good naturedly, even to answering gross insults in the kindest manner; always saying: "I will pray for you, you can't prevent

Men of Faith

Reverend William Bradford Dodge. Photo by Janovsek and Poruhn.

that!" [When] some would sneer at him and tell him to leave he would go with the remark: "I will pray for you," and go off singing one of his favorite hymns at the top of his voice. "Ye angels who stand around the throne and view Immanuel's face" was his favorite. He sang it with his whole soul, and interspersed it with loud "amen's" and similar outbursts. . . .

The next day he called at our house. I was called in to entertain him and be entertained, and this is the way it turned out; I found him in one corner of the room and my wife in another she looking very serious, and he wringing his long slender hands, swaying his body and groaning as if in deep pain.

He stopped long enough to shake hands, then renewed the groaning and other performances, with an occasional burst of song or praise. This was kept up for some time, when he said, "Let's pray," and down he went on his knees and prayed loud and long.

Eventually Martin's cheery persistence won the hearts of the locals, and his familiar cry "Let's pray!" invited not only awkward foot shuffling and attempts to escape but bowed heads and some participation.

Ministry could seem thankless at times, its duties physically taxing and scarcely remunerative for the often uneducated backwoods preachers who worked only for the joy of it; they were seldom paid for the Lord's work. Methodist Bishop Francis Asbury wrote of the plight of the traveling itinerant:

Aug 29, 1797. Many of our preachers have suffered want, hunger, labour, lodging, rocks, rivers, mountains, wilderness, preaching in the Southern States, night and day. Many young men . . . have [been] tenderly brought up where they have had servants to do the drudgery [and] it is wrecking their slender systems.

March 30, 1808: Think of the many hours I must be on horseback, when I only ride 3, or at most, 4 miles in an hour. In many places we have only solitary woods for retirement. In towns and cities . . . I visit only the houses of God, and my friends that are sick. I do not go from house to house to talk, and eat, and drink. And . . . our travelling connexion [the itinerant minister] is kept poor. We have almost 600 preachers . . . and our funds and collections yield us possibly 6 or 7000 dollars a year. . . . Every conference in the Union is insolvent. . . . We had to thrust out of our preachers into the extremities, and some preachers and their wives have to draw, almost their whole salary from the conferences.

Despite the drawbacks, Asbury was intensely satisfied with his outreach. He wrote on July 19, 1815: "I stand astonished at myself and the goodness of God that I have been kept alive and moving.

During my ten months indisposition I have rode upon horseback two thousand miles in the worst of weather, south and west, and yet [still] I am an unprofitable servant. I have not done my duty."

Clerics with congregations concerned themselves with worries about propriety, dress, donations, and degree of conviction. Preachers sized up congregations for support, both financial and personal, and in return bore the scrutiny of their flock. "I do abominate whiskers on anybody, but on a minister they become intolerably annoying," griped Israel Lord, who objected to hirsutism in clerics. He admired the Baptist pastor James W. Capen, whom he described as "young, tall, has a fine figure, scrupulously neat and tasty in his dress, affable and easy in his manners, has not the shadow of a whisker, and above all, appears unassumingly pious."

The temporary rector of the Trinity Church Episcopal congregation in San Francisco was a "plain, good man," wrote General E. D. Townsend, "[n]ot a popular preacher, [or] a man with much talent," but one who ministered to plain folks and respectfully dressed accordingly, in a plain suit, white shirt, and simple pair of shoes. Conversely, a stand-in rector, Mr. Moore, was a stylish man with "considerable vanity and a very imprudent . . . way of talking." Worse, he adopted an "odd style of sermons calculated to excite people against him." In a "sarcastic and bitter . . . manner" he exhorted people with "portions of the lessons where the words 'charity,' 'false brethren,' and the like occurred," slyly watching their effect upon the guilty. As a substitute he was invited to preside only until someone else could be ordained. Although soon asked to step down, he refused, ignoring the congregation's growing aversion, After much hubbub, along with repeated invitations to leave, one day "Mr. Moore went to Church with his surplice under his arm and found it closed . . . he had been shut out."

Ministers, like other men, faced a litany of discontent from peevish parishioners to other ministers. Grudges set in, as when John G. Fee accused Brother Williams, a fellow pastor and superintendent of Camp Nelson, Kentucky, of being a mere "Bandbox" Christian, who might drop his duties at any inconvenience—namely, "the rough & tumble of camp life." In Fee's view, according to historian Richard Sears, Williams was inadequate to "pull the people . . . out of the mire & filth of sin & suffering."

Father Craft, hero of the Wounded Knee fight.

With few local entertainments, people might view the church as theater and the pastor as the leading man. In cities, where ministers abounded, if a cleric failed to entertain, he could be asked to leave. Episcopal Minister Bert Foster was continually shocked at the disloyalty of western parishioners, men and women who flocked after "personalities," changed churches on whim, and were unwilling to support earnestness over inspiration, departing if a sermon failed to be snappy.

Franciscan missionary, Reverend Oderic Derenthal, with a collection of traditional religious objects.

example he had set. . . . He was judged by his neighbors while in these melancholy moods as being insincere, hypocritical and mysteriously secretive."

Yet for others, sanctity ruled. "I was born into an atmosphere of pungent and invigorating Puritanism," wrote Hubert Howe Bancroft. "Preparations were made for the Sabbath as for a solemn ovation. The garden was put in order, and the sheep driven to their quiet quarters. The house was scrubbed, and in the winter fuel prepared the day before. All picture-books and scraps of secular reading which might catch the eye and offend the imagination were thrust into a closet, and on the table in their stead were placed the bible, *Memoirs of Payson*, and *Baxter's Saints' Rest*." Men might claim not to care for religion yet recognized its calming influence. Bancroft heard one father say, "For myself, I care not for dogmas and creeds, but something of the kind is necessary for women and children [or else] society would fall in pieces."

While evangelists sprouted like barley, laypeople were busy spreading the word as well. America was a Christian nation, where the question "Are you saved?" was as common as the request "Pass the salt." Sundays were sacrosanct even when traveling, and conflicts inevitably arose when some preferred hunting to a quiet day of prayer and reflection. On the wagon train of Ephriam Green, the party "remained in camp . . . and had preaching it being Sunday." On another train, emigrant Alonzo Delano noted "what a blessing to have one day in seven to rest" although "some of the boys cant resist the temptation to fish and hunt on Sunday." One man, Tyle, found temptation great when they camped "near a stream abounding in trout." "Although he will curse & swear [he] will neither fish, hunt, clean his gun or anything of the sort [on] Sunday."

Others also had a hard time balancing secular and religious expectations. Traveler W. G. Johnston, for one, was occasionally confused.

On the plains, the Sabbath with us, and with most emigrants had been as another day, and we scarcely knew of its arrival, having become careless as to the obligation to refrain from labor. Personally, however, I knew of the return of the sacred day, and was aware too that I was acting in disregard of a father's express coun-

For some, faith and society were tightly interwoven, as men, such as the Methodist preacher Parson King, grappled with vice. His "inordinate love for liquor" was noted by his neighbor, Kansas Constable John R. Cook: "Periodically, he would get as full as a goose, and about as silly. When sobering up he would be struck with the remorse of a guilty conscience, for the sin he had committed and the

sel, given me before starting—to do no work on the Sabbath. "Sunday work" said he, "never prospers." I always feel, however, that it would have been utterly useless for me even to raise my protest. In the mines I do not remember that it was ever suggested to rest on that day; but by silent, common consent we refrained from labor as we had all been accustomed in our far off homes.

Observing the Sabbath prompted endless arguments. When Jochen Hanse-Peter, a farmer, ran after a a passel of squirrels raiding his berries, his wife, Freeka, complained. Hunting on Sunday? "Now see here, mother," he retorted. "Don't I have to protect my crop as well on Sunday as any other day? What is the use for me to go after them thieves tomorrow morning, when they have eaten up my berries today? Don't the Savior say that it isn't right to wait until Monday to pull the ass out of the ditch when he falls in on Sunday. What is the use to pull him out on Monday when he is drowned?" She mused: "Jochen can quote scripture when it suits his purposes, but when it comes to find a text that is against his conduct, he is as dumb as an unhatched egg—he doesn't know any Scripture then."

Two great waves of religious reform swept through America. The Great Awakening, which occurred with dramatic suddenness in the early eighteenth century, made salvation and biblical interpretation personal, rather than through the aegis of clerics or church. Revival continued through the Second Awakening, which commenced in the 1790s and surged past the turn of the century. Evangelical fire spread west, onto the frontier, sparking men of every culture, profession, and persuasion, from Ohio to Kansas to California. Itinerant preachers spread over hills and valleys, their saddlebags bulging with church newspapers, magazines, hymnbooks, and religious leaflets. They were faith's emissaries to America's backwoods, bearing both the Good News and local news, settling disputes, comforting the sick, encouraging the fearful, and solemnizing marriages along the way. In the Methodist Church alone, nearly 4,000 circuit riders and 7,730 local preachers swelled the church's ranks, transforming it from a small splinter faction in 1775 to the largest Protestant denomination eighty-eight years later.

By the late 1800s the camp meeting had become an institution, mimicking the largest camp meeting held in August 1801 in Cane Ridge, Kentucky. Hundreds of the faithful assembled, and the combined forces of preachers, singers, musicians, exhorters, and even politicians, attempted to compensate for ignorance, widespread illiteracy, and prevalent violence. Preachers made emotional appeals to save souls and bring grace to an unruly land. Revivals became the standard technique for recruiting church members. "The Methodist preachers were the pioneer messengers of salvation in these ends of the earth," said Peter Cartwright, the most famous of the early Methodist circuit riders.

The old-fashioned revival, wrote diarist H. C. Bailey, also functioned as an egalitarian space where "the richest and the poorest, the most learned and the ignorant, all met on a common level, to have a good time and respite from life's routine of cares and drudgery." If there were any social or financial distinctions before the meeting, they were left at home.

Nevertheless, the frontier seethed with dissent. Denominations and creeds met, compared chapter and verse, then scrambled for ascendancy. Like an evangelical shoot-out, Catholics and Protestants reviled each other and were particularly at odds when it came to evangelizing Indians. "The French priests were in the habit of telling their Indians to have nothing to do with the 'Bostons,' for if they came and settled on their lands, they would bring the American religion with them, which was a false religion. The French priests have always left their missions and gone off with the Indians whenever they have gone to war with the whites," noted General E. D. Townsend in 1852. This infuriated the general, who railed against white men who could side with Indians against their own race. "I would break up the Jesuit missions in the Indian country, if I had a chance!"

A difficult task, given the inroads made by centuries of settlement and conversion by the Catholic Church. James O. Pattie, a trapper adventuring through the West from Kentucky to New Mexico from 1824 to 1830, observed the Mission St. Thomas in California, a "plantation" of a thousand Indians so large that "thirty beeves" were killed for food each week, then their hides and tallow sold for goods. Pattie described a life of ease enjoyed by the church fathers. "The beautiful plain . . . was literally covered with horses and cattle

Daniel Sylvester Tuttle, first Episcopal bishop of Montana, 1867–1881. Photo by F. W. Guerin.

belonging to the mission. . . . The wild oats and clover grow spontaneously, and in great luxuriance, and were now knee high. . . . The old superintending priest . . . showed himself very friendly, and equally inquisitive. He invited us to sup with him. . . . We sat down to a large table, elegantly furnished with various dishes of the country. . . . The priest said grace at the close, when fire and cigars were brought in by the attendants, and we began to smoke. We sat and smoked, and drank wine until 12 o'clock."

Not all Catholics had it so easy. Polish settlers at Panna Maria, Texas, suffered from starvation, were stricken by early deaths, and worried till senseless about a profusion of rattlesnakes. No sooner did their parish priest, Franciscan Father Leonard Moczygemba, "comfort and calm" them with prayers and wise counsel than, as they gathered to sip soup together, slithering down from the roof fell the very cause of their despair: a rattlesnake! To the Poles, this omen seemed a venomous confirmation that neither God nor nature had use for Catholics, or anyone, in hostile terrain.

Other Catholics stayed the course, although Protestants found their rituals too strange for their taste. "We saw a type of humanity that for downright superstition beats anything," confided hunter John R. Cook, witnessing Mexican Catholics waving the image of Christ in the air to quell storms or invoke rain. "When doing penance these superstitious beings . . . were compelled by their priests to shoulder crosses, with timbers large as railroad ties, and march around the church for a given length of time." Other penitents had to "crawl bare-kneed on beans strewn on hard ground."

Catholics priests were well-educated men, tending to religious longings they hoped to scatter among the faithful. Many had come to the priesthood after heeding a childhood call; who could argue with divine summons? Other conversions proved more difficult. Take the case of the novice in a Trappist monastery in Illinois whose turning toward God was a Saul of Tarsus affair. Wrote a fellow monk, Dom Urban Guillet:

> As a soldier he had cursed all priests and religious, condemning them all to the bottom of the sea tied to the Pope's neck. He used to say that he preferred to burn quickly rather than to become a Trappist. But he resisted God in vain. How could he be at peace and resist the Omnipotent? The very moment of his rebellion was used to conquer him. The more he laughed, the more he swore, the more he cursed, the more he heard in the depths of his soul a voice louder than his own telling him to join the Trappists. . . . He cried out only to silence this voice, and the more persistently the latter urged him until it was heard. He still resisted eight days longer, but he was obliged to surrender in spite of his pride and his grand title.

Catholicism demanded obedience as well as constant self-scrutiny, keeping track of character, piety, humility, and personal strength. Even though Dom Urban encouraged the young novitiates, he confided in a letter to his monsignor that one Father Marie Bernard had "not been sufficiently humiliated when in the novitiate." He suspected the younger prelate of the sin of pride, as well as a deep confusion that was, he believed, the result of pursuing his faith in America, a land of turmoil.

Along with worship, the priest must surrender to church directives, putting personal preferences aside. Thus, when the French Trappist monk Urban Guillet was ordered by his superiors to leave his peaceful monastic existence and travel to Kentucky to build three monasteries, he reluctantly complied, although completely lacking worldly experience. Somehow, the first monastery was constructed, but Dom Urban was confounded by the world of finance. He wrote to his monsignor in May 1810:

Monsignor:

I am greatly obliged to you for [the money] because an unfortunate bankruptcy occasioned my losing a note for 500 dollars which I was to have drawn on arriving. . . . I clearly understand that Your Excellency holds me somewhat at fault. . . .

Members of Chinese Presbyterian Church, Los Angeles, California, 1895.

Reared in the monastery of La Trappe in France . . . I saw the superior leave the monastery only once . . . and I unthinkingly assumed that I could follow his example. But I was not long in discovering that I was mistaken. With scarcely two and a half dollars in the treasury I had to support my brethren and build three monasteries. . . .

The first business operation I undertook brought on a lawsuit because I unwittingly bought some stolen wood. I [ignored] five court summons, but finally was obliged to appear, otherwise they would have taken me from the monastery by force. . . . Soon after the Prior and the Procurator were killed when some planks fell on them while they were working on the building. . . .

It is true I am hardly fitted for [this] task. I can only repeat what our General told me when he appointed me Superior. Having declared to him my ignorance and inability: "My son," he replied, "for lack of a horse I must use a donkey."

Dom Urban suffered severe personal crises, one year to the next. Although his monsignor tried to calm his fears, "I cannot understand how you could have imagined that God destined me for something great," Urban protested. "My letters should be enough to show you that I am capable of nothing. The lack of success of our small foundation should leave no doubt on this point. A clear miracle was necessary to make me undertake the office of superior, especially when my General told me that for lack of a horse he was obliged to use a donkey. But it would take several miracles to make me believe myself good for something. The resurrection of a dead man would not be enough."

The Catholic faith struck deep among its believers, and those raised in its precepts often proved unwavering. Patrick Breen, a Donner party survivor, lived out his faith in the worst of circumstances, as the first storm of the winter struck one month early. The panicked emigrants hurriedly made tents out of wagon canvas and shivered in the cold, flimsy shelters. While the days wore on, food as well as the hopes of the eighty-nine trapped emigrants dwindled, yet Breen stayed optimistic as with fading strength, they managed to cut down trees and gather firewood or listlessly probe through the deep snow in the hope of finding one of the buried frozen cattle for food. As hope dwindled, Breen's faith emerged. Wrote C. F. McGlashan, a member of the group: "Breen was a devout Catholic. During the darkest hours of trial the prayers were regularly read. That this might be done during the long weary evenings, as well as by day, pieces of pitch pine were split and laid carefully in one corner of the cabin, which would be lighted at the fire, and would serve as a substitute for candles. Those of the survivors who are living often speak of the times when they held these sticks while Mr. Breen read the prayers."

Breen's diary was faintly scratched letters on eight sheets of letter paper, roughly trimmed and folded into a book of thirty-two pages.

Thursd 24th [1846] Rained all night & still continues poor prospect for any kind of comfort spiritual or temporal may God help us spend the Christmas we ought considering circumstances

Friday 25th Began to snow yesterday about 12 o'clock snowed all night & snows yet rapidly . . . offerd our prayers to God this Christmas morning the prospect is appalling but hope in God Amen. . . .

Thursday 31st Last of the year, may we with Gods help spend the comeing year better than the past which we purpose to do if Almighty God will deliver us from our present dredful situation which is our prayer if the will of God sees it fitting for us Amen.

January 1st 1847 We pray the God of Mercy to deliver us from our present calamity if it be his Holy will Amen provisions getting scant dug up a hide from under the snow yesterday.

Thursd. 14th sun shining brilliantly renovates our spirits prais be to God, Amen.

Tues. 19th Peggy & Edward sick last night by eating some meat that Donlan threw his tobacco on, pretty well to day (praise God for his blessings)

Wednsd. 10th Milt Elliot died last night at Murphys shanty about 9 o'clock . . . God help spring will soon smile upon us.

Frid. 12th We hope with the assistance of Amighty God to be able to live to see the bare surface of the earth once more. O God of Mercy grant it if it be thy holy will Amen.

Tuesd. 23 shot Towser [dog] to day & dressed his flesh. Mrs. Graves came here this morning to borrow meat dog or ox they think I have meat to spare but I know to the contrary they have plenty [of] hides. . . .

Frid. 26th Mrs. Murphy said here yesterday that she thought she would commence on Mil. [one of the party members] & eat him. I don't know that she has done so yet, it is distressing The Donners told the California folks that they commenced to eat the dead people 4 days ago, if they did not succeed that day or next in finding their cattle when under ten or twelve feet of snow & did not know the spot or near it, I suppose they have done so ere this time.

Sund. 28th 1 solitary indian passed by yesterday come from the lake had a heavy pack on his back gave me 5 or 6 roots resembling onions in shape taste some like a sweet potatoe, all full of little tough fibers. . . .

At the end of the ordeal, forty-five had died, and a party of fifteen who had left to find help had "stripped the flesh from the bones" of four dead companions and, "averting their eyes and weeping," commenced to eat. The rest of the parts were labeled so that none would eat his own kin, as the remaining party stumbled on. Breen, who had not traveled with the splinter party, remained behind with his family, who were nothing more than "living skeletons" when a rescue party finally appeared.

✢ ✢ ✢

BREEN WAS A man of faith, and many such existed outside orthodox religion, often in the granges, covenants, meetinghouses, and utopian communes scattered throughout the West. Just as the desire for independence drove men west, so the desire to share goals and cooperate drew them together. "We covet no man's silver or gold," announced a circular for the Brotherhood of Man, a communitarian group whose near-religious fervor unified disparate believers throughout the West, drawing in as members the Harmony Society of George Rapp, the celibate Pietists, the Society of Separatists of Zoar, and more. In most groups, mysticism, as well as guiding principles based on social evolution and progress, prevailed. Strong leaders stressed communitarianism, guided by cooperation, with the addition, in some cases, of free love.

In some retreats, the communal ethos was secular, embracing socialist visions by denying private holdings, the antithesis of the frontier settler and farmer. Generally small and short-lived, such groups seemed to prey on the soaring idealism of the times before sputtering to a halt, usually from lack of supplies and technology.

By the mid-1830s there were Dunkers, or Brethren, descendants of sixteenth-century Pietist mystics who believed in the doctrine of universal salvation. Dunker farmers came across the mountains into Kentucky and the Old Northwest, an area that lay between Ohio, Mississippi, and the Great Lakes, settling in clans, worshiping in barns and homes throughout Ohio, Indiana, and Illinois.

By the mid-1800s a Separatist society had sprung up at Zoar, there was a Mormon village at Kirtland, Ohio, and a group called the Owenites was at Yellow Springs and Oberlin Community, all part of communitarian practices rooted in religious experience.

The turmoil of the Civil War fostered Berea, a nonsectarian church identified by its founder, Reverend John Gregg Fee, as "almost Pentecostal, with a diversity in which were 'persons from the East, the West, the North, the South . . . male and female, soldier and citizen, and every grade of complexion from the fairest Caucasian to the darkest African.' I thank God I have lived to see this day!" Fee was thrilled at the success of such an egalitarian effort in a slave state such as Kentucky, where he worked with black refugees at Camp Nelson during and after the Civil War. An ardent sympathizer of the black population, he devised a method of oral instruction based on listening; much of slave life had been based on learning by listening. He advocated "kind social mingling" and believed that ex-slaves would learn only through "conformity to their [earlier] habits." His belief that social equality was the keystone to education seemed revolutionary to post–Civil War white educators. Fee wanted to "avoid the idea there must be separation" between the races, founding a "school for humanity" in which black and white would learn together. In fact there were many examples of cross cultural compassion; some religious men took their callings seriously. Reverend Scofield, also stationed at Camp Nelson, witnessed the starving families of black Union soldiers, who were freezing, without enough clothing, in the bitter cold. Of the 400 counted in November 1864, 102 had died by February. Scofield traveled north in the dead of winter to get them clothing, forging through the snow as far as Peterboro, New York, to procure blankets and a stove.

Utopian members sought mental and moral uplift and, like many contemplatives, were horrified by slavery and the mistreatment of the Indians. They also protested worldliness, particularly in the church. But such efforts were extremely difficult to maintain and took deeply motivated men to lead, to inspire for the long-term, men such as James Gilruth, gigantic in stature, weighing over 250 pounds, and so strong, his followers maintained, he had thrown an ax over the steeple of a courthouse. A Methodist circuit rider, religiously "convicted" in 1823, Gilruth, along with cofounders Henry O. Sheldon and John Baldwin and thirty initial families, was disenchanted with local ministries and dreamed of a spiritual oasis, "a Christian community governed by the express words or laws of the New Testament." Over objections from the traditional church, Gilruth talked to friends and others about a backwoods retreat, a commune loosely based on the Shakers' Union Village, Ohio. When his community was finally built, Gilruth's constitutional preamble advised: "We taked the Scriptures in their plain, grammatical sense for the laws of this Association." Those rejected from the clan were the vain pleasure takers of the world, "whose God," he claimed, "is their belly." Plain men and women utopians wore dark, shapeless clothing, a gesture of nonconformity that symbolically rejected the world while signifying the joy of inward conversion. Clothes evoked humility and membership in a specific group.

Religious pluralism flourished in the West. Public debates and political momentum grew from revivals and camp meetings, and Christian identity was forged in the plains, farmlands, and deep forests of the frontier as priests and clerics witnessed to their faith among the faithful and the unchurched alike. The Christian couriers who traveled, ministered, starved, exulted, and sometimes suffered utter defeat, only to resume their course and try again, lived out their commitment in ways sometimes epic, sometimes futile, yet as they spanned westward, their horizons expanded in a geographical sweep comparable only to the companion changes within American politics, sociology, and culture itself.

Part 6

MEN AT WORK

Photo on previous page: Colfax, California, depot crew, ca. 1880s.

13

DOCTORIN' MEN

❖

The doctor was busily employed in dealing out whiskey and appeared
to have a good run of custom in that way.—*Emigrant*

✧

My friends, before your very eyes I will demonstrate these remedies. . . .
Come closer! Let me help you!—*Dr. Philipe Lamereux*

MEDICINE IN THE 1800s was a rambunctious and unpre-
dictable arena, where the unschooled were healed by the
unlicensed, and any man with nimble fingers, a bagful of
cutters, pliers and thread, an ax, and a trusty Colt Peacemaker could
set up a practice. House calls were made by foot, canoe, buckboard,
and extreme effort, which included carrying a medical bag replete
with roots, herbs, calomel, a lancet, cupping glasses, crude surgical
instruments, and, upon occasion, a jar of leeches. Until the 1850s the
field of medicine was unregulated, and basically treacherous—particularly for patients. The most talented surgeons in the country
might speed through resections, ligations, and other complicated
operations with relative ease, but most physicians performed only
minor surgery and tried to avoid "heroic" measures like amputation,
learned during the Civil War, in which limbs were hacked like tree

branches, conditions were unsanitary, and instruments unsterilized.
"The marine sponges had been used in prior pus cases and had only
been washed in tap water," admitted an early surgeon. When tools
fell to the floor, a quick rinse in a basin of tap water would, he
hoped, make them passably clean.

Most early doctors had learned medicine as apprentices. There
were no medical schools west of the Alleghenies until 1810, when
the Transylvania Medical College was founded in Kentucky, and
1820, when the Ohio Medical College sprang up in Cincinnati.
Schools were poorly staffed since doctors struggled financially and
could not neglect their practices long enough to teach. Private medical schools were essentially diploma mills, asking only a high school
education and the enrollment fee, with a brief, standard course of
study of one to two weeks. In 1845, licensing requirements had been
lifted from most schools, and the ill-trained, unwashed medical offspring of such institutions were more terrifying than the diseases
they hoped to cure. Men with little more than glib tongues and
folksy manners could qualify as doctors; medicine was almost considered a layman's pursuit. Typical was John Marsh, a Bachelor of
Arts graduate from Harvard who had always *wanted* to study medicine and in the freewheeling anonymity of the gold rush frontier
claimed that he had. Surely his degree from Harvard would carry
him through, since "no one in California could read Latin anyway."
Dr. Henry Hoyt, still a medical student, found that "there were no

Unidentified doctor, ca. 1880 Photo by Stellman.

thy, included pediatrics, gynecology, physiology, and materia medica, with later forays into anesthesiology, metabolism, serology, cardiography, roentgenology, endocrinology, aseptic surgery, and preventive medicine.

The general public generally shied away from medicine, turning to its practitioners only when necessary. "Nobody we knew ever underwent an operation," recalled San Franciscan Harriet Levy. "Cousin Lenore was going to die because she had refused to have one. . . . She lived for fifty years and we all rejoiced because she had outwitted the doctors." On the other hand, common sense prevailed when a cowhand at the XIT Ranch broke his leg. "When I got out to the ranch . . . the boys were taking turns . . . pulling on Huffman's leg. They would take a turn of 30 minutes each and sit with one foot in Huffman's crotch to hold him and pull upon his leg with both hands. At the same time they kept pouring cold water over it . . . when I got there the bone was in place as good as I could have done and all I had to do was place splints upon it."

People often feared the doctor. From surgery to childbirth, heroic measures, often surgical, maimed and killed reluctant patients, while bizarre practices were touted as "scientific." One, advanced by a medical doctor, cautioned against breathing through the mouth, thus ingesting germs. Mastectomies to excise visible tumors were explored as early as 1840, and amputation during childbirth was common; the arm of a fetus, extended through the vagina and complicating the birth process, was commonly lopped off until the number of disfigured children and a growing aversion to the technique caused the process to fall into disfavor. One physician, Indiana practitioner William A. Lindsay, found that the process, at least in one case, made delivery easier:

Was called to see Mrs. Thornton on the night of the 14th Nov. 1839 . . . by Dr. Joel Bugg. . . . On arriving I learned that Dr. Bugg had been in attendance some 36 hours. . . . [Dr. Bugg] ascertained that there was an arm presentation, which by any skill or effort could not be altered . . . in all events after the removal of the Arm at the shoulder I was unsuccessful in turning or getting holt of a foot. . . . On consultation it was agreed that the exhibition of the Ergot should be tried, which was [given] in doses

laws regulating the practice of medicine and surgery," so he "decided to locate in some lively town and practice," selecting Deadwood, North Dakota, for his "adventure."

Medicine split into two branches: allopathy, or treating a disease with agents producing effects different from the disease, and homeopathy, or administering minute doses of medicine that would, in larger amounts, actually cause the disease. Both concepts of healing were as competitive as decency allowed, with highly charged criticism concerning both. Dr. Israel Lord observed the "race" of the two rival branches and proudly reported, as if scoring a sporting event, that "Homeopaths have been beyond compare the most successful. They cured at the outset, when the Allopaths lost almost every patient." Allopaths pointed to their own successes. By 1860 practitioners of both had flooded into the country's nearly forty training institutes and a handful of national medical schools to study disease diagnosis and anatomy. Advanced studies, usually in allopa-

every 15 to 20 minutes; and in about 2 hours from this time she was delivered of the child.

Not only could doctors be butchers—witness the rampant surgeries of the Civil War—but it was well known that medical schools obtained their anatomical subjects by grave robbing. In nineteenth-century Ohio alone nearly five thousand bodies were used for anatomical instruction in one ten-year period, and an undetermined number of them dug from graves. "A good method of preparing a skeleton after dissecting is to bleach the bones under water for a year or so," noted Dr. Henry Hoyt, who packed up his bones in "an ordinary shoebox" and sank them in the middle of a lake. Such ghoulish practices aroused public protest, and mobs stormed the school whenever a body was found missing. In 1845 the buried remains of Eli Tarbell vanished from his resting place. Word spread, and an angry mob surrounded Willoughby College, demanding the return of Mr. Tarbell, whose body had been hidden for safekeeping in a nearby barn. Horace Ackley, professor of surgery at Willoughby College, was forced to stand them off at the head of the stairs, waving a loaded small cannon, threatening to blast away the intruders if they advanced. Meekly the mob withdrew, convinced that the scrappy physician was as good as his word. Soon thereafter Mr. Tarbell was mysteriously returned to his final resting place.

Rural distrust of doctors was linked to the expense of professional medicine; settlers considered themselves caretakers of their own well-being. Thus, when North Dakotan Helge Anderson fell

Unidentified Kansas physician, ca. 1880s.

quishes disease without drug or lancet. . . . Everything is accomplished by the potency of a charm," observed James Hall. Folk medicine was the purview of snake oil vendors, shrewd salesmen, and water witchers, who healed by touch, potion, powder, suggestion, and folklore. "Kiss a donkey," claimed one folk dictum, "and a toothache will vanish." Whooping cough vanished by breathing into the mouth of a live fish, while to cure asthma, the afflicted must spit into a frog's mouth. People bought small eye stones to slip under the upper eyelid to cure eye distress or sank sore feet into hot horse manure. Also effective was a frontier remedy cited by historian Madge Pickard: "To cut a square from the door facing where the person gasped for breath. Take out a chunk of wood, cut a lock of hair off the person, and place it back in the hold; then cover it up with a chunk of wood."

Sometimes Indian remedies were the best. In Clallam County, Washington, Queet Indian William Penn sent a message to his brother Morton that his legs were so badly swollen that even the white doctor couldn't help. Morton rode up the Bogachiel River to the Hoh River, left his horse, crossed, and walked to the Queets River, where he "chewed yew tree needles and made them into a plaster which he applied to his brother's legs. This relieved the pain immediately and the patient recovered. The remedy had been bought from a Canadian Indian for ten dollars."

Self-help ranged from the Graham cure—eating unmilled flours for digestive purity—to magnetic rings, electric corsets, vaporizers, a device called the Health Jolting Chair, and water cure resorts, where patients were invited to bring their own supplies. Phrenology, the "reading" of someone's personality by head size and temperament, was popular, although it did have critics. Jacob Murray, writing to his friend Uriah Oblinger in Nebraska, reminded him of "how Emfry Ely Moses and all the other Phrenologis are getting along. We talked some on Phre[nology] and Temperament . . . he says he does not beleve the doctrine for Jo and Sabra have a baby and they are both of the same temperament consequently [the] doctrine cannot be true."

The desire to treat symptoms without medical advice, or its attendant expense, gave rise to legions of snake oil salesmen, tincture vendors, and self-proclaimed spiritualists promising ready cures. William P. Burt was fascinated by medicine shows and joined one:

and shattered his right arm in two places above the elbow, he blinked, bit his lip, and resolutely went about his business, even attending a school board meeting, where he sat impassively, thinking about his pain. After a sleepless night he grudgingly decided to go to the doctor—a great sign of weakness as well as an expense.

In religious times, faith was preferred to physic, and medical men with bona fide degrees and scientific acumen were bypassed by tonics, pills, nostrums, and the magical ministrations of the spiritual healer. "Your faith doctor . . . practices without diploma, and van-

When the train pulled into Wahoo, Nebraska . . . I found the "Big Sensation Medicine Company" was all that the name implied. It was not only big, it was colossal . . . [with] a 60-ft. round top . . . and ornately draped stage. Near the entrance was a candy and lemonade stand. . . . Across the front of a small tent near the main entrance was a banner announcing "The King of the Forceps." There were twenty-eight people including a twelve-piece band [and] during the entertainment there was a fifteen-minute session given over to the extraction of teeth. The medicines sold by this company were compounded from the formulas found in an old-time publication, *A Doctor in Your House*, and were, of course, home made.

After leaving the Big Sensation, Burt joined the Shaker Remedies Advertising Units, traveling and performing throughout Colorado:

The salesmanship was at times uncanny. The man had a most profound superstition regarding the "first bottle sold." It had to be sold from the stage and by him, otherwise—in his opinion—the efforts of the other sales agents would be unrewarded.

There must have been some hypnotic power in the make-up of this lecturer, for he had a most annoying habit of looking over his audience until he had absolute silence, then—before starting his lecture—announce[d] in a confidential whisper the exact person who would buy that "first bottle."

His build-up was classic. With tear-filled eyes . . . and a voice trembling with emotion, he would tell a story of some helpless infant, or beloved parent who had passed away, and add—"I don't mean to say this remedy would have saved that poor one, but I will tell you that had a bottle been in the house it would have prolonged life until the doctor arrived," then with his eyes fixed on the selected buyer, he would yell—"And wouldn't you give a dollar to save a life by buying this bottle?" And in a flash of a second the important "first bottle" would be sold from the stage by the lecturer.

Even cowboys filled their saddlebags with homey remedies such as Indian Cough Cure, Autumn Leaf Extracts, Simons Liver Regula-

tor, Ocean Weed Heart Remedy, Prompt Parilla Liver Pills, and the ever-popular Swamp Root. Anything titled "Indian" had allure; the creators of Kickapoo Indian Sagwa, Indian Cough Cure, and Kickapoo Indian Worm Killer, were John E. "Doc" Healy and Charles H. "Texas Charlie" Bigelow, who swore that their production was "at all times under the Indians' personal supervision, they alone possessing the secret of its combination." Bracingly high in alcohol content, even the concoctions produced by the most reputable of America's potion producers, the United Society of Believers in Christ's Second Appearing (the Shakers), were barely disguised bar drinks. Newspapers touted claims by traveling vendors and medicine show outfitters, mostly male. Dr. Gibbons was a favorite in the *San Francisco Chronicle* in 1909: "This old reliable and most successful specialist . . . still continues to cure all Debility or Diseases wearing on body and mind. All stages of weakness consequent upon the errors of ignorance of the sexes and skin diseases successfully treated. The afflicted should call upon him. . . . The Doctor cures when others fail. . . . Persons at a distance may be cured at home."

Another popular healer, Dr. Morel, promised that "private disease, blood, skin or nervous trouble" would vanish under his touch and was so confident of success that he promised, "You may pay me after I cure you."

Despite skepticism, the tonics occasionally worked, as witnessed by Dr. Scepter Patrick from Indiana, who nearly died while traveling West.

I was taken with the cholera . . . and there was not a man near me who understood dealing out a dose of medicine, except one cursed fool of a pepper doctor. I was vomiting, purging and suffering all the tortures of the infernal regions, when I told the steam doctor to give me a large dose of calomel, camphor and opium. But he urged me to take a dose of number-six. "Give me calomel or I am a dead man." I replied. But the fool kept talking about number-six, number-six, till, finally, to satisfy him . . . I told him to pour it out—hoping that after taking *his* medicine, he would be willing to give me mine. He immediately poured out a double dose of his *liquid fire*, and I took it down. I thought I should surely die, for the remedy seemed worse than the disease. I

thought my whole insides were on fire, and I roared out, "Water, water! For heaven's sake, or I shall be burnt up." But there was not a drop of water in the camp, nor any within a mile. "Well, then, give me brandy, anything; fire, turpentine, live coals; I am dying!" All were very much alarmed, and the doctor jumped to the brandy jug, and poured out half a glassful—another quadruple dose of number six—thus adding fuel to the flames; and now I thought I was surely gone. But it stuck. It stopped my vomiting in a short time, and then he was willing to give me my medicine; and that stuck, too; and operated finely. The disease was finally checked, and I got well; and after all, I don't know but the fellow's number-six was beneficial to me.

Doctors were summoned, but grudgingly. Thus, when North Dakota settler Ole Dovre was attacked by quinsy, death, to him, seemed inevitable. He propped himself carefully in a rocking chair and waited to bleed his life away. Hours later he tired of the process and demanded a doctor, recounted his niece, Barbara Levorson. A doctor was roused, remedies were applied, and the family members who had assembled for his supposed death "trudged homeward again, feeling much better now that the doctor had been there and said he would be all right again."

With so much reluctance on the part of patients, payment was often sketchy to nonexistent, leaving doctors frequently in debt. In 1776 Dr. Antoine Reynal was only the third surgeon in St. Louis.

Much of his time was spent on collections, including an unsuccessful attempt to bill for a mission of mercy. Like others of his profession, he had difficulty balancing humanitarian instincts with appropriate payment. One frustrated healer, David Long of Cleveland, finally ran a notice in the *Cleveland Herald* in 1819 in an attempt to collect his debts: "Last Notice—Those persons who are indebted and do not call and settle their accounts by the 10th of January next, may expect to pay costs. Cleveland, Dec. 28, 1819. David Long."

Some patients tried trickery to circumvent payment. Colorado physician Henry Hoyt recalled a summons he got to "go ten miles over the mountains": "I responded on horseback and found a man with an arm badly shot up. I fixed him up, was paid a flat fee in dust—very little money was in circulation at that time in the Black Hills—and returned home. The day after, I went to the bank and to my dismay was told that a good part of my dust was phony . . . as a result of this experience I provided myself with a bottle of testing acid, so this trick was never duplicated."

Doctors in Santa Fe in the 1840s "soon gave up medical practice" because their patients, both the "destitute and the affluent[,] liquidated their bills by saying *Dios se lo page*—May God pay you."

Payment in kind was the frequent fate of the rural doctor, and the pigs, cattle, and chickens that arrived in exchange for doctoring launched hundreds of physicians as small farmers. Others simply abandoned their work and took to the gold mines, hoping to make up in a week or month what they had lost over the years. Dr. Thomas M. Logan, writing to a fellow physician in the East in 1850, described the lives of doctors in California. He had seen "M.D.'s driving ox teams . . . laboring in our streets . . . serving at barrooms, monte tables, boarding houses, etc., and digging and delving among the rocks and stones." Wrote Colorado physician Henry Hoyt: "My income diminished, and it was not long that I was . . . flat broke. As a solution I applied to W. C. Bill Moore, superintendent of the LX Ranches, for a job. My first duty as a cowboy . . . was to construct a large corral . . . but my hands were now soft and this job produced quite a crop of blisters." His income had soared during a smallpox epidemic, and then "smallpox faded away and there was little for me to do."

Doctors proved in communities made adequate livings, and some could even afford frills, such as gold watches and fobs or the luxury of an occasional silk cravat. Usually medical status afforded a modest yet passable life, as noted by Elizabeth Therese Baird, a Frenchwoman living in Wisconsin in the 1820s. While canoeing and camping with a party of settlers on the Wisconsin River, she chanced upon a house hidden away in a remote clearing. "The house aroused our curiosity. . . . It was a small log structure, and everything about it was exquisitely neat. . . . We peered into the windows, and in the bedroom we saw the nicely made bed, and on the pillow lay a night cap with embroidered strings. . . . [We learned it] belonged to Doctor Madaria."

The best physicians were curious as squirrels, always gathering up bits of new information, fascinated by what nature, circumstances, or other cultures had to offer. An Arizona physician, Dr. Pfefferkorn, found that mescal leaves were an infallible antiscorbutic, that hierba anis, when boiled, cured inflammatory fevers, and that herbs were effective as laxatives, snakebite antidote, poultices, and internal concoctions. For a sore throat there was *garrotillo*, a poultice of maize. Isaac Lord explored Native American healing and cited the case of an Indian woman who doctored her naked infant, apparently dying from an inflammation of the lungs: "She held it on one hand with its face up, and dripped warm water from the fingers of the other into its mouth and over the face, so fast as almost to suffocate it. In about five minutes the child breathed freely, did not cough, and seemed entirely easy. Perhaps this practice may cure Diggers [Indians] and might kill Yankees. Don't know." The baby's final therapy was to be wrapped in cloth and tied up like a package, then "handed over" to a young Indian, who rolled him about on the ground, playing toss and tumble with the squirming infant.

Whether Lord ever used the technique himself is unknown, but he did remember it. He was piqued as a scientist by everything in nature, whether it seemed cruel or not. On the westward passages through Oregon and California he noticed the oxen that staggered and groaned as they fell to the ground, unable to go farther, and sat down beside one to "see how philosophically an oxen could die." As the beast lay limply in the sun, the doctor, tired and sleepy, "sat listlessly watching his motions. . . . His bones seemed to bend out and his wrinkled skin to swell, and a sound like the shrill whistle of the wind through a broken casement became a low muttering." Two

Minnesota medical class, cadaver lab, 1892.

hours later the doctor left, satisfied that the ox had breathed its last and "was only a pile of skin and bones after all . . . a bovial collapse."

The lively spirit of inquiry prompted Colorado's Dr. Henry Hoyt, whose stock of medicines was limited, to "rack his brain" for something to allay the itching of a smallpox victim. "One thing that was plentiful was gunpowder and knowing it consisted of charcoal, saltpeter and sulphur I tried an experiment. I added water, made a paste, and had it spread over the entire body. It was a decided success."

Relief of pain was a doctor's foremost concern, and in most cases, compassion was his operating modus; why else pursue such an often thankless profession? Each physician had his own way of taming pain. Before anesthesia, a doctor used a stick in the mouth for biting down or ample supplies of liquor, with which the patient could "cheer up." A merchant's receipt of August 14, 1789, lists supplies delivered to

the local army barracks. "Then recd. of Colo. Clark one Bagg & two pounds of Jasuits Bark twenty pounds of sugar & One Kegg of wine which I delivered the Doctor for the use of the Hospital at Cahocas likewise one Kegg of Brandy for the use of the fatigue of my Companys. Jos. Bowman"

"Some had a general fear of anesthesia," wrote Oregon physician Urling Coe, particularly when it came to childbirth. "Some thought it might be detrimental to the baby; and others thought it forbidden by the bible. Most of the old pioneers considered it cowardly to want an anesthetic to ease labor pains . . . [but] I always [gave] my patients chloroform when their pains became severe." He would "pack a large wad of cotton" in the bottom of a drinking glass. The cotton was drenched with chloroform, and the patient could self-administer. Said Coe of one woman patient: "Her hand relaxed and she dropped the glass before she took too much."

More dangerous was opium, and addiction to the popular drug plunged its users into a dreamy, private ether world where none responded, none remembered, and many were part of a troubled population beset with rheumatism, arthritis, neuralgia, and assorted other pains. "Opium smoking was the dark countercurrent of Westward expansion," wrote historian David Courtright, and much of it came from a medical establishment barely able to keep abreast of diseases that seemed willful as grizzlies.

Medical help, both scarce and often ineffective, left people to kill their pain on their own, with whatever opiates they could find. According to Courtright, the spread of the hypodermic during the 1860s and 1870s made it easier to administer drugs, and chronic conditions called for frequent drug use. Wrote Dr. Gibbons of San Francisco, of a patient, Mr. A.: "I meet him frequently as he drives through the streets. . . . He manifests no desire to stop and talk. . . . I have not the least doubt that he is still sticking happiness into his skin at the rate of six or eight punctures a day." Mr. A. had his own memories of such "happiness": "He [Gibbons] made an opening in the skin with a lancet, and injected it with a common glass syringe. The relief was so great that I came forthwith to San Francisco and bought me a syringe and went to using it on myself. I continued to use it every day, and then more than once a day. . . . My neuralgia is entirely gone. I have had none of it for a year or more, but I can not

do without the injections. I suffer terribly when I am not under their influence."

Army Lieutenant John Spring found himself addicted to laudanum after several months of illness, having lost forty pounds and been dosed daily with castor oil and laudanum. His physician, surgeon Smart, was concerned and "spoke like a father" to him about giving up the opiate: "I don't believe in the so-called process of tapering off. I will put you in a room by yourself, where you can burn a light all night and read the interesting books I am going to send you. The steward will give you a spoonful of brandy from time to time to

subdue the nervousness." Despite "intense nervousness and cravings," Spring "withstood all temptation" and survived his drug dependence.

⌁ ⌁ ⌁ ⌁

EMERGENCIES FLARED UP on the frontier, quick as lightning. "A sick man died in some of the houses last night. Poor chance here for the sick," wrote Israel Lord. "I heard muttering and low cries in a dark corner," recalled Colorado physician Charles Fox, far in the outback to attend to a young boy.

There on a pile of skins and old sacks I saw a form covered with an old coat. . . . There was a boy of fifteen. I asked for a lamp. I pulled the coat back, and held the lamp closer as I knelt down. One glance was enough! The swollen pustular face, the delerium, the fingers scratching the face, and the smell, were enough. Confluent smallpox! I had seen many cases like it before. I did what I could, put lard on the scarred and bleeding face, and tied the hands to protect the eyes. I told the family what it was. No one spoke. I was getting up from my knees when bang! A bullet hit the logs just over the boy, knocked out the chinking between the logs, and scattered splinters all over us. At this point the business was mixed up with smallpox and a little war. The old grandmother piped up in a a shrill voice "The Lord will provide."

A cholera epidemic demanded every available medical skill and still resulted in a litany of deaths. Dr. Israel Lord cited tragic events from October through November, 1850:

8th. . . . witnessed the terrible struggles of a man lying on the levee dying of cholera. This is the first case I have seen. . . .

Oct. 20. Hot day. A man died of cholera in the baker, back of our boarding house. People are just beginning to realize that cholera is here.

Oct. 21. Several cases of cholera yesterday, and all fatal. It seems to strike *dead* at once. A man found lying on the ground in 11th street, and died shortly after . . . yet most of the M.D.s in town deny the presence of cholera. . . . Said to be seven cases fatal yesterday. I doubt if that is more than half. . . . The heated city is a living, moving toiling mass of men and animal, crawling like maggots in the filth, and breathing an atmosphere filled with poison and dust.

Oct. 24. A dozen or fifteen cases yesterday . . . mostly fatal.

Oct. 25. Fifteen to 20 died yesterday—some dozen reported.

Oct. 26. Twenty-three cases of cholera certain.

Oct. 27. I suppose from 30 to 40 died yesterday. It is impossible to determine exactly.

Nov. 12. A woman died last night of cholera at the next corner above. Was apparently in good health three hours before. Another died this evening in the room opposite the one I occupy—killed by the medicine, I doubt not. . . .

Nov. 13. . . . I believe I forgot to report the death of Thomas Wygant of Flag Creek, Lyonsville Co., Ill. He died of cholera supervening diarrhea (chronic). . . . Not quite as warm today.

Pestilence and disease were fueled by almost complete ignorance of hygiene, disease, or germs. In Phoenix, "saloons put their spittoons to soak in irrigation ditches drained by water used by the citizens for drinking and culinary purposes." One physician, Warren E. Day of Prescott, Arizona, scoffed at the idea of contagion. As long as a person was "two feet removed from the patient and a current of air [was] was in motion," no disease would spread. In San Francisco in 1871 a jury recommended that surgery should be practiced in a separate room rather than in the open wards where everyone could watch. Dr. Israel Lord "went up to Sutter's Fort to see a sick man in the Sacramento Hospital. . . . There are too many patients (not less than 60) crowded into the principal room. They are mostly fever patients, or rather were; more than one half of them having diarrhea consequent on, or in connection with, fever. The floor is covered with . . . rush matting, which retains all the filth and effluvia falling upon it. The air in the room is very offensive. The mortality is very great, and probably ever will be here."

❖   ❖   ❖   ❖

WHO WERE THE men who took to medicine? Many were inventive. When Dr. Urling Coe was forced to make a forceps delivery alone, he invented a special harness to use. "It had large leather cuffs to go around the thighs with an adjustable metal bar between them to hold the thighs wide apart. From the thigh cuffs a leather strap ran

up over the shoulders and held the knees up to the chest with the thighs flexed on the abdomen." Doctors were often thoughtful and with a deep sense of compassion, not unlike the physician who ministered to young George Conklin of Ohio when he broke his leg in three places. The first doctor consulted promptly decided to amputate. A second said the same thing. His father, however, was not convinced, and called in an old doctor named Wiley, who said he could save the boy's leg.

The first thing he did was to make a box a little larger than my leg, with the board on one side enough longer than the box to reach from my hip to my armpit. Putting my leg in the box, he bound its long side so tightly to my body that the box could not move. Then . . . he bound the leg in splints, after which he filled the box with bran, packing it so carefully under and around my leg that no part of my leg or foot touched the box.

There I lay with my leg in that box for two months. At first I suffered a great deal of pain . . . and I was obliged to lie in one position all the time. It was no uncommon thing to wake up in the night and find the mice nibbling the bran. The two months seemed like two years, but at last the day came when the old doctor dug out the bran and took off the box and splints. My leg was as stiff as a stick and black as coal. It did not seem possible that it could ever be of any use again. But in a few days the doctor came, bringing some pieces of board which he called "playthings." He showed me how to lift my leg and support it. . . . After a few days the weight of the foot would bend the knee slightly . . . by such methods I gradually regained the use of my leg.

Dr. Lindsay recorded the degree of concern a physician could show. Conscientious doctors might spend hours, even days, at the bedsides of the ill. "Such was the joy & satisfaction consequent to my efforts [in a childbirth] that the parents named their son for me." In another difficult childbirth case, Lindsay "remained with the patient all night, and in the latter part of it she seemed to get some rest. This was the only concern I had in the case, as she was quite an enfeebled delicate female, and her recovery was tedious." When death struck, he tried to be matter-of-fact. "She was first attended by an experienced female midwife, and first & last by 3 or 4 physicians who, of the number, had a good Set of accouchery Instruments. Yet amidst all this array of skill and general experience she was not saved."

Compassion flowed easily to a medical man's own family, as they too were faced with the loss of children, wives, and relatives from every manner of disease or accident. When the wife of Dr. Lindsay, "an industrious and hard working woman," fell into delicate and declining health, he was angry. He had loved her for twenty-one years and seen her labor alongside the family servants, washing clothes side by side with the washerwoman, and had chided her about "laboring beyond her strength." Although sickly, she was resolute and "seemed not to heed" his advice. On the day of her fatal and unidentified illness, someone had given the doctor a shoat as a gift, and "she chose to do the principal work herself of cutting it up &

salting it away. She remarked that salting away the pork had chilled her very much."

In recording the events of her death, Lindsay wrote: "I can assure my children . . . that [my] mind is laboring under a heavy load of sorrow; and expects long to mourn. . . . For to him she has truly ever been an affectionate & dutiful wife & helpmate . . . [and] he is happy that she is gone to a more blissful clime. It cannot be otherwise that one possessing so much virtue, piety, & sterling merit, has gone to join the society of those who are truly happy."

Eventually medical science improved. Anesthesia and antisepsis came to be used in hospitals, and an array of precise new instruments was invented. Medical examining boards and four-year medical schools gradually raised the caliber of physicians in practice, and doctors were increasingly required to be licensed. On the frontier, some men found medicine a passport to adventure, while others were conscientious practitioners, whose hardworking servitude to the Hippocratic Oath kept pace with people's changing attitudes toward health and medicine.

14

Land Grabbers and Entrepreneurs

THE WEST WAS ripe for magic. Lured by visions of free land and gold, hopeful emigrants were quick to embrace the West's promise, even after being walloped by its reality. Credulity ruled, and there were plenty to take advantage, including charlatans, such as Jefferson Randolph Smith. Smith wrapped twenty-, fifty-, and hundred-dollar bills inside the paper covers of some poor-quality cakes of soap, and people flocked to buy them. The lucky "winners" were always Soapy Smith's shills, who gasped and cried out in delight at their winnings, then secretly returned the money after the show. Another carnival type, Manuel Blaso, or Old Blazes, rumbled around New Mexico in 1883 in "hell on wheels," a carriage as gaudy as a circus bandwagon, three windows cut into each side, drawn by six plumed horses, announcing his tables of roulette, faro, and dice.

Water was key to farming success, and any man who purported to hold the "secret" to rainmaking, either preventing or provoking a heavenly downpour, was completely revered. Charles Mallory Hatfield preyed upon the vulnerabilities of drought dwellers, particularly in Southern California in the early 1900s. According to historian Richard Dillon, Hatfield's success at producing precipitation using "evaporating tanks" mounted on towers, filled with churning, bubbling chemicals, earned him such rainmaking status that he quickly became a folk hero. Known as the great "Moisture Accellerator," he blasted the clouds from below with airborne waves of carbonic acid gas, supposedly seeding them to rain. Cannily he would allow himself up to sixty days' leeway before the rains. He studied weather charts with all the skill of a meteorologist, sensing when the skies were about to break, and acted swiftly and accordingly. Unlike snake oil vendors or others involved in more psychosomatic aspects of healing, Hatfield often was accurate in predicting rain, once in

A. J. Smith, Jefferson County, Nebraska, 1886. Photo by Solomon Butcher.

such sheets and torrents that the Otay Dam above the city of San Diego burst wide open, causing enormous property damage and loss of life.

Also popular was the dowser, whose supple, forked fruit tree branch quivered eagerly at the hint of underground water, a precious commodity to the frontier farmer. Few dared sink wells without having first located hidden springs, and witchers were in demand.

Another "magic" came from the quick-fingered reaping of the land speculator, a farm mortgage broker on the frontier who could turn distant vistas into chopped-up parcels, their ownership usually disputed, riddling the plains with strife and dissension. Government land giveaways drew shifty men of singular purpose bent on instituting themselves between the system and its beneficiaries. Why allow land to go for free when a dollar could be made? "The excitement of the time I cannot describe," wrote Elizabeth Therese Baird as land offices sprang up to handle the surge in Wisconsin. "The land office . . . was established here in 1835; and the first government land sale that took place brought many moneyed men to Green Bay.

Many came from Milwaukee, some from Chicago, and more from Detroit. They were the leading business men of those places," wrote Baird. William B. Ogden, the "railroad king," bought "largely of land at government prices, and would sell the same property at auction, in the evening. The purchases were made for speculation."

Wrote James H. Rinehart from Iowa in 1845:

Each sale was for lands in certain townships, and on advertised dates, and all the settlers would be present when the sale began. They were organized for mutual protection against outside land speculators. There were usually one or two "shoulder strikers" and if a land speculator made a bid on a squatter's claim he would be punched at the butt of the ear by one of the heavy weight officials, and then by another until he would find himself entirely outside the circle of bidders. Thus they were soon schooled in the "unwritten law" and made no more bids on lands held by squatters.

Speculators were viewed with scorn. They were grasping, covetous, intrepid, and ruthless, and nothing stood between them and the realization of their dream, the full settlement of the American West. They suffered the ongoing hatred that the frontiersman usually reserved for tax collectors and absentee landlords as they invaded the local land offices, studied confused and tangled land titles, then slapped together provisional organizations to register claims for town lots and homesteads. As a territory rose up, with its elected legislature and laws, towns were laid out in all directions, some with structures, others marked only by high hopes and a maze of stakes in the buffalo grass. Successful promoters formed vigilance committees, with each member able to hold all the unclaimed land he chose, provided he would promise to work on it. According to John Young Nelson, "The penalty for jumping a claim was hang by the neck till dead, dead, DEAD. "

The average pioneer wanted good land, well situated, with "credit extended over enough years to permit payment from the proceed of his farm." The speculators could provide both. Large corporations had frontier agents, usually traders or hunters who sought out the richest regions and preempted them for their employers. Such companies could also provide credit, giving the frontiersman enough time to buy himself into the clear.

The Homestead Act in 1862 guaranteed free land to anyone willing to improve and live on it. To borrow on the land, the homesteader could pay $1.25 an acre and receive his title under the Preemption Act. Eventually all available lands were acquired—unfortunately, many by land-grant corporations and private speculators. Ultimately, the lure of such cheap land was clouded by complaints that the "first-rate" land had vanished, and for bargain acreage the farmer had to go far beyond civilization, often to scanty or uninhabitable areas, to settle.

Speculators combed the frontier for "secondhand" lands, virgin acres no longer owned by the state or federal government but held by corporations or other speculators. Thus the last remaining prime sites sold well above the government prices. In Iowa, the most popular immigrant destination of the 1860s, the 1862 census reported some fifteen million acres owned by nonresidents, making the land eligible for speculation and sales at three dollars an acre or greater.

No acres, even those owned by churches or clerics, were sacrosanct, as Dom Urbain Guillet, a French Trappist monk, learned. Guillet was in Kentucky presiding over twenty-five workers building a monastery when "the government threw us into the greatest anxiety by seizing the title to our land. Neighbors of a few days standing, more furious than bears, squatted on the land, and because we had no [clear] title to invoke against them, they seized the greater part of the tract. My community . . . begged me to go to Congress and obtain a clear title to the land."

Armed with a letter of recommendation from his monsignor, he went to Washington, where he found that in order to keep the community lands, he would have to raise orphans at the institute, and raise them in ways unacceptable to the order. The child residents could not be selected by priests but would be state-appointed and would have to be cared for until they were twenty-one.

"I consulted several of the Senators and Representatives of the nation. The Federalists are of the opinion that since I wish to purchase, there is little risk of refusal if I ask for a great deal of land. Once I have clear title I shall be able to sell part of the land at a slightly higher price in order to pay for the rest. . . . The Democrats, on the contrary, are of the opinion that if I petition for a great deal of land I shall be taken for a speculator and that I shall obtain no land at all."

He decided to "embrace the spirit of both" ideas since he should "certainly have a great deal of trouble paying" even with "credit for twelve years." He petitioned for four hundred acres of land, a piece "large enough to show the importance of our institution and at the same time . . . too small a parcel for anyone to suspect" him of land speculation. His monsignor chided him: Wasn't the "400 acres of land . . . enough to supply their needs for many years"? Dom Urbain, however, feared that the government might again reject their title, and they would "be obliged to move again."

Like a wounded buck, Guillet was nipped at and worried by "families of rogues" hovering nearby, even on the land itself, waiting for the priests to lose their title. "[The squatters] are doing all they can to locate near us or even on our 400 acres in case the title should be rejected."

In his next letter, dated November 1810, Father Guillet had caught the speculating spirit. Writing to the monsignor in Quebec from his mission in St. Clair County in the Illinois Territory, he wondered if instead of asking Congress to allow him to buy land, he shouldn't "register titles secured from various individuals . . . [unclaimed] title-deeds that were gifts made by the nation to soldiers since the [Revolutionary] war"? The idea was sound, and the priest proceeded with his plan. Eventually these titles were added to the original four hundred acres.

＋　＋　＋

LAND SPECULATION GREW so rampant that the government made occasional attempts to stem the incessant trading by passing national land laws, beginning with the Ordinance of 1785, designed to undercut speculators' functions. Subsequent land acts of 1796 and 1800 gradually reduced the minimum amount of acres that could be purchased by an investor. The Land Act of 1796 raised the minimum price per acre to two dollars, giving a year's credit and a 10 percent discount for cash payment, terms that were still unattractive to the settlers. The new Land Act of 1800 reduced the minimum amount of land to 320 acres, establishing credit for a period of four years. Settlers continued to beg for relief through preemption, or "purchase before the sale," the means by which thousands of acres of land were settled by the homesteading population. "The people who will migrate to the Westward . . . will be a people little able to pay taxes," wrote Thomas Jefferson in 1776. "By selling the lands to them, you will disgust them. . . . They will settle the lands in spite of everybody." Although the federal government sold acres for cash only, state lands were frequently sold on credit terms, and the credit was usually given by landed corporations and by private speculators. Credit was usually offered for only a year or two.

The frontiersman naturally wanted free access to the earth, but free land would destroy the economic and political values of the country. Preemption was the compromise. The government "pardoned" the squatter for his illegal settlement and gave him the right to buy it at a greatly reduced price. The Homestead Act freed up so much acreage that many speculators ended up as loan brokers or working for large land-buying corporations. Wrote Henry Brokmeyer in St. Louis 1856:

The real estate agent offered me ten dollars for the option upon the adjacent fifty feet of ground. . . . I told him that it was not for sale.

I could not understand what the fellow was lying about. He offers to pay me money for an object which with the same breath he declares to be worthless. I have since learned that these men do a considerable business in selling property, on the usual terms, as they call it, that is, one-third cash and the balance in one and two years, the deferred payments being secured by deeds of trust. Then if default is made . . . they sell and buy in the property. Upon examining the abstract of title that had been furnished to me, I found that this had actually occurred with the property that I bought.

Land leasing was also common, and owners might become inadvertent landlords. Brokmeyer received a letter from his friend Mr. Pheyety informing him that "all the Dutch of the prairie have migrated into [Brokmeyer's] neighborhood." They had "started with seven plows" and in three days "had twenty-three going." They had built two houses in one day, "with roof and doors complete," and two more under construction. The subsequent conversation was recalled by Brokmeyer:

"What does it mean, Henry? Are these men really on your land?"

"I think they are, Mr. Pheyety. I left them there last Sunday, and I think they are there yet and likely to stay for the next five years at least."

"With twenty-three plows?"

"I expect there are more by now. They think that prairie can't be broken to advantage after this month. They are in a hurry. The season crowds them."

"And you have leased the land for five years?"

"Yes. They fence the land; build the necessary farm buildings for four farms, into which the tract is divided. They break the land and put it into good cultivatable condition, and for doing this they have the use of it for three years from last Friday. Then for the two following years they pay me seventy-five cents an acre per year for the land under cultivation."

Speculators, like the debt-ridden men they often fleeced, found frequent financial disaster in their western land ventures. According to historian Ray Allen Billington, "speculators as a group generally lost money and the chief gainers were the small farmers." One disappointed speculator, writing in 1831, had bought land through the Galveston Bay and Texas Land Company while in New York. Arriving in Texas to claim it, he was told that his twenty thousand acres had been fraudulently sold to a local man as well. The speculator, William Austin, "was confident that the government would never recognize the . . . title for the land" and soon learned that his "worst fears were too well founded, and that all [his] hopes were fallacious."

✦ ✦ ✦ ✦

THE FEDERAL GOVERNMENT owned most available land other than those acres deeded by Spanish land grant, the ownership of which stirred up intense greed and rancor. "The whole of this beautiful country is claimed by half a dozen semi-savages under Spanish or Mexican grants," wrote Israel Lord in California in the 1850s, echoing the popular, anti-Hispanic sentiments of the day. Why, men wondered, should the Spanish have such huge tracts? "The Yankees doubt the validity of these [claims]. . . . I should judge that they are

putting their doubts to a practical test for their own special benefit." Lord believed that the government should "reduce every land claim in California to a limited quantity, say 320 acres, and only to actual settlers." He, and others, believed that "California [was] claimed by a very few lazy, idle, worthless individuals" who boosted the price of acreage far beyond the means of most farmers.

The Spanish landowners were overwhelmed by this flood of land-hungry Americans, who camped out on their great haciendas, refusing to leave, simply taking over. Antonio Berryessa, one of the final survivors of a large landowning family, recounted his downfall:

In the year 1846 Carlos Weber was persecuting us, threatening to take away our horses, and we (some young fellows and myself), in order to avoid this wicked, cruel and bloodthirsty man, who

had caused so many evils to the country, took the horses to the rancho San Pablo, where we thought they would be safe from the threats and connivance of Weber to steal them. Such was not the case, however, for when we had been there with them for two weeks, Weber attacked us with his men at a time when we had the horses all together in the corral, and took them away by force. Not only this, but, besides taking from us 35 to 40 fine horses, he also left us without saddles and rifles, threatening to kill us if we offered any resistance. After leaving us afoot, they went to the other buildings of the rancho and there did the same thing, taking by force horses, saddles and bridles, robbing and committing thousands of atrocities against the Castro families. They entered the houses by force, opening trunks, taking out and carrying off what there was in them.

When they were satiated with so much crime, they went to

Man selling remedies, ca. 1890s.

the neighboring ranchos where they did the same thing. I, along with my mother . . . went to take the news to my father, who was at the Milpitas rancho. We all traveled on foot at night, undergoing thousands of hardships and frights by reason of the streams which were very swollen and the roads which were in very bad condition.

After three days of painful travel, we arrived at Milpitas. When my father [heard] of the theft of his stock of horses and other things, he told us that things had gone very badly with him there, too, since the same Weber party had put Jose, my brother, out on

the road, had taken away the only horse that remained to him and thrown out on the ground a sack of flour which he had ordered brought on it.

. . . My father then became very sad and ill. He had no peace, for his great fear that Weber's men and others . . . would still persecute him and cause him further injury. So it was that he lived in this continuous state of anxiety. . . .

During the years 1849–1850 . . . thousands of adventurers from the United States seized possession of land holdings by force. They were called "squatters." A great number of these fell upon Milpitas and took possession of lands belonging to my father, fencing these in, except for one small holding. Besides this they shot his horses and sheep. All these misfortunes affected my father to such an extent that he began to lose his mind.

Speculation and complicity were rampant, as cited by an early settler in Clinton, Iowa, Daniel H. Pearce:

Some of the . . . gentlemen of elegant leisure, followed the business of making claims and selling them to emigrants as they came through. As soon as a new settler arrived, the above named gentry would ascertain his "pile" . . . and would then have a claim to suit the newcomer's purpose and purse, and, if he demurred paying anything to them . . . they would soon convince him of his error. He would be summoned to appear before a justice of the peace as a trespasser . . . [and] the magistrate issuing the summons belonged to the fraternity, and the poor settler would have to sell out or leave, and even if he went, would have to go a poorer if not sadder man.

For the hopeful, the skilled, and the plucky, the West offered bountiful opportunity to seize upon a likely notion, round up investors, and try out an idea, often buying cattle or killing, skinning, and selling buffalo, even striking up a lively commerce in buffalo bones. Anything was salable to those who would buy, as John Young Nelson noted. He became a trader huntsman, selling wild meat to a boardinghouse for ten cents a pound. "Every day I went out, and I killed more than I can carry. . . . I used to bring in from three to six deer a day, until at length the supply was greater than the demand . . . [and] I was making over twenty dollars a day. . . . When I had saved up three hundred dollars I gave up hunting, bade my friends adieu and tramped [away]. . . ."

Another frontiersman, John Cook, looking for gain, "cast his lot" with a partner for a summer buffalo hunt, bought a new wagon and harness, hitched their horses together, and the two were ready to "share and share alike all the expenses, and the same with the profits. . . . We hired a Mexican called Pedro to skin buffaloes at 20 cents per hide, and . . . the boy . . . continued on at $25 per month,

work or play. We bought our flour, groceries and ammunition . . . and after counting out the price of my saddle, wagon, harness, and some clothing, I had just $106 left from all sources." By Cook's calculation, he would kill and skin twenty-two buffalo a day for forty-one days, which, at 25 cents per hide, would earn $225.50.

For the lively, the forthright, and the quick, the real "gold" in the gold rush was found outside the mines. "The Fosters . . . have amassed some twenty thousand dollars or more," reported Israel Lord, "but not by mining. They have bought and sold and packed and ranched and dealt in any and everything that would turn a penny into their pockets."

Men hardly lacked for work. Moreover, since not all had the funding or the enterprise to start a company, by scanning the classifieds in any metropolitan newspaper, they could find myriad prospects, including, from the *San Francisco Chronicle* in 1910: "by silvering mirrors at home in your spare time; any one can easily make $4 daily"; "Learn show-card writing by mail. No former experience necessary"; "ten live canvassers wanted for well-established business." No one knows if the work proved profitable—only that it existed in greater diversity than in previous generations.

Even without great profits, the independence of western men's lives brought them, in their own minds, success. "When twelve years ago, I landed upon the wharf of the city of New York, after a seven weeks' voyage across the Atlantic, I was seventeen years old; had twenty-five cents in my pocked and . . . three words of the English language in my head. I had not relative, friend or acquaintance upon the continent," wrote Henry Brokmeyer in 1856. "To-day I landed upon the wharf city of St. Louis. I have a full dollar left and . . . I am the master of three trades, with splendid health." He believed in achieving small, reasonable goals:

I make skillets. With this work and skill I earn four dollars a day. I furnish him [a cook], and ten thousand like him, with skillets, and they furnish me with the things to fry. . . . If they produced nothing to fry, nobody would want a skillet. No, then, what does he get? I get four dollars a day, and he gets fifty cents, thirteen dollars a month and board. If the board is worth thirteen dollars a month, he gets a dollar a day, the year around. For this he works, from daylight to dark, from six to six in the winter, and from four o'clock in the morning to seven o'clock at night in the summer. On these conditions he furnishes the things to fry, and I the things to fry them in.

Two months ago I had to look for a job. . . . I found that the molders . . . earned as high as five and six dollars a day [so] I determined to turn apprentice, to learn something, in order that I might be able to earn something. It was my privilege to do this. . . . I earn more with the same amount of labor than the farm hand, the shoemaker, the harness maker, the tanner or the currier; more in fact than any mechanic in any other vocation. I want to do as well as my neighbor, and if I can, a little better.

For the Wolf brothers, shopkeepers in Sonora, California, innovation and advertising meant increased sales. "Wolf Brothers . . . thank their patrons and inform them they are now prepared to sell *Cheaper* than any other place in the mining region, and even in San Francisco—because they pay no rent . . . and get their goods directly from the Western States and Europe. Call and convince yourself of the fact at their *Fire-proof store.* Always on hand a large assortment of *Fancy Staple and Foreign Dry Goods.*"

Settler James H. Rinehart recalled his first enterprise: "I was large enough to drive a span of horses and haul goods from Keokuk to Oskaloosa [Iowa], 125 miles. For the stores [for] $1.00 per hundred. . . . I visited the country twenty years later . . . when railroads were running in all directions. . . . Yet some of the old farmers were setting in their fine upholstered chairs, cursing the railroads which they said were just ruining the country."

Homesteader Ole Dovre decided to go into the restaurant business:

The restaurant I bought in Dickinson (N. Dakota) was the only one in town, except for one run by a Chinese fellow at the railroad depot. When I took possession I realized what a run-down place it was. Only men ate there; mostly they were workers for the railroad and other firms, cowboys and a sprinkling of gamblers. This crowd was too rough for women, but my idea was to make the cafe nice enough for anybody.

I locked the door and for five days I cleaned papered, painted and threw away all the junk and replaced it with new things. . . .

Business seemed good, but the profits were small. Most night cooks were men I got from an unemployment office at St. Paul, Minnesota. They gave me trouble, mostly from drinking. They were drunk at a bad time. My day cook was an Irish woman, Maggie Reagan. Every morning at 7 am she was there; at 7 pm she was gone. . . .

One night cook we got from St. Paul was Sing, an excellent pastry cook. His specialty was baking cakes. One day he made a wedding cake, topped by a bride and groom. It was a beauty. But the ingredients had cost eleven dollars and nobody in town was getting married. So we told Sing to bake no cakes other than those we ordered. That didn't set well with him.

A more unusual occupation was that of goose herder. When arrows of geese winged south to winter nesting sites, they crossed the great plains and valleys of California, often dipping down to nip at grain stalks and eat the kernels, ruining crops and calling for the skills of the goose herders, an occupation that appeared in mid-nineteenth-century America and apparently vanished soon after. Geese were a greedy threat to grain crops, and their heavy bodies, flapping through the skies each autumn, had to be routed away from fields, to avert crop loss.

Herders patrolled the grain fields from the earliest light, shotguns ready, stocked with sacks full of shells. At the first sound of honking, the initial round was fired, and the herder's job—to startle geese wherever they flew—began. He worked five months of the year, during goose season, from November into April.

Equally humble was the life of the frontier bee hunter. Wrote Gottfried Duden on June 16, 1826:

Yesterday, as I was roaming through the forests in my usual manner, I came upon two bee hunters. . . . They proceeded as follows: They chose their first stand on the ridge of a hill between two valleys. They lighted a small fire in a spot free of trees and placed honeycombs on it so that the wax produced a column of smoke without being consumed by the fire. A strong odor of honey spread in all directions and in a short time attracted all kinds of flying insects and also some bees. Now it was the business of the hunters to keep their eyes fixed on the lure, [i]n order to be able to watch the bees as they flew away. Soon three of them rose and flew away in the same direction. This was noted as accurately as possible. . . . Then one of the hunters took a glowing coal and walked about two hundred paces farther on the same ridge, leaving his companion.

When the nest was found, the honey was raided, providing tidy sustenance for this backwoods entrepreneur.

"No European poverty prevails here," wrote Gottfried Duden, an idea about the West held sacred by land speculators and small businessmen. Flawed as the speculators were, historian Ray Allen Billington pointed out, promoters and speculators still shared with trappers, traders, and pioneers credit for the country's westward expansion, thus earning them an important place in the nation's history, along with legions of self-made men, the country's new entrepreneurs. As for the self-made men, whether hunter, carpenter, tailor, or skillet maker, they found opportunity in the West, forging from difficulty a direction for the future. And even those unable to succeed financially could claim the notion of freedom in the West.

15

TINKERERS, TEACHERS, BOOKISH MEN, AND POLITICIANS

It will be a source of astonishment to many, who reflect that I am now a member of the American Congress,—the most enlightened body of men in the world,—and that at the age of fifteen, I did not know the first letter in the book.
—*Davy Crockett*

It has always been my belief . . . that a man with a good head is better off than one with a good purse.
—*Conrad White to Henry Brokmeyer*

An American could no more live without making speeches or hearing them, holding office or voting somebody else into office . . . than he could without his newspaper. . . .
—*J. Ross Browne*

I have tried many occupations, and there is no kind of work . . . so wearing as literary labor.
—*Hubert Howe Bancroft*

WHO KNEW WHERE the practical mind stopped and imagination took over? The West begged invention; "making do" was the ethic that sprang from necessity. The discovery of good, rich mud meant that a potter could build a wheel for throwing, creating an abundance of crocks, sauerkraut jars, syrup jugs, flower pots, plates, and mugs. Sturdy logs served to convert a grove of trees into architecture.

Craftsmen thrived in the backwoods. Their art and skill were sometimes as simple as transforming a lock of hair, delivered by a lovelorn young woman to a jeweler, into a watch fob for her beloved, a traditional statement of love among early settlers. Braiding was idly pursued by cowboys, farmers, homesteaders, ranchers, even prisoners, who, at day's end, during the dark and cloistered winter months, might sit, smoke, and braid stiff strands of horsehair into hackamores, fly switches, bridle reins, hatbands, and lariats. Hairs of varied hue were woven in three- or four-plait design, expertly shaped by skinning knife, punch, and pliers. Beautiful designs were achieved by Mormon men serving prison time for polygamy, according to historian Austin Fife.

Invention knew no bounds. Martin, the second cousin of Barbara Levorson's father, fashioned skis for the snowbound family in North Dakota "made entirely by hand (from two boards) and when they were ready to bend they were soaked in a wash boiler full of hot water on the kitchen stove. Then they were dried in a frame that held them bent to the desired degree. All the work was done in the kitchen."

The West seemed to release men's inventiveness. Dr. William Thomas, traveling west in 1849, was amazed to see a wagon clip the Cherokee Trail with a homemade "roadometer," designed to calculate mileage. It "consisted of three small cogwheels attached to the back part of the waggon bed so that the hub of the waggon wheel operates upon the first cogwheel, and that upon the second the waggon turns often enough round to make a mile." A farmer, according to the *San Francisco Chronicle* of May 15, 1910, patented a "cover for milking pails that admits the milk" through a cloth-covered strainer. The cover flipped off for cleaning and even "kept impure air from entering the pail." German ironmonger Henry Brokmeyer set a sponge in a wire mask to protect himself from fumes released by the acids he used in molding skillets.

The quieter cousin of innovation was repair, and success lay with the man who could patch together his equipment. Homesteader Barbara Levorson's father seemed a wizard at this. "If it were some wooden piece such as a doubletree, his store of oak from Minnesota usually held a suitable piece. Then he would get down on his knees and trace the contours of the broken part on a new piece of oak. Then came the laborious shaping of the hard oak with dull tools. Repairs on harness or hard machinery could be needed any day, and papa did them carefully. I have seen harnesses held together with bits or rope or twine."

America was ready for new ideas, new crops, new professions. "Pard predicts that there will grow wheat and fruit in the valleys and California will be a rich and big State, and he tells me that he is thinking of investing five thousand dollars in real estate in the Bay," wrote Carlisle Abbot. Luther Burbank, in the summer of 1875, set out for California with nothing more than ten potatoes; his namesake potato was a variety of his own invention. After selling the seed rights to a merchant in Marblehead, Massachusetts, for $150 and paying $140 for his fare west, Burbank arrived in Santa Rosa, California, with $10 left. But dreams were bountiful, and they led to his invention of many new plant species: the Shasta and Alaska daisy, the calla lily, the fire poppy, and even spineless cactus, designed to feed cattle.

Quaker physicist and nurseryman Henderson Luelling, hearing

Unidentified toolsmith at work.

the adventures of Lewis and Clark, also dreamed of planting trees in the Willamette Valley, south of the Columbia River, bounded by the lush Cascade Range, and, according to members of the Lewis and Clark Expedition, "the only desirable . . . settlement on the western side of the Rocky Mountains." On April 17, 1847, he set out with his wife and eight children, the youngest named Oregon Columbia, with nursery stock of eight hundred to one thousand young trees and shrubs in two long wooden boxes, snugly fitted into the wagon bed. Racks were constructed to keep the cargo from being eaten by cattle. Another major concern was keeping the lone family protected from Indians. At one point a war party charged toward them, then stopped short at the sight of a wagon overflowing with trees. Trees were protected by the Great Spirit, and Luelling's load of apples, pears, quince, plums, cherries, grapes, and berry bushes was granted safe passage west. He settled south of Portland and grafted the first fruit stock ever to come to the mild climate of the valley. Settlers eagerly purchased every tree.

→ → ← ←

Knife repairman, ca. 1870. Photo by Stellman.

THE GOLD BOOM prompted inventions of its own. "A scientific cuss in Nevada has formed a company to get the gold out of quartz by a new method and is selling shares like hot cakes at ten dollars a share. He is going to build a furnace and melt the gold out of the rock. It may be all right, but I don't know anything about quartz mines," wrote Carlisle Abbot. Precious metals demanded mills, built with enormous labor and expense by importing heavy timber for joists and beams from the flanks of the mountains, while lugging the impossible machinery by switchback up and across steep peaks. A roasting furnace in Reese River, Nevada, built in 1864, stirred the hopes of the silver miners. Broiling away in the cold, its brick walls covered with blankets to keep in the heat, the oven extracted "first class chlorides" as well as lesser gradients.

Ignorance was no deterrence. The "scientific cuss," a "worthy professor," according to Abbot, "knew nothing about quartz mines or quartz mills . . . but like a brave man he went to work, and by dint of algebraic equations, trigonometry, geometry, and an occasional reference to Plato and Aristotle, he built a quartz mill." At its completion the professor was "in ecstasies." His "mill wheels flew around with a tremendous clatter; his battery battered up the quartz at an amazing rate; his amalgamating pans made the finest of suds." However, the grease he used to make the machinery work happened to carry the gold away with it, while the flood of 1862 swept down the Sierra Nevada, flushing away cabins and farms, forcing the professor to "abandon his mill and seek refuge in a hole which he and his friends burrowed in a neighboring hill," where he lay blockaded until spring, reading his beloved Plato or "philosophizing to his fellows like Diogenes in his tub."

The highly intelligent metal molder Henry Brokmeyer read Hegel and other classical authors and contemplated their philosophy while fashioning griddles, skillets, and treating plates. "I finished the 'Illiad,' " he wrote in 1856. "My job went on nicely—but somehow I could not get rid of Homer." Meanwhile the foreman of his shop began to bring him problems. "Show me how to use this thing," he asked. "I found upon applying the instrument that it had a thin place . . . three inches in one direction. One end of this defect was located within an inch of one of the gates, the place where the iron is poured in, and therefore a very serious defect, that would obstruct the flow of the metal. Upon testing further, I found that this space was . . . below the standard thickness of the gate, and declared the pattern worthless." The foreman was astonished; even his best men had failed to find the problem. "This is a service that we can not accept for nothing," the foreman insisted, handing Brokmeyer a check for one hundred dollars. Brokmeyer, newly energized, then realized that he could apply paint or varnish, which would bring the thin spot up to standard. "There is money in it [for you] the foreman insisted," recalled Brokmeyer.

June 23, 1856

I wanted to test my experiment with the pattern. The truth is . . . I had no trouble in finding the mastic that I need for the operation. . . . The only difficulty is . . . not to change the weight of the casting, or at least, not to increase it.

June 24

The result was all that could be desired. . . . The foreman . . . had the pattern and casting taken over to the office. . . . I found him examining the pattern with a lens.

"This is most excellent, Henry," said he, "I can find no trace of the patch. I can not detect it by the sound, either."

"There is a way of detecting it," said I. "By washing it off. I have stuff in my room that will take it off in a very short time."

"You don't say so! Now tell me, Henry, what will you take for the secret of making that paste?"

"Nothing," said I. "I will doctor every defective pattern you have."

June 27

Was sent for by the foreman at nine o'clock and had to explain to the proprietor the method of doctoring the defective patterns. He seemed so much interested that I went to my room for some more paste and tools and set to work on the No. 6 bottom pattern. . . . He then asked me about its durability. Would it chip off?

"And now what must I pay you for the use of the material? My foreman tells me that you propose to keep the paste for use in our shop exclusively. What do you earn on the floor?"

Jacob Brodbeck, maker of early flying machines. Courtesy Mr. E. E. Brodbeck.

I told him my average earnings per week. . . .

He turned to the foreman and directed him to have my name put on the payroll of the pattern makers. . . . Then, pointing to a room adjoining the foreman's office, he said:

"Have that room cleared of the old rubbish and furnish Mr. Brokmeyer with whatever he needs to arrange it for his work."

Brokmeyer, a scholar and academic, had chosen to work in a skillet foundry because he had made a firm calculation about how he could earn money there.

"What led you to the study of philosophy?" his employer asked. Brokmeyer replied, "When a person has a clear conception of general meanings . . . it shows him how to look for the rest."

Technology forged ahead, bringing with it the enjoyment of rail

Charles Henry Beever, using a B & H pear burner, patented by him and George Hindes, Fri County, Texas, ca. 1890s.

Unidentified man at work at desk.

travel in Pullman cars so speedy that it prompted wonder and awe— with moving parlors, dining rooms, bedrooms, even servants to attend to all needs. The three thousand miles from Chicago to San Francisco unrolled like a ribbon, as plains and mountains vanished behind. On some cars, there was a house organ, and music rang out as the train crested over the mountains.

Men also reinvented themselves in a quintessential feature of American life, politics. With little entertainment to be had, political dissension drew arguments and crowds. Issues too minor to note in the city flared up in rural settings. Candidates paraded their integrity, intelligence, and superior positions, challenging one another like prairie gladiators. Politics seemed strangely akin to the national penchant for gambling. Politics prompted excess, noted J. Ross Browne, citing two men of Austin, Nevada, who were equally confident of success as the town mayor. One enthusiastic supporter swore that if Buel, his candidate, were elected, he would carry a very heavy, over-two-hundred-pound, sack of flour from Clifton Street to Upper Austin, a steep, uphill trek. If the reverse occurred, then his opponent, Gridley, must lug the sack downhill. When the mayor was reappointed, "Go to it, Gridley!" was the rousing cry, as the good-natured loser shouldered the huge bag and set forth, flanked on each side by mounted horsemen "carrying high in the air the flag of the Union." Gridley reached Clifton with the sack, followed by an immense surge of miners and merchants, who watched, spellbound, as Gridley auctioned it off for the enormous sum of three thousand dollars. Startled at the sack's success—and the fact that he got to keep it after the auction—he staged a second auction the next day, earning seventeen hundred dollars. Now geared up, he sold the same sack in Virginia City for eight thousand, in Sacramento for ten thousand, and in San Francisco for fifteen thousand, testimony to a booming economy and a prevailing spirit of civic-minded cooperation, since no one bothered to keep the sack. Aglow with success, Gridley returned to Austin, found financing, and started a bank, impressed beyond measure with the American way.

Another to enjoy politics was Davy Crockett, who assured his constituents that they would be taken care of when he was reelected to the Tennessee legislature:

When I set out electioneering, I would go prepared to put every man on as good footing when I left him as I found him on. I would therefore have me a large buckskin hunting-shirt made, with a couple of pockets holding about a peck each; and that in one I would carry a large twist of tobacco, and in the other my bottle of liquor; for I knowed when I met a man and offered him a dram, he would throw out his quid of tobacco to take one, and another. . . . I would out [sic] with my twist and give him another chaw. And in this way he would not be worse off than when I found him. . . .

Crockett's promises charmed his constituents. He beat his opponent by 247 votes and was later returned as a member of the legislature, in 1823 and 1824. Elected to Congress in 1827, he won renown as the canebrake congressman, a representative of the dawning age of the common man, the triumph of pure democracy over the European class system.

⊁ ⊁ ⊱ ⊱

BOOKS PROVIDED A quieter source of entertainment than politics. Helge Anderson, a Norwegian settler in North Dakota, was an "an avid reader and had a store of books" that he passed out to anyone interested, including young pioneer Barbara Levorson. A Wyoming homesteader Samuel Emlen recalled, "Most of our time has been spent in our little house reading novels which we borrow. . . . I think I have read more novels since I have been here than in the past five years."

Engrossed with the recording of history in the Pacific states, historian Hubert Howe Bancroft loved reading but disdained collecting books. "Bibliomaniac I was not. This, with every other species of

Patent Office, ca. 1880s.

lunacy, I disliked. I know nothing morally wrong with one possessing the money . . . to hunt down old [relics] and buy them. . . . But it is a taste having no practical purpose in view, and therefore would never satisfy me." Yet fate intervened. Bancroft was astonished to discover nearly five hundred bulky volumes of original documents lodged in the office of the U.S. Surveyor General in San Francisco, the forgotten archives of the secular government of Spanish California. Most were in Spanish, some of it "very bad Spanish, poorly written, and difficult to decipher," along with bundles of papers at the missions throughout California. Compelled to collect, Bancroft "succeeded in getting together some fifty or seventy five volumes . . . the origin of [his] library, sometimes called . . . the Bancroft Library." Still, he maintained: "[N]ot half the books printed are ever read; not half the books sold are bought to be read."

Nor did poetry have much influence on the American imagination. "Should Byron come here and publish for the first time his

Tinkerers,

Teachers,

Bookish Men,

and Politicians

213

Man named Anderson standing with cotton-lifting machine he invented, Sherman, Texas, 1920. Courtesy Jean Sellstorm.

Childe Harold," wrote Bancroft, "[i]t would not find buyers enough to pay the printer." Equally difficult was newspaper life. Perhaps one of the riskiest professions in the West was editor of a small-town newspaper, where opinions teetered between the activities of the vigilance committees, which were illegal, and the bandits that roamed through the unsettled West. John Young Nelson described the state of the *Rocky Mountain News* in Denver:

> It was full of scathing articles against the gamblers and blacklegs; in fact, the paper was run in the interest of the Vigilance Committee and law and order. The composing offices were in a log shanty, and the printers had to set the type with their six-shooters and double-barreled guns lying on the benches beside them. . . . The editor's name was Byers. . . . He never showed outside his door whilst these articles were appearing. The rowdies were always on the lookout for him, and directly he made any movement to leave his house half a dozen bullets would bury themselves in the woodwork.

Men of great intelligence sprouted up in rural settings, from Abraham Lincoln to the McGuffey brothers, sons of a Scottish frontiersman and an ambitious, stern, and fierce Irish mother, raised in a clapboard shack in rural Ohio, authors of America's most popular children's textbooks, *McGuffey's Readers.* The elder, William, "ate up knowledge, and his memory was prodigious." He attended a small school opened by a Presbyterian minister and soaked up all the Latin he could. There were no organized schools in the West until 1825, and at fifteen he set out with his newly won certificate to be a traveling teacher, drumming up "subscription scholars" to pay by the course. William was marked by a religious calm and deep sense of concentration. Alexander, sixteen years younger, was first a teacher before turning to the law, a profession that was considered disreputable during colonial times, but that he sensed would afford him the grace, ease, and luxury to which he knew he could grow accustomed. He grew into an elegant cosmopolitan, an attorney versed in civil and ecclesiastical law, who traveled in Europe and collaborated with his brother to write the popular series of schoolbooks.

William thirsted to teach. Living among unruly, uneducated

Teachers J. H. Richards (left), Reverend H. R. Voth (center), J. H. Schmidt (standing), and Abraham Suderman (right), Darlington Indian Mission School, Indian Territory (later Oklahoma), 1890.

backwoodsmen, he believed that young minds, if sparked early enough, would seek greater enlightenment. He believed educated youth would do good in the world as they tried to advance. To most, his idea of a sound education in the backwoods was laughable. William's own life was an example of his ideas. He attended high school and college, followed by years of costly theological training. Despite the odds, his genius carried him through one school after another, until he became a professor in ancient languages and was ordained into the ministry in 1833. As headmaster of Ohio University he was paid fifteen hundred dollars a year but still fretted about children's education. Approached by the publisher Winthrop B.

Smith about writing a series of schoolbooks for children, he quickly agreed. The historic little books—a primer, four readers, and a speller—appeared in 1837. They were filled with enticing pictures of children skating, swimming, flying kites, and playing ball, unlike the dour textbooks that harkened back to Greek history. William was convinced that if children could read for pleasure, they would absorb learning and moral instruction. A light and joyous presence shone through each book, and children nationwide poured over "Harry and the Guidepost," "George Washington and His Little Hatchet," and "The Arab and His Horse." The books even touched on forbidden subjects, such as madness, torture, and death, suitable for

First county school in Tripp County, South Dakota. Photo by Fred Hulststrand.

older children only "if expressed with force or beauty." To stimulate the imagination was to capture heaven, and once engaged, the imagination would work for the best.

Some children went no further than the *Fourth Reader* but, in their setting, were enriched by this version of belles lettres. William, dreamer and visionary, saw his work satisfy the intellectual hunger of illiterate pioneers; the total sales were estimated to have been 122 million. The brothers received only a lump-sum payment of five hundred dollars, and, for William only, a "barrel of choice hams" at Christmas, as well as "shawls and breastpins" for his wife. Ever the scholar, he simply shrugged.

The work of the educator was uphill. Men of every level, including multitudes of wandering illiterates, had taken to the road. "I noticed a sign nailed to the corner, 'Bred for sail,' " wrote John D. Young. "Both words [were] spelled as wrong as possible, however that did not make any difference. We knew what it meant and were bound to have some."

In some company, education was seen as effete, and male teachers were rare as gold. The pay was low, the hours were long, and most men looked elsewhere for their income. "The young men receive from $2.25 to $5.00 per day for manual labor, and they seem to have forgotten that school-teaching is any longer a profession. Several schools in the county (Kentucky) have not been taught for two or three years, and many must wait until some of the teachers have closed their schools."

Finding room and board was also difficult. "Uncle Ole had a lot of men come [and board] and he also boarded the teacher, season after season. It was almost impossible to find boarding places for teachers. Houses had no spare rooms and mothers were burdened with so much work every day that they refused to take the extra responsibility of boarding a stranger."

As gold income faltered and farming proved without profit, men were increasingly drawn to rural teaching, a step up from farm labor, which gave them some salary, community respect, and the right to exercise strong discipline. Occasionally, "strong" got out of control, noted John Young Nelson, who reacted to the punishment of a fourteen-year-old girl, described as "silly" and assailed by her teacher. "In the afternoon he took to whacking her because she could not pronounce some word, and the more she tried to do as she was told, the more he confused her."

Young Nelson "stood it" for as long as he could but was revolted by the increasing intensity of the "severe hits with his cane across the shoulders and arms. This was more than I could stand," he recalled, "so I went for him with my slate, and broke it over his head." Still not satisfied, Nelson seized a log from the bench and "gave him the soundest hiding I was capable of." Terrified that the man had died, Nelson ran away and went to live with his uncle, a "mean, psalm-singing, contemptible specimen of a man, who would skin a flint in everything he did," but at least "it was better than being arrested for murder."

Occasionally, students resisted, as did the Indian pupils of Alanson Wesley Smith, called to open an Indian school in La Push, Washington. Going hut to hut, he recruited his class by begging the Indian families in poverty-stricken Chinook to think of their children's education. Indians feared white schools, where many children became ill and where white customs and language made children feel foreign in their own culture. The La Push Indians finally agreed, however, and the children were forced into attendance. They were embarrassed and awkward. Their toes became stuck in large cracks in the floorboards, causing them pain as they tried to dislodge them. Smith's one small victory—that the boys agreed to wear western clothes—occurred only when the boys realized that a spanking hurt less when they were so dressed. Smith seemed mired in perpetual conflict. Once a group of angry Indian parents surrounded his house after he had punished a student. Another time a seventeen-year old boy tackled him around the legs when he was told to change seats. When the boy refused to let go, Smith banged him on the head with his slate, uncharacteristic punishment that so infuriated the youth he tried to get his classmates to kill the teacher.

✦ ✦ ✦ ✦

NO MATTER THE persuasion or profession, western men were self-made, and their success stories, although episodic and not universal, established the popular image of manifest destiny. Many came and faced the cruel whims of a harsh environment, and those who stayed on, in peaceful professions—literary, scientific, educational, even political—were truly unsung heroes of their time.

Part 7

N A T I V E   A M E R I C A N S

❖

Photo on previous page: Unidentified Apache. Photo by H. Buehman.

16

NATIVE AMERICANS
ON THE LAND

❖

I like to be near the Indians. They are good neighbors and are always finding something [interesting] in the way of fish or animals.
—*Robert Hunter Fitzhugh*

✦

They held a potlach but called it Christmas.—*Evelyn Tinkham*

✦

Everything in this world talks, just as we are [talking] now—the trees, rocks, everything. But we cannot understand them, just as the white people do not understand Indians.—*Nomlaki Indian*

✦

Our prairies were once covered with horses as the trees are covered with leaves. Where are they now?—*Porcupine Bear*

THE WEST ROILED with upset and cultural clashes, usually arising from Yankee rapaciousness, always resulting in change, native dislocation, and land loss. The multiple ways in which Native Americans and Anglos encountered each other, usually through their men, is a sorrowful tale in the history of the West. Indian men of the plains, once nomadic buffalo hunters, intent upon

survival, commerce, and family building, fell powerless to the invasion of the white settlers and the military. Indian aggression flared as one treaty after another was broken, buffalo vanished, and settlements sprang up. While settlers forged west, members of the 250 or so remaining tribes were scattered and forced onto bleak reservations to live in hostile dependency. As Anglo needs grew, the idea of allowing Indians autonomous nations faded away. The tribes were pushed farther and farther west, first by President Andrew Jackson in the 1830s, then by the Indian Wars from 1865 to 1891. Spears and flint gave way to an onslaught of powder and steel, symbols of a culture clash so ruthless as to rend apart an entire continent.

Displaced tribes had been granted 7.5 million acres reserved in perpetuity under U.S. treaties, which the U.S. Senate refused to ratify. Thus the areas were never established, nor were the Indians paid for their original lands, preempted by the federal government. Instead tribes were herded onto reservations, which were basically government almshouses, where they were deprived of the rights of citizenry, exploited for their labor, and often ruined with alcohol. Worse, the Vagabond Act of 1850 stated that Indians who were perceived as loiterers could be forced to become servants, legally justifying the practice of forced Indian labor on farms and in the mines. The Indian population in California alone declined by 50 percent from 1846 to 1856 and by 82 percent between 1848 and 1880. The reservation system forced Indians to adopt Western culture and

Unidentified Inuit man, Nome, Alaska, 1904.
Photo by Wilfred McDaniel.

and salmon-fattened Pacific coast tribes to the coastal Indians of California, the diggers.

In the turmoil of conquest and decimation, could one race face another with vision and not just react with fear? Margaret Hecox doubted that the "savage instinct could ever be eradicated from the wild man's breast." According to Harriet Bunyard, "How detestable they are, all the men riding and the women walking and carrying the load. There was a Pemore Indian here today. He had his face painted and long strings of beads in his ears. He was very friendly, but all he wants is a chance to steal our stock." Thought Hattie Wilson: "The Osage Indians used to come to our camp frequently . . . and [once] an Indian chief asked for some of my mother's fresh bread. She gave him a roll. He stuck his finger through it and handed it back, much to our disgust." To Gertrude Burlingame, they were "red devils," while Mary Gettys Lockhard had the "fixed idea that Indians rose up from the ground at times and killed everybody in sight."

For their part Indians wondered at the white men, who wore tight, binding clothes, lacked exercise, and feared the dark, avoiding danger and even sunlight! The Indians believed in simplicity and were fascinated by superfluities of the whites, such as eyeglasses, pocket watches, bric-a-brac, tidies, ruffles, and pleats.

The record of cross-cultural confusion goes back to the first interactions. Brother Heckewelder, a Moravian missionary in 1789, wrote: "The Delaware were a race of men . . . who would not admit that whites were superior beings. They regarded them as a mixed race, therefore a troublesome one. . . . They thought the [whites] might have been sent to them . . . for some great and important purpose. They, therefore, welcomed them, hoping to be made happier by their company. It was not long however, before they discovered their mistake." James Ross Larkin, in 1857, figured out his own method of interacting with Indians. "I was called by an old chief to come to him, which I did. . . . He made signs & spoke to me & seemed to signify that he was going to fight the Americans. . . . I had Harpers [magazine] for September with me, containing a number of cuts engravings of Indians. I showed them to the old man & the Squaw & a lot of children soon gathered around to take a look at such a novelty—They were very much pleased with the sights."

Despite all fears, by 1860 there were only 362 recorded deaths

placed them at the mercy of government officials who were often corrupt. Also, peoples of different tribes and languages were forced to live together, creating deep unhappiness. Only in 1887 did the Dawes Allotment Act allow displaced Indians to qualify for land allotments, breeding deep distrust and unresolved, simmering, anger. The Indians felt the indignity of being given back small allotments of the land they once had freely lived upon.

Nearly three thousand tribes existed before the influx of Anglos. All were diverse in habit, temperament, and outlook, from the fleet horsemen of the Great Plains, matrilineal tribes of the Southwest,

of whites by Indian attack, although more than 250,000 emigrants had traveled west by then, and other stories were told: accounts of Indian compassion, sharing, and goodwill; of Indians who piloted settlers across treacherous crossings or forded rivers in advance of the main party. Levi Jackman, a Mormon emigrant in 1847, described the Sioux his party encountered outside Chimney Rock. "So far they had met only two Sioux, a man and his wife, both definitely friendly. Now they encountered 35 of them—magnificent, clean, well-dressed, noble-looking, many cuts above the demoralized Omahas or their thievish Pawnees. The Saints were universally impressed, extended overnight hospitality to the chief and his wife, and gave them a thrill by letting observe the moon through Pratt's telescope. Truly gentlemen and ladies," said Jackman.

Indians believed in frankness, truthfulness, and integrity. To give their word was sacred; they *hated* liars. Indian men trained themselves around weakening emotions. They had no self-pity and believed strongly in the dictates of fate. In 1903 Theodora Kroeber recorded an old Mohave warrior, recalling a council of 1850, at which the Mohaves were discussing fighting the whites:

> I have heard that these whites are everywhere on all sides. You have heard that too. Nevertheless you want to fight them. Well, we will follow your counsel—we will go to fight. That is what we want. We are not like mountains; we do not stay forever. We are not like the sky, always there; not like the sun or moon—we die. Perhaps in a year, in a month, in two or three days. I want to die fighting. Well, how many times do you expect to die? You die once and do not come alive again. We will fight with you and die too. No one likes to die. If you like it, why not tie your hands and feet together and jump into the river? No one does it that way; that is killing yourself. So you say you want to die soon? Well, good, we will go along and help you.

Had the settlers looked farther, they would have found small, democratic societies, their ethic of independence similar to that of the European settlers, with tribes that functioned in an orderly fashion. Each village, even small settlements with only a few families, had its own chief. He might have only nominal power, and occa-

Unidentified Plains Indians in front of tent, ca. 1885.

Unidentified Plains Indians looking at photographic negatives.

sionally a potent shaman could exert more influence than the chief leader. Recalled Apache John Rope:

I was born at a place between old summit and Black River and I don't remember much till we were living at Cedar Creek, west of Fort Apache. I can remember playing as a child there with the other children. At that time we had lots of corn planted, and our people were digging a ditch and making a dam in the creek to water the ground. The men and women worked together, digging with sharp pointed sticks. . . . The men did this work, and when it was done they tied bear grass and dry bark into the tripods at first in bundles. Then they laid bear grass lengthwise along the upper side of the tripods from one to another. Over the bear

grass they packed the dry inner bark of cedar and cottonwood, the men and women both working. . . .

The head man (chief) of a community was always the first to get the use of the village water. After him came the others.

Supreme leader or wise counselor, the chief had a position of dignity, which made the treatment of Chief Truckee, leader of the Paiute nation, even more humbling, a sad story of white and Indian interaction, told by the chief's granddaughter, Sarah Winnemucca. Instead of fearing the white settlers, Chief Truckee, acting on a vision, welcomed them. "My white brothers—my long-looked-for white brothers have come at last . . ." he announced. The next year a great number of settlers arrived, and Chief Truckee went to greet them.

When our white brothers were going away they gave my grandfather a white tin plate—it was so bright. They say that after he left, my grandfather called for all his people to come together, and he then showed them the beautiful gift which he had received from his white brothers. Everyone was so pleased; nothing like it was ever seen in our country before. My grandfather thought so much of it that he bored holes in it and fastened it on his head, and wore it as a hat [and] held it in much admiration. . . .

That same fall, very late, the emigrants kept coming. . . . [Our white brothers] could not get over the mountains so they had to live with us. . . . My people did not seek to kill them . . . no, no, far from it. During the winter my people helped them. When they saw the tin plate, they laughed at the chief, and he was ashamed. He took the plate from his head and put it away, although he never gave up on his "White Brothers."

Chiefs in the California culture had no real power, other than to offer good advice in a persuasive manner, as did a Wintu chief who advised his members: "Do right; don't get into trouble; help your neighbor." Likewise, said an Atsugewi chief to his tribe: "Get up and do something for your living! Be on your guard! You have to work hard for your living. There may be a long winter, so put away all the food you can."

Indian men seemed at ease with women, and both sexes took part, or at least shared a lively interest, in tribal decisions. White onlookers, such as Californian Gertrude Atherton, scorned Indian men because while "squaws did what work was done the bucks basked in the sun for eight months in the year." Still, there was often social and political accord between the sexes. "The men never talk without smoking first," wrote Nevada Paiute Sarah Winnemucca. "The women sit behind them in another circle, and if the children wish to hear, they can be there too. The women know as much as the men do, and their advice is often asked. We have a republic . . . the council-tent is our congress and anybody can speak who has anything to say, woman and all. They are always interested in what their husbands are doing and thinking about. And they even take part in the wars. They are always near at hand when fighting is going on, ready to snatch their husbands up and carry them off if wounded or killed."

Gender equality also graced the art of food preparation. Cooking was generally a woman's task, but with frequent good-natured exceptions. Often men were assigned vegetable handling. The Yana man prepared the roasting pits, gathered firewood, and cooked the roots, gathered by the women. Michahai and Waksachi men of Eshom Valley, California, gathered and roasted the yucca cooperatively, then divided it. Men were quick to pick up pine nuts and also picked corn. Among the Wintus, acorn shelling by the fire at night gave young men a rare opportunity to visit women.

Meat preparation was primarily masculine in northern California, while drying meat was feminine. In the Northeast, with the Modocs and Atsugewis, cooking meat was solely the man's job. With the Yokuts, if women were out gathering, the men prepared the food; the reverse took place if the men were away.

Most California Indians tended toward cooperative assistance rather than inflexible labor dichotomy. The Wintus had arrowmakers, but because they worked only part-time, it might take six months to manufacture twenty arrows. Miwok men spent about ten days making a bow. Because of the time and effort required to make their own equipment, Indians placed great value on it.

Men of all tribes sought love, languished from love, and considered marriage and children vital. Marriage customs differed among the many tribes. Some would cohabit to establish suitability, finally "marrying" only when their compatibility was clear. Among the Shawnees and Delawares, the marriage contract was binding only as long as the husband and wife wanted it so. But because marriage brought together lineage and property and history, the union was not taken lightly. If a woman left her husband, she was authorized by law to take all the personal property she possessed at the time of the marriage, and the husband had no claim to it. One interpretation of the Sun Dance is that the male suffered during the ceremony to symbolize a woman's giving birth.

Men who languished from unreturned love might pine and mourn for months, while forbidden love or stealthy liaisons often led to forced separation, angst, depression, and even in some cases suicide. A botanist named Pursh, at an Onondoga village in 1807, observed a number of Native Americans using a plant called *Cicuta maculata* "to poison themselves when they have an inclination of going out of the world." In 1838 a traveler named Dearborne was told by a Tonawanda Indian that skunk cabbage, the "fatal root," although sweet in taste, caused violent spasms and death and was eaten in order to die. "[L]ove unrequited," he understood, "was a common cause for suicide."

Infidelity was despised by all and, when discovered, could result in the faithless woman's expulsion or maiming. Punishment also fell upon adulterous men, who made restitution by accepting physical injury or paying heavy fines. Sanctions were brushed aside in the case of wife sharing, considered a simple courtesy by many, especially among the Pueblo culture. Captive women routinely became second wives to their conquerors, yet wife stealing among men of the same tribe was a murderous offense. A Blackfoot named Apikuni recalled a tug-of-war held over Crow Woman, who was tanning a buffalo hide when a drunken Cree came along, "picked her up, and started off with her." Apikuni interceded and subdued the man, but only when joined by a second Blackfoot.

Bachelors were rare in most Native American tribes. To forgo children was to reap pity, for through offspring, a man could gain influence. A childless man was invisible in the Kiowa-Apache culture, as in others.

An unwed male was the berdache, a dress-wearing male who performed women's work and was often homosexual yet was readily accepted by the tribe as a member of a "third gender." One such was We'wha, a tall Zuni, his hair rolled tight, who dressed in a long cotton gown, and listed his occupation as "Farmer, Weaver, Potter, Housekeeper." According to historian Will Roscoe, the first two were male occupations, the second two, female. Becoming a shaman or a berdache was often a way for a person not conforming to the "personality norm" of the group to express himself. Among some tribes, berdaches acted as undertakers.

Transvestism and homosexuality were tribally recognized among many Indians as a special condition, given to a youth during a dream. Such third gender men often dreamed of women's tools, often their metates. If a dreamer became a shaman, his power would be greater than that of a heterosexual.

Part of a male's life was gambling. Indians of all tribes enjoyed gaming, using cylinders of cougar or deer bones or wood wrapped in grass for a guessing game, or shaking dice made of acorns to guess numbers. Gambling games were played with pebbles. But they must have sensed the dangers of overbidding, indicated by a gambling myth of the Maidu tribe in California, observed by Stephen Powers.

There lived near Chico a tribe of Indians whose chief was Kiunaddissi. Two old men of the north came down and gambled with him. They had four short pieces of bone, two plain and two marked. They rolled them up in little balls of dry grass; then one of the players held up one of them in each hand, and the other held up his. If he matched them, he counted two; if he failed to match them, the other counted one. There were sixteen bits of wood as counters, and when one got the sixteen he was a winner. The old man used a trick. His arms were hollow, and there was a hole through his body, so that he could slip his pieces across from one hand to the other and win every time. Kiunaddissi wished to bet bows, arrows, shell-money, etc., as usual, but the man would not bet anything but men and women. So he won Kiunaddissi's whole tribe from him, and carried them away to the north, to the ice-land.

Men and boys also enjoyed target shooting with bow and arrow and tossing around wicker balls to catch, while young boys enjoyed the clover game, in which they stood in circles and tossed pellets of green clover from one to another to be caught in the mouth. Whoever's mouth was open widest was likely to win; a variant was to play the game with eyes shut, increasing the difficulty.

Tribal gatherings, held by flickering firelight, fueled by aromatic smoke and roasted game, were occasions for revelry, tales of heroism, and, in many cases, comic playacting, as observed by Powers in his California travels. Snidely he wrote that Indian displays were "inferior" to the American circus: "The Indians themselves admit that they never witnessed . . . a handspring or a somersault before they became acquainted with the Americans." Yet, he wrote, the "tumbling and tomfoolery" went on all night, and filled the tents and huts with "irrepressible laughter." He said of the Maidu tribe:

The performer . . . is more properly a clown than a tumbler or an athlete. One performance is to pretend that a bear has crawled under the hollow slab which is used for a drum. . . . Seizing something which is supposed to represent his tail he twists it until Bruin roars lustily. Then he binds up straws and splinters into a bundle . . . and with prodigious effort . . . tries to carry it, but falls sprawling all along on his belly, crushed to the earth by his enormous burden. Next, he offers somebody an [empty] basket of soup, pretending that it is very, very heavy. He smells it and smacks his mouth over it, and makes motions as if taking swallows of it and licking his lips. . . .

Another performance is acrobatic. . . . The clown, fantastically arrayed in feathers and paint, climbs a pole and hangs head downward from a cross bar and sings, while a company dance underneath. Four men stand close together and join hands; then four others climb up on their shoulders, standing up, and four more on top of these; then those underneath walk about, and the twelve join in singing.

The quest for food—ideally fresh or smoked salmon, corn, peas, potatoes, pumpkins, onions, wheat, camas roots, watermelon— never ended. "The camp is full of Indians," noted Helen Carpenter of the Nevada Paiutes. "We got some fish from them, they also brought a few wild ducks. After seeing the entrails of one thrown

away, an Indian picked them up, threw them on the fire barely long enough to warm, and then greedily devoured the dainty morsel." She watched them enjoy sugarcane, its leaves and stalks "covered with tiny green bugs that puncture the plant and then get caught in the oozing sweetness. The Indians scrape off sugar and bugs and eat without any further preparation. Some of our party tried eating 'Indian sugar' before they knew that a goodly portion was bugs."

Indian men dealt in items of value: buffalo robes, dressed elk and deerskins, lariats, ropes, and bows and arrows. A California hunter might pound a moccasin on a rock to call a hunted sheep within arrow range, the animal mistaking the noise for the sound of two rams locking horns. Sometimes sheep were rounded up and driven past hunters lying in ambush. Among desert tribes, snake and lizard meat, as well as coyote meat and that of other unpalatable scavengers, the buzzard and the vulture, was considered taboo. Indian men poisoned fish by throwing the stems and leaves of the soap plant or doveweed into shallow, quiet pools to stun or stupefy the fish. Others survived on acorns. Wrote Arizona Apache John Rope, or Tlol-dil-xil:

> We used to gather acorns all the way from Oak Springs . . . to Rocky Creek. When the acorns were ripe, we climbed the oak tree and shook the acorns to the ground where they were picked up and carried back to camp in baskets. After a while we always

Native Americans on the Land

227

Cheyenne converts, "native helpers," at Mennonite conference, Freeman, South Dakota.

sent someone back to Cedar Creek to see how the corn was getting on. If the corn were ripe all our people would pack up the acorns we had gathered and move back to harvest the corn. . . .

We boys used to hunt rats with bows and arrows. . . . The way we got the rats was by one boy poking a long stick into a rat's nest, while the other boy would stand at the opposite end. When the stick was poked in, the rat would come to the door and stick out his head; then the boy would shoot him. . . . The rats to be eaten were put in the fire and all the hair burnt off. Then they were skinned and either roasted or boiled. It was the same with rabbits.

Singing, charming, making incantations were some ways the hunter lured animals into his range. Paiute men found game through charms and incantations, according to John Rope:

Every morning early, when the bright morning star could be seen, the people sat around the opening to the circle, with my father sitting in the middle of the opening, and my father lighted his pipe and passed it to his right, and the pipe went round the circle five times. And at night they did the same thing.

After they had smoked the pipe, my father took a kind of drum, which is used in this charming, and made music with it. [The drum] is used for antelope charming. It is made of the hide of some large animal, stuffed with grass, so as to make it sound hollow, and then wound around tightly from one end to the other with a cord as large as my finger. One end of this instrument is large . . . and it tapers down to the other end, which is small, so that it makes a different sound in the different parts. My father took a stick and rubbed this stick from one end of the instrument to the other, making a penetrating, vibrating sound, that could be heard afar off, and he sang, and all his people sang with him.

After that the two men who were messengers went out to see the antelopes. They carried their torches in their right hands, and one of them carried a pipe in his left hand. They started from my father's wigwam and went straight across the damp to the opening; then they crossed and one went around the second circle to the right and the other to the left till they got on the other side of the circle. Then they crossed again, and one went round the herd of antelopes one way and the other went round the other way, but they did not let the antelopes see them. When they met on the other side of the herd, they stopped and smoked the pipe, and then they crossed, and each man came back on the track of the other to the camp, and told my father what they saw and what the antelopes were doing.

This was done every day for five days, and after the first day all the men and women and boys followed the messengers, and went around the circle they were to enter. On the fifth day the antelopes were charmed, and the whole herd followed the tracks of my people and entered the circle where the mounts were, coming in at the entrance, bowing and tossing their heads, and looking sleepy and under a powerful spell. They ran round and round inside the circle just as if there was a fence all around it and they could not get out, and staid there until my people had killed every one. But if anybody had dropped anything, or had stumbled and had not told about it, then when the antelopes came to the place where they had done that, they threw off the spell and rushed wildly out of the circle at that place.

My brother can charm horses in the same way.

General E. D. Townsend, traveling through California in 1851, observed that "when the wild cattle are required for beef, native Californians, mounted on their tough little horses, and armed with their lassoes, are sent out for them. Their skill in throwing the lassos is wonderful. They pursue some particular animal . . . and entangle their fore-feet, horns or hind-feet, as they choose. . . ."

Indians saw themselves as an integral part of nature. To them, animals had intelligence equal to man's and even souls, as well as human qualities and emotions. In many mythologies, animals were believed to have inhabited the earth before man and gotten the world ready for him. Animal providers made food accessible and also initiated the food supply for men, the plant's role was to nourish both men and animals; and the human role was to gather plants and hunt animals as necessary for food. All respect went to them, often assisted by fasting-induced visions, dreams, or hallucinations triggered by ingesting jimsonweed or tolache (datura). Some tribes believed that humans became animals after death.

All over the West, rituals of supplication and appreciation, ceremonies of thanksgiving for the animal's life being given for food, took place. These translated into some ceremonies in which the hunters had to be physically clean, washed, without sexual union for some time, bathed in fragrant smoke, to make themselves acceptable to the deer, which then allowed themselves to be shot.

What to say about a people who have been represented primarily by critics, usually Anglo Americans with the ability to write their impressions and fears, and seldom by the Indians themselves? The record of their lives has too often been told as white men have perceived and distorted them. Only the Indians themselves could truly tell of the Indian man's devotion to his family, courage under fire, and capacity for friendship and compassion.

REFERENCES

❖

Abbot, Carlisle S. *Recollections of a California Pioneer.* New York: Neale Publishing Co., 1917.

Abbott, E. C. *We Pointed Them North: Recollections of a Cowpuncher.* New York, Toronto: Farrar, Rinehart, 1839.

Allen, Barbara. *Homesteading the High Desert.* Salt Lake City: University of Utah Press, 1987.

Ambrose, Stephen. *Nothing Like It in the World: The Men Who Built the Transcontinental Railroad 1863–1869.* New York: Simon & Schuster, 2000.

Asbury, Francis. *The Journals and Letters of Francis Asbury,* vol. 4, ed. Manning Potts. London: Epworth Press, Nashville: Abingdon Press, 1958.

Athern, Robert G. *The Mythic West in Twentieth Century America.* Lawrence: University of Kansas Press, 1986.

Atherton, Gertrude. *California: An Intimate History.* New York and London: Harpers and Brothers Publishers, 1914.

Austin, Stephen F. *The Austin Papers,* vols. 1 and 2, ed. Eugene C. Barker. Annual Report of the American Historical Association for the Years 1919 and 1922, Washington. Austin: University of Texas Press, 1926.

The Backwoods Preacher: An Autobiography of Peter Cartwright, the Backwoods Preacher, ed by W. P. Strickland, L. Swormstedf, and A. Poe. Cincinnati: L. Swormstedf and A. Poe, 1856.

Bailey, H. C. "California in '53." Typed manuscript of reminiscences. Bancroft Library, University of California, Berkeley.

Baird, Elizabeth Therese. "Reminiscences of Life in Territorial Wisconsin 1824–1842." State Historical Society of Wisconsin, 1900.

Bancroft, Hubert Howe. *The Works of Hubert Howe Bancroft,* vol. 39. San Francisco: History Company Publishers, 1890.

Barette, Leonore. *Thumbpapers: Sketches of Pioneer Days.* Eugene, Ore.: Lane County Historical Society, 2001.

Barry, T. A., and B. A. Patten. *Men and Memories of San Francisco in the "Spring of '50."* San Francisco: A. L. Bancroft & Company, 1873.

Becker, Carl. "Kansas," *Turner Essays in American History.* New York: Henry Holt and Co., 1910.

Beckwourth, Jim. *Mountain Man, Indian Chief: The Life and Adventures of Jim Beckwourth,* written from his own dictation by T. D. Bonner, ed., with introduction, Betty Shepard. New York: Harcourt, Brace & World, 1968.

Billington, R. A. *Westward Expansion: A History of the American Frontier.* Albuquerque: University of New Mexico Press, 2001.

Bird, Isabella L. *A Lady's Life in the Rocky Mountains.* New York: Putnam, 1879.

Bolton, Herbert Eugene. *With the Makers of Texas: A Source Reader in Texas History.* Austin, Texas: Gammel-Statesman Publishing Co., 1904.

Booth, Edmund. *Forty Niner: The Life Story of a Deaf Pioneer.* Stockton, Calif.: San Joaquin Pioneer and Historical Society, 1953.

Booth, J. M. Letter, private collection of Frank Q. Newton, lent by Robert Chandler. Wells Fargo History Museum.

Borthwick, John David. *The Gold Hunters.* New York: International Fiction Library, 1917.

Bowman, Joseph *Old Cahokia,* ed. John Francis McDermott. Belleville, Ill.: Buechler Publishing Co., 1949.

Breen, John. "Pioneer Memoirs." Typescript manuscript. Bancroft Library, University of California, Berkeley.

Breen, Patrick. Handwritten manuscript. Bancroft Library, University of California, Berkeley.

Brokmeyer, Henry C. *A Mechanic's Diary.* Washington, D.C.: E. C. Brokmeyer, 1910.

Brooks, Connie. *The Last Cowboys: Closing the Open Range in Southeastern New Mexico, 1890s–1920s.* Albuquerque: University of New Mexico Press, 1993.

Rabbit drive, Fresno, California, 1870.

Brown, John Evans. *Memoirs of an American Gold Seeker*. Fairfield, Wash.: Ye Galleon Press, n.d.

Brown, Richard M. "Meet Anyone Face to Face and Keep the Bullet in Front." *Montana: The Magazine of Western History* (Spring 1992).

Browne, J. Ross. *Mining Adventures in California & Nevada, 1863–1865*. rep. Balboa Island, Calif.: Paisano Press, 1961.

Bruner, Jacob. Jacob Bruner Papers. Ohio Historical Society, Columbus, Ohio.

Bryant, Edwin. Biographical sketches of Edwin Bryant Crocker. Bancroft Library, University of California, Berkeley.

Bunyard, Harriet. "Diary of a Young Girl from Collin County, Texas." Henry E. Huntington Library, San Marino, Calif.

Burt, William P. "Back Stage with a Medicine Show Fifty Years Ago." *Colorado Magazine,* vol. 19 (July 1942).

Byers, William N., and John H. Kellom. *Hand Book to the Gold Fields of Nebraska and Kansas*. Chicago: D. B. Cook & Co., 1859.

Carlisle, Ann Carmichael ed. *Hunter: The Yukon Gold Rush Letters of Robert Hunter Fitzhugh, Jr., 1897–1900*. Montgomery, Ala.: Black Belt Press, 1999.

Carpenter, Helen. "A Journal across the Plains in an Ox Cart, 1857." Henry E. Huntington Library, San Marino, Calif.

Carter, Henry Washington. "My Journey to California, 1857–1858." Manuscript. Bancroft Library, University of California, Berkeley.

Cave Johnson Coutts diary, August 22–September 1, 1846. MS C-E 118, Bancroft Library, University of California, Berkeley.

Chandler, Dr. Robert J. "California Stagecoaching: The Dusty Reality," *Dogtown Territorial Quarterly 2001, no. 47* (Fall 2001).

Clack, Tommie, and Mollie Clack. *Pioneer Days . . . Two Views.* Abilene, Tex.: Reporter Publishing Co., 1979.

Clinton, De Witt. Correspondence and papers. Bancroft Library, University of California, Berkeley.

Coe, George W. *Frontier Fighter: The Autobiography of George W. Coe,* as related to Nan Lillary Harrison. Albuquerque: University of New Mexico Press, 1934.

Coe, Urling. *Frontier Doctor.* New York: Macmillan, 1939.

Colt, Miriam Davis. *Went to Kansas.* New York: L. Ingalls & Co., 1862. rep. Readex Microprint Corp., 1966.

Conant, Roger. *Mercer's Belles.* Seattle: University of Washington Press, 1960.

Conklin, George. *The Ways of the Circus, Being the Memories & Adventures of George Conklin.* New York: Harper, 1921.

Cook, John R. *The Border and the Buffalo,* ed. Milo Milton Quaife. Chicago: Lakeside Press, R. R. Donnelley & Sons, 1938.

Courtright, David. "Opiate Addiction in the American West, 1850–1920." *Journal of the West,* (July 1982). vol. 21, no. 3.

Courtright, M. D. "Letheomania: The Result of the Hypodermic Injection of Morphis." *Pacific Medical and Surgical Journal,* vol. 12 (1870).

Craven, J. J. Unpublished letters to his wife, 1849–1891. Manuscripts Division, Library of Congress.

Crawford, Lucy. *Lucy Crawford's History of the White Mountains,* Morse ed. Boston: Appalachian Mountain Club, 1978.

Crockett, David. *A Narrative of the Life of David Crockett.* Lincoln: University of Nebraska Press, 1987.

Cushing, Frank. *The Correspondence and Journals of Frank Hamilton Cushing 1879–1884.* Albuquerque: University of New Mexico Press, 1990.

Custer, Elizabeth B. *Tenting on the Plains.* Williamstown, Mass.: Corner House Publishers, 1973.

Danhof, Clarence H. "Farm-making Costs and the 'Safety Valve,' 1850–1860." *Essays on the History of the American West,* ed. Stephen Salsbury. Hinsdale, Ill.: Dryden Press, 1975.

Unidentified laborers, California, ca.1880s.

Preacher in the back of a wagon with Bible, ca. 1870. Photo by Stellman.

Daughters of Dakota, vol. 2, ed. Sally Roesch Wagner (Yankton, S.D.: Daughters of Dakota, 1990).

Day, Dr. Warren E. "Physiological and Medical Observatories in Early Arizona," *Arizona Weekly Miner,* April 13, 1878, Frances E. Quebbeman. *Medicine in Territorial Arizona.* Phoenix: Arizona Historical Foundation, 1966.

Delano, Alonzo. *Life on the Plains and among the Diggings.* Auburn and Buffalo: Miller, Orton & Mulligan, 1854. rep. Readex Microprint, 1966.

Demarest, David. Diary. Bancroft Library, University of California, Berkeley.

Dick, Everett. *The Sod-House Frontier 1854–1940.* Lincoln, Neb.: Johnsen Publishing Co., 1954.

Dillon, Richard H. *Humbugs and Heroes.* San Francisco: Bookpeople, 1983.

Dittrick, Howard. *Pioneer Medicine in the Western Reserve.* Cleveland: Academy of Medicine, 1932.

Drake, Daniel. *Physician to the West: Selected Writings of Daniel Drake on Science and Society.* Lexington: University of Kentucky Press, 1970.

Duden, Gottfried. "Report on a Journey to the Western States of North America," manuscript. Columbia: State Historical Society of Missouri and University of Missouri Press, 1980.

Duffield, George. *National Union: The Test of American Loyalty.* Detroit: Frank Raymond, 1864.

Dunbar, William. *Life, Letters and Papers of William Dunbar.* Jackson: Press of the Mississippi Historical Society, 1930.

Emlen, Samuel. Letters to his sister, 1870. Bancroft Library, University of California, Berkeley.

Emmons County [North Dakota] *Historical Society Newsletter,* vol. 4 (July 1976).

Emrich, Duncan. *It's an Old World Custom.* New York: Vanguard Press, 1949.

Enrique Cerruti interview with Thomas Knight for Hubert Howe Bancroft. Bancroft Library, University of California, Berkeley.

Erdoes, Richard. *Saloons of the Old West.* New York: Alfred A. Knopf, 1979.

Fife, Austin E. "Folklife and Folk Arts in the United States Exhibit." Merrill Art Gallery and Special Collections Library, Utah State University.

Foster, Reverend Bertram. *In Alaskan Waters.* Philadelphia: Penn Publishing Co., 1925.

Fougera, Katherine Gibson. *With Custer's Cavalry.* Lincoln: University of Nebraska Press, 1987.

Fox, Charles Gardiner. *Doctor at Timberline.* Caldwell, Ida.: Caxton Printers, 1946.

Franz, Joe B., and Julian Ernest Choate, Jr. *The American Cowboy: The Myth and the Reality.* Norman: University of Oklahoma Press, 1955.

Fuller, Henry C. *A Texas Sheriff.* Nacogdoches, Tex.: Baker Printing Co., 1831.

Galloway, James Hezlep. James Hezlep Galloway diary. MS CF 191, Bancroft Library, University of California, Berkeley.

Garland, Hamlin. *The Long Trail.* New York, London: Harper & Brothers, 1935.

Garcia, Andrew. *Tough Trip through Paradise,* ed. Bennet Stein. New York, Houghton-Mifflin, 1967.

Giller, C. H. Letter to L. P. Griswold, 1857. E. A. Wiltsee Collection, Wells Fargo Bank, No. 374, Gregory's Express Pocket Letter Book, Frame 135.

Goodwin, Grenville. "Experiences of an Indian Scout: Excerpts from the Life of John Rope, and 'Old Timer' of the White Mountain Apaches." *Arizona Historical Review,* vol. 7, no. 1 (January 1936).

Green, Ephriam. *The 1848 Trail Journal of Ephriam Green,* ed. Will Bagley. Salt Lake City: Prairie Dog Press, 1991.

Green, Jerome A. *Colonel Nelson A. Miles and the Great Sioux War, 1876–1877.* Lincoln: University of Nebraska Press, 1991.

Grey, William. *A Picture of Pioneer Times in California* (San Francisco: W. M. Hinton Co., 1881).

Guillet, Edwin C. *The Great Migration.* New York, London, Toronto: Thomas Nelson and Sons, 1937.

Haines, James. "Social Life in Central Illinois in Pioneer Days." Speech, Springfield, Ill., January 25, 1903. Pekin: Illinois Historical Society, 1905.

Halgouet, Jerome de. *Citeaux* (St. Louis, Mo.: Bellefontaine Abby, 1910).

Hall, James. *Letters from the West, 1828.* London: Henry Colburn, New Burlington Street, 1828.

Hall, Robert. dictation from Robert H. Hall, Rawlins, Wyoming, 1885. MSS PM 23, Bancroft Library, University of California, Berkeley.

Hand, Wayland D. "Plugging, Nailing, Wedging and Kindred Folk Medical Practices," ed. Bruce Jackson. *Folklore & Society: Essays in Honor of Benj. A.* Hatboro, Pa.: Botkin, 1966.

Haney, William J. *The Mountain People of Kentucky.* Cincinnati: Robert Clarke Co., 1906.

Harte, Bret. *The Luck of Roaring Camp.* Oakland, Calif.: Star Rover House, 1983.

Hayes, Lorena. Personal journal. MS 0615, Bancroft Library, University of California, Berkeley.

Hecox, Margaret. *California Caravan: The 1845 Overland Trail Memoir of Margaret M. Hecox.* San Jose, Calif.: Harlan-Young Press, 1966.

Heizer, Robert F., and Albert B. Elaser. *The Natural World of the California Indians.* Berkeley: University of California Press, 1980.

Helskell, Hugh Brown. "The Diary of Hugh Brown Helskell." Manuscript. Bancroft Library, University of California, Berkeley.

Hine, Robert V. *Josiah Royce: From Grass Valley to Harvard.* Norman: University of Oklahoma Press, 1992.

Hofstadter, Richard. *Anti-Intellectualism in America.* New York: Charles Scribner's & Sons, 1944.

Hopkins, Sarah Winnemucca. *Life among the Piutes: Their Wrongs and Claims,* ed., Mrs. Horace Mann. Boston: Cupples, Upham and Col, N.Y.: G. P. Putnam's Sons, and by the author, 1883.

Hough, Emerson. *The Story of the Outlaw: A Study of the Western Desperado with Historical Narratives of Famous Outlaws,* New York: Outing Publishing, 1969.

Howard, W. C. Dictation from W. C. Howard, 1887. BANC ms. P-O 115:23, Bancroft Library, University of California, Berkeley.

Hoyt, Henry F. *A Frontier Doctor.* Chicago: Lakeside Press, 1854; rep. Cambridge: Riverside Press, 1929.

Hulbert, Archer. "The Methods and Operations of the Scioto Group of Speculators." *Mississippi Valley Historical Review,* vol. 2 (June 1915).

Ingersoll, Ernest *Knocking round the Rockies.* Norman: University of Oklahoma Press, 1852.

Johnson, Overton, and William H. Winter. *Route across the Rocky Mountains: With a Description of Oregon and California, Their Geographical Features, Their Resources, Soil, Climate, Productions, &c.* Lafayette, Ind.: J. B. Semans, printer, 1982.

Johnston, William G. *Experiences of a Forty-Niner.* Pittsburgh, self-published: 1855.

Karolevitz, Robert F. *Doctors of the Old West.* Seattle: Superior Publishing Co., 1967.

Keleher, William A. *The Fabulous Frontier: Twelve New Mexico Stories.* Santa Fe, N.M.: Rydal Press, 1945.

Kirkland, Caroline. *A New Home, or Life in the Clearings.* New York: G. P. Putnam's Sons, 1953.

Knight, Thomas. "Statement of Early Events in California, 1870." MSS 70/118, Bancroft Library, University of California, Berkeley.

Kroeber, Theodora. *Almost Ancestors: The First Californians.* San Francisco: Sierra Club, 1968.

Lamar, Howard A. *The Reader's Encyclopedia of the American West.* New York: Thomas Y. Crowell Co., 1977.

Larkin, Jack. *The Reshaping of Everyday Life, 1790–1840.* New York: Harper & Row, 1988.

Larkin, James Ross. *James Ross Larkin on the Santa Fe Trail,* ed. Barton Barbour. Albuquerque: University of New Mexico Press, 1990.

Larpenteur, Charles. *Forty Years a Fur Trader on the Upper Missouri: The Personal Narrative of Charles Larpenteur 1833–1872.* Minneapolis: Ross & Haines, 1962.

Leckie, Shirley A. *Elizabeth Bacon Custer and the Making of a Myth.* Norman: University of Oklahoma Press, 1993.

Levorson, Barbara. *The Quiet Conquest: A History of the Lives and Times of the First Settlers of Central North Dakota.* Hawley, Minn.: *Hawley Herald,* 1974.

Levy, Harriet. *920 O'Farrell Street.* New York: Doubleday & Co., 1947.

Lewis, Merriwether. *Original Journals of the Lewis and Clark Party,* 1804–1806. ed. Reuben Gold Thwaites. New York: n.p., 1904.

Lincoln, Abraham. *Uncollected Works of Abraham Lincoln: His Letters, Addresses & Other Papers.* Elmira, N.Y.: Primavera Press, 1947.

Lindsay, William A. *The Journals of William A. Lindsay,* ed. Katherine McDonnell. Indianapolis: Indiana Historical Society, 1989.

Lindsey, David. "A 'Backwoods Utopia': The Berea Community of 1836–1837." *Ohio Historical Quarterly,* vol. 65 (1987).

Locke, Jonathan F. "Personal Letters, 1832." Manuscript. Bancroft Library, University of California, Berkeley.

Lockett, Jim. *Settling the Land of Promise: Stories of Pioneer Men, Women & Children Who Laid a Firm Foundation for Years to Come.* McMinneville, Ore.: J & R Lockett, 1994.

Long, James Larpenteur. *The Assiniboines: From the Accounts of the Old Ones Told to First Boy,* ed. Michael Stephen Kennedy. Norman: University of Oklahoma Press, 1961.

Lord, Israel Shipman Pelton. *A Doctor's Gold Rush Journey to California,* ed. Necia Dixon Liles. Lincoln and London: University of Nebraska Press, 1995.

Love, Nat. *The Life and Adventures of Nat Love, Better Known in the Cattle Country as Deadwood Dick, by Himself: A True History of Slavery Days.* Los Angeles: s.n., 1907.

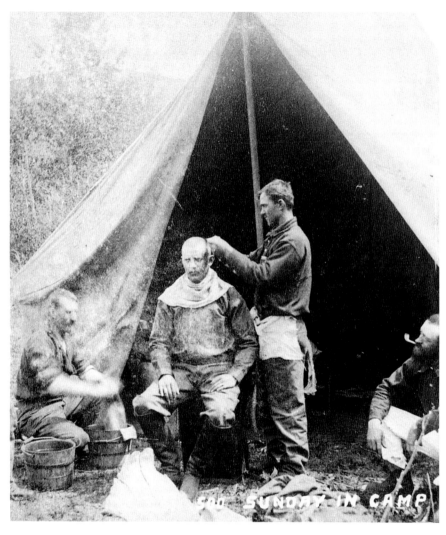

Sunday haircut in camp, Colorado, ca. 1870s.

Luchetti, Cathy. *Children of the West.* New York: W. W. Norton, 2001.

———. *Home on the Range: A Culinary History of the American West.* New York: Villard, 1993.

———. *Under God's Spell: Frontier Evangelists 1772–1915.* San Diego: Harcourt, Brace, 1989.

Lyman, George D. *John Marsh, Pioneer.* New York: Chautauqua Press, 1931.

McClellan, Guy. *The Golden State. A History of the Region West of the Rocky Mountains.* Philadelphia: William Flint and Co., 1876.

MacGowan, Michael. *The Hard Road to Klondike.* London and Boston: Routledge and Kegan Paul, 1962.

McGraw, Nellie Tichenor. "My Early Days in San Francisco." *Pacific Historian* (November 1961).

McKnight, George. Letter written from Columbia, California, in 1851, to brother John. E. A. Wiltsee Collection, Wells Fargo Bank, No. 374, Gregory's Express Letter Book, Frame 64.

"Manners and Morals," William Bradford diary. Manuscript Collection. Bancroft Library, University of California, Berkeley.

Marcy, Randolph B. *Thirty Years of Army Life on the Border.* New York and Philadelphia: J. B. Lippincott Co., 1963.

Marryat, Captain C. R. *Travels and Adventures of Monsieur Violet in California, Sonora, and Western Texas.* New York: Harper & Brothers, 1843.

May, Richard Martin. May family genealogy. Unpublished manuscript, private collection of James C. Simms, San Francisco, 1903.

Mather, R. E. *Scandal of the West: Domestic Violence on the Frontier.* Oklahoma City: History West Publishing Co., 1988.

Matthews, Mary McNair. *Ten Years in Nevada, or, Life on the Pacific Coast.* New York: Baker, Jones & Co., 1880.

Moore, Arthur K. *The Frontier Mind.* New York: McGraw-Hill, 1963.

Mossman, Isaac Van Dorsey. "A Pony Expressman's Recollections." *Oregon Native Son,* vol. 2, no. 6 (1899).

Nelson, Oliver. *The Cowman's Southwest: The Reminiscences of Oliver Nelson,* ed. Angie Debo. Lincoln: University of Nebraska Press, 1953.

Oblinger, Uriah W. "Family Letters, 1862–1912." Letter from C. S. Bishop to Uriah W. Oblinger, November 8, 1889; letter from C. H. Bumgardner to Uriah Oblinger, November 26, 1889. Nebraska State Archives and Library of Congress "American Memories."

O'Reilly, Harrington. *Fifty Years on the Trail: The Adventures of John Young Nelson.* Norman: University of Oklahoma Press, 1963.

Osterud, Nancy Grey. *Bonds of Community: The Lives of Farm Women in Nineteenth Century New York.* Ithaca: Cornell University Press, 1991.

Owen, Rev. Isaac. Manuscript. Bancroft Library, University of California, Berkeley.

Parkman, Francis. *Chronicles of Colorado.* Boulder, Colo.: Roberts Rinehart, 1984.

Pattie, James O. *The Personal Narrative of James O. Pattie.* Philadelphia: Lippincott, 1967.

Phelps, Andrew. Phelps family papers, 1852–1878. BANC-MSS 74/188, Bancroft Library, University of California, Berkeley.

Pickard, Madge, and R. Carlyle Buley. *The Midwest Pioneer: His Ills, Cures & Doctors.* Crawfordville, Ind.: R. E. Banta, 1945.

Pike, Zebulon. *The Journals of Zebulon Montgomery Pike: With Letters and Related*

Documents, ed. Donald Jackson, vol. 2. Norman: University of Oklahoma Press, 1966.

Powers, Stephen. *Tribes of California.* Berkeley: University of California Press, 1976.

Prendergast, Thomas F. *Forgotten Pioneers: Irish Leaders in Early California.* San Francisco: Trade Pressroom, 1942.

Priest, Loring B. *Uncle Sam's Step Children: The Reformation of United States Indian Policy, 1865–1887* (New Brunswick: Rutgers University Press, 1942).

Pyeatt, John Rankin. *Cherokee Trail Diaries,* vols. 1 and 2, ed. Patricia K. A. Fletcher, Dr. Jack Earl Fletcher, Lee Whitely (Caldwell, Ida.: Caxton Printers, Ltd., n.d.).

Quebbeman, Frances E. *Medicine in Territorial Arizona.* Phoenix: Arizona Historical Foundation, 1966.

Radin, Paul. *The Autobiography of a Winnebago Indian.* Berkeley: University of California Publication in American Archeology and Anthropology, 1920.

Relación de Antonio Berryessa, dictada a D. Emilia Pina, para la Bancroft Library, 1877, Recorded by Erskine Greer. Bancroft Library, University of California, Berkeley.

Reno, Marcus A. *The Official Record of a Court of Inquiry Convened at Chicago, Il, Jan 13, 1879.* Pacific Palisades, Calif.: n.p., 1951.

Riley, Glenda. "Torn Asunder: Divorce in Early Oklahoma Territory." *Chronicles of Oklahoma,* vol. 68, no. 4, (Winter 1989–90).

Rinehart family story. Manuscript. Personal collection of Steve Thaw, Rinehart family.

Robinson, Sarah T. D. *Kansas, Its Interior and Exterior Life.* Boston: n.p., 1856.

Ronan, Margaret. *Frontier Woman: The Story of Mary Ronan.* Missoula: University of Montana, 1973.

Rosicky, Rose. *A History of Czechs (Bohemians) in Nebraska.* Omaha: Czech Historical Society of Nebraska, 1929.

Russell, Osborne. *Journal of a Trapper,* ed. Aubrey L. Haines. Portland: Oregon Historical Society, 1955.

Ruxton, George Frederick. *Adventures in Mexico and the Rocky Mountains.* Self-published, 1849.

Schultz, James Willard. *Blackfeet and Buffalo: Memories of Life among the Indians,* ed. Keith C. Steele. Norman: University of Oklahoma Press, 1981.

Sears, Richard. *A Utopian Experiment in Kentucky: Integration and Social Equality at Berea, 1866–1904.* Westport, Conn.: Greenwood Press, 1996.

Serra, Junipero. *Writings of Junipero Serra,* ed. Antonine Ibesas O.F.M. (Washington, D.C.:Academy of American Franciscan History, 1955).

Sieberts, Bruce. *Nothing Like Prairie and Sky: Life on the Dakota Range in the Early Days.* Norman: University of Oklahoma, 1970.

Siringo, Charles A. *A Texas Cowboy.* Lincoln: University of Nebraska Press, 1979.

Smith, John E. *Pioneer Reminiscences.* Fairfield, Wash.: Ye Galleon Press, 1996.

Smythe, H. *Historical Sketch of Parker County and Weatherford, Texas.* St. Louis: Louis C. Lavat, 1877.

Abe Warner in his Cobweb Palace, San Francisco.

Snyder, Eugene Edmund. "C. S. Price As I Remember Him." *Oregon Historical Quarterly,* vol. 92, no 2. (Summer 1994).

Solano, Isadora. "Reminiscences of a Princess, Isidora Solano." Bancroft Library, University of California, Berkeley.

Spicer, Edward, ed. *Perspectives in American Indian Culture Change.* Chicago: University of Chicago Press, 1969.

Springs, John. *John Spring's Arizona,* ed. A. M. Gustafson. Tucson: University of Arizona Press, 1966.

"Statement Taken April 11, 1885," manuscript. Bancroft Library, University of California, Berkeley.

Stephens, Charles. "Trying for a Change: Sixteen Years in the White River Valley, NV." *Nevada Historical Society Quarterly,* vol. 56, no. 2 (Summer 1982).

Stephens, Lorenzo Dow. *The Dealings of God, Man, and the Devil.* St. Louis: privately published, 1849.

Still, Bayard. *The West: Contemporary Records of America's Expansion across the Continent 1607–1890.* New York: Capricorn Books, 1961.

Stoner, Anna Louisa Wellington. *Letters by Lamplight: A Woman's View of Everyday Life in South Texas,* ed. Lois E. Myers. Waco, Tex.: Baylor University Press, 1991.

Stratton, Joanna. *Pioneer Women: Voices from the Pioneer Frontier.* New York: Simon & Schuster, 1981.

Stritecky, Vavrin. "Letters of Marie and Vavrin Stritecky, 1913–1934, ed. Marilee Richards. *South Dakota History,* vol. 11, no. 4 (Fall 1981).

John Thornburn reminiscences. Handwritten autobiography, 1864. Montana Historical Society.

Timmons, William. *Twilight on the Range: Recollections of a Latterday Cowboy.* Austin: University of Texas Press, 1971.

Toqueville, Alexis de. *Democracy in America,* ed. Richard Heffner. New York: Mentor Books, 1955.

Townsend, E. D. *The California Diary of General E. D. Townsend,* ed. Malcolm Edwards. N.p.: Anderson, Ritchie & Simon, 1970.

Tullock, James Francis. *The James Francis Tullock Diary 1875–1910,* comp. and ed. Gordon Keith. Portland, Ore.: Binford & Mort, 1979.

Turner, Frederick Jackson. *The Significance of the Frontier in American History.* New York: Ungar, 1963.

Twain, Mark. *Mark Twain's West.* Chicago: R. R. Donnelley & Sons, 1983.

Twitchell, R. E. *Leading Facts of New Mexican History,* vol. 1. Alburquerque: University of New Mexico Press, 1969.

Tyro, Smith. "History of the Dugen Valley." *Washington State Genealogical and Historical Review,* vol. 2, no. 2 (Spring 1984).

Unruh, John D. *The Plains Across.* Urbana, Chicago, and London: University of Illinois Press, 1978.

Walker, Captain Samuel. *Samuel H. Walker's Account of the Mier Expedition,* ed. Marilyn McAdams Sibley. Fort Worth: Texas State Historical Association, 1978.

Wayland, Doc. Quoted in Matlock Correspondence, Yellow House, Texas, 1887. The Haley Museum, Midland, Texas.

Whitewolf, Jim. *The Life of a Kiowa Apache Indian,* ed. Charles S. Brant. New York: Dover Publications, Inc.

The William Thomas Prestwood Enciphered Diary 1808–1859, ed. Nathaniel Clernroy Browder. Raleigh, N.C.: n.p., 1984.

Wolfe, Patrick B. *Wolfe's History of Clinton County, Iowa.* Indianapolis: Ralston Printers, 1911.

Wyatt, Steve M. "Flax and Linen: An Uncertain Oregon Industry." *Oregon Historical Quarterly,* vol. 95, No. 2 (Summer 1994).

Young, John D. *John D. Young and the Colorado Gold Rush,* ed. Dwight Smith. Chicago: R. R. Donnelley & Sons Co., 1969.

Zanjini, Sally. "Hang Me If You Will: Violence in the Last Western Mining Boomtown." *Montana,* vol. 42, no. 2 (Spring 1992).

PHOTOGRAPH CREDITS

PHOTOGRAPH

CREDITS

INDEX

Page numbers in *italics* refer to illustrations.

C

Young, John D., 13, 34, 35, 37, 40, 50–51, 57, 61, 65, 67–68, 69–70, 92–93, 96, 119, 129, 216

⟶ Z ⟵

Zanjini, Sally, 76
Zoar, Ohio, 182
Zunis, 226